NLP II
The Next Generation

Enriching the study of the Structure of Subjective Experience

Robert Dilts

and

Judith DeLozier

with

Deborah Bacon Dilts

Meta Publications
P.O. Box 1910
Capitola, California 95010
(831) 464-0254
FAX (831) 464-0517
E-Mail: metapub@prodigy.net
Homepage: http://www.meta-publications.com

Library of Congress Card Number 2010922378
I.S.B.N. 0-916990-49-4

Contents

Dedication

This book is dedicated with affection and respect to:

The co-founders of NLP

Richard Bandler and John Grinder

who initiated us into this great adventure and encouraged
us to be confident, courageous and creative in our own
exploration of the structure of subjective experience.

The creative spirit of

Milton H. Erickson
Virginia Satir
Fritz Perls and
Gregory Bateson

who taught us through their example how to be pioneers
of human potential.

The legions of

NLP Practitioners,

Master Practitioners and

Trainers

throughout the world

who have created the fertile and generative field that has
made new generations of NLP possible.

Acknowledgments

We would like to acknowledge:

Stephen Gilligan for his profoundly important contributions to the evolution of Next Generation NLP. Stephen was one of the members of the original group of students studying with Richard Bandler and John Grinder at the beginnings of NLP. He has since gone on to develop his own ideas through his work on Self-Relations and the Generative Self.

A number of the core ideas presented in this book regarding generativity, the three minds (cognitive, somatic and field) and their associated principles and elements, archetypal energies, centering and the idea of sponsorship were originally developed by Stephen in his seminal work on Self-Relations (1997). The rich cross-fertilization between Self-Relations and NLP can be seen the book *The Hero's Journey: A Voyage of Self-Discovery* (Gilligan and Dilts, 2009).

We also want to acknowledge:

Gabrielle Roth, creator of the 5Rhythms® (who shares a common mentorship with Gregory Bateson), for continuing to champion the deep importance of movement and connection with the body as key to the process of change.

Richard Moss for making the transformative power of awareness, presence and connection so clear.

Teresa Epstein for working so diligently over the years to provide the NLP University context in which we can all continue to generatively collaborate.

Sandra Bacon for lending her expert proofreading skills to this effort.

Michael Dilts and Claire Sage for their steady support and editing assistance with the cover.

Preface

At the conclusion of our book *NLP Volume I* (1980), we authors (Dilts, Grinder, Bandler and DeLozier) promised a second volume, *NLP II*, which would present more concrete applications of the concepts, principles and distinctions we laid out in that first introduction to NLP. We claimed the second book would "explore more specifically how to apply Neuro-Linguistic Programming to your work and everyday life."

For a variety of reasons, *NLP Volume II* never materialized. This was partly because we authors all had busy lives and were intensely involved in developing and experiencing those applications about which we had pledged to write. As time went on, life took us in separate directions. We have never all been together again in the same way as we were in those early days, and the project to produce *NLP II* "got lost in the shuffle."

Another factor was that the field kept developing so rapidly that it was difficult to select a particular group of processes that we felt most characterized the history and potential of NLP. New challenges and opportunities stretched us to find resources and solutions that constantly brought innovations touching the very foundations of the field.

While all four of us original authors of *NLP I* have continued to travel extensively throughout the world, teaching NLP and contributing to its evolution and development, we (Robert and Judith) have maintained a close personal and working relationship, culminating each year in our summer residential programs at NLP University at the University of California in Santa Cruz.

Over the years, we have frequently ruminated on the vision and promise of an *NLP II* made all those years ago. People within the field have also continued to ask, "Where is *NLP Volume II?*" At times, we have attempted to fulfill the promise in other ways. We spent four years writing the *Encyclopedia of Systemic NLP and NLP New Coding* to cover the rich variety of NLP models and applications and to honor the intellectual history of the fascinating field of NLP. In our work, we have sought to preserve the spirit of the original ensemble of students studying and developing NLP in small groups in the Santa Cruz mountains with Bandler and Grinder.

Four years ago, we decided the time had come to finally complete our commitment to a second volume. In our view, there was clearly something new to say. This book *NLP II: The Next Generation* is a result of that decision.

The book has gone through various evolutions over the past several years and would not exist without the energy and support of Deborah—a 5Rhythms® dance teacher, psychotherapist and Psychosynthesis trainer as well as an interpreter—who has been an important contributor to a number of the new developments presented in the later chapters.

Deborah's connection with NLP began in 1994 when she interpreted John Grinder into French in Paris, where she has been living since the early 1980s as an American expatriate. Since that time, she has interpreted many other NLP trainers, including David Gordon, Charles Faulkner, Lynne Conwell, Robert McDonald and, of course, Robert and Judith.

Since 2005, Deborah and Robert have been developing programs bringing together Deborah's background in body-oriented transformational practices, such as the 5Rhythms®, and principles of NLP. (Robert and Deborah were married in 2008.) They have applied these new developments in workshops and seminars throughout the world as well as with Judith at NLP University in California.

The collaboration between the three of us (Robert, Judith and Deborah) has been characterized by enthusiasm, creativity and inclusiveness. We hope that all these qualities come forth in this book and provide you readers with a new appreciation of the depth, richness and potential of NLP.

Robert Dilts
Judith DeLozier
Deborah Bacon Dilts
August, 2010
Santa Cruz, California

A New Generation of NLP

Background and Overview of NLP

This book is about significant new developments in Neuro-Linguistic Programming. *Neuro-Linguistic Programming (NLP)* is an approach to understanding human behavior, and a set of explicit skills and techniques derived from that approach. Originated by Richard Bandler and John Grinder in the 1970s, NLP examines the patterns or *"programming"* created by the interaction between the nervous system (*"neuro"*) and language structures (*"linguistic"*), and their influence on our bodies and behaviors. From the NLP perspective, it is this interaction that produces both effective and ineffective behavior, and is responsible for the processes behind both human excellence and pathology.

Bandler and Grinder defined Neuro-Linguistic Programming as *the study of the structure of subjective experience.*

The term *study* implies ongoing research and inquiry. In the field of NLP, this takes place primarily through the process of *behavioral modeling*. Many of the skills and techniques of NLP were derived from observing the patterns of excellence in remarkable performers from diverse fields including psychotherapy, business, art, science, law and education. The purpose of this type of examination is to discover *the differences that make the difference* between poor, average and exceptional performance.

The notion of *structure* implies an emphasis on *process* as opposed to content. That is, the modeling processes of NLP focus more on revealing *how* people do what they do rather than describe *what* they are doing. NLP is not so interested in the details of what decisions people make, what they learn or what they create, but rather in the *process of how* they decide, learn and create. In fact, NLP co-founder John

Grinder has claimed that all of the techniques and formats of NLP have essentially arisen from asking the questions "How do you know that?" or "How do you do that?" NLP distinctions allow us to look past the behavioral content of what people do to the more invisible forces behind those behaviors; to the structures of thought, belief and emotion that allow people to perform effectively or interfere with that performance. NLP contains a set of procedures and distinctions that are uniquely suited to identify crucial *patterns* of thought, motivation and behavior so that they may be put into pragmatic and testable implementations.

Central to the NLP modeling process is its emphasis on the structure of *subjective experience* (i.e., thoughts, beliefs, emotions, inner representations, etc.) as opposed to "objective reality." At the foundation of NLP is the presupposition that "The map is not the territory." That is, our inner maps and models of the world in which we live are necessarily different from the world they portray (just as a map of a city is not the city and the menu is not the meal). The inner representations we generate through our nervous systems and language patterns inherently contain generalizations, deletions and distortions with respect to the "reality" they are intended to reflect. It is these inner maps and models, however, that actually determine how we experience and respond to the world in which we live.

The study of the structure of subjective experience, then, is grounded in our personal, ongoing *sensory experience* (what and how we actually see, hear, feel, smell and taste) rather than coming from theories and ideas about external "reality." As an example, in its exploration of spiritual experience, NLP is not interested in presenting a theory, philosophy or set of belief systems about spirituality. Rather, NLP examines the *structure* of people's *subjective experience* of the spiritual; i.e., *How* do we experience being a part of something beyond ourselves and what are the ramifications of experiencing it that way?

The modeling process of NLP is concerned with *instrumental* questions such as: How can one influence a particular subjective experience? How can one use it? How can one make more or less of it? What types of processes enhance or interfere with that subjective experience?

In summary, NLP is an approach to studying human behavior that provides:

1. An **Epistemology** – A system of principles and distinctions for organizing knowledge about ourselves and our interaction with the world

2. A **Methodology** – Processes and procedures for gathering and applying that knowledge

3. A **Technology** – Tools to aid in the application of that knowledge in order to achieve particular results

The Evolution of NLP

NLP was originated by John Grinder (whose background was in linguistics) and Richard Bandler (whose background was in mathematics and gestalt therapy) for the purpose of making explicit models of human excellence. Their first work, *The Structure of Magic, Vol. I & II* (1975, 1976), identified the verbal and behavioral patterns of therapists Fritz Perls (the creator of gestalt therapy) and Virginia Satir (internationally renowned family therapist). Their next work, *Patterns of the Hypnotic Techniques of Milton H. Erickson, M.D., Vol. I & II* (1975, 1976), examined the verbal and behavioral patterns of Milton Erickson, founder of the American Society of Clinical Hypnosis and one of the world's most widely acknowledged and clinically successful psychiatrists.

As a result of this earlier work, Grinder and Bandler formalized their modeling methods and their own individual contributions under the name "Neuro-Linguistic Programming" to symbolize the relationship between the nervous system and language and their consequences on our experience, physiology and actions.

According to NLP, the basic process of change involves:

1) identifying the *present state* of the person, team, organization or system, and

2) adding the appropriate *resources* to lead that person, team, organization or system to some

3) *desired state.*

Present State + Appropriate Resources ⟶ Desired State

The distinctions and techniques of NLP are organized to help identify and define present states and desired states of various types and levels and then to access and apply the appropriate resources to produce effective and ecological change in the direction of the desired state.

Through the years, NLP has developed some very powerful tools and skills for communication and change in a wide range of professional areas including: coaching, counseling, psychotherapy, education, health, creativity, law, management, sales, leadership and parenting.

The function of any Neuro-Linguistic Programming technique is to enrich, or add to, one of the three properties of effective behavior – that is, having: a) a rich model of the world, in particular of desired outcomes; b) full access to all of our sensory experience; and c) flexibility of internal responses and external behavior.

The many, many explicit techniques and procedures that make up the behavioral technology of NLP are presented in the ever-growing number of books, recordings and seminars that represent the development of the field of Neuro-Linguistic Programming. There are also many techniques that have not been transformed into written or recorded representations, and many still in the process of being refined and developed.

NLP is now in its third decade as a field of study and has evolved considerably since its beginnings in the mid 1970s. As we write these lines, it has been exactly 30 years since the publication of *NLP Volume 1* (Dilts, Grinder, Bandler, DeLozier, 1980). Over these years, NLP has literally spread around the world and has touched the lives of millions of people. At our NLP University programs in California, people come from more than 35 different countries from all over the world each year to learn to be NLP Practitioners, Master Practitioners and Trainers. Many more thousands of people are trained in NLP each year in specialized NLP Institutes throughout the planet.

As a third generation of NLP developers, trainers and practitioners move into the world, it is also time to acknowledge a new generation of NLP. In doing so, we must address two fundamental questions:

1. What makes it a "new" generation and not simply a variation of an existing generation of NLP? (This is a similar question to what makes a plant or animal a new biological species and not simply a variation of already existing species.)

2. How do we know the discoveries or structures proposed by the new generation are a "part of" NLP and not something else? In other words, what distinguishes an NLP model or method from those of other fields?

What Makes Something NLP?

We will begin by addressing the question, "What makes something (specifically, a technique, format, model or set of distinctions) a part of NLP?"

NLP processes and procedures address an impressive range of topics and issues. Our *Encyclopedia of Systemic NLP and NLP New Coding* (Dilts & DeLozier, 2000), for example, covers subjects such as: treatment of phobias, traumas and emotional disorders; techniques for learning spelling, foreign languages, creative writing, accelerated reading, algebra, etc.; leadership and management skills; methods for strategic planning, team development, and organizational development; formats relating to physical healing, creativity, conflict resolution, motivation and many, many others. NLP covers a scope of applications far beyond other psychological and behavioral models such as psychoanalysis, Gestalt, Transactional Analysis, Psychosynthesis, even cognitive psychology.

Clearly, NLP is not defined or bound by any particular area or topic of application. Given the wide range of techniques and models of NLP, it is indeed intriguing to attempt to define what makes something part of NLP.

This is a fundamental "epistemological" issue. The term *epistemology* comes from the Greek words *epi* (meaning "above" or "upon"), *histanai* (meaning to "set" or "place") and *logos* (meaning "word" or "knowledge")—i.e., "that upon which we set our knowledge." An epistemology, then, is the fundamental system of distinctions and assumptions upon which one bases and generates all other knowledge. As Gregory Bateson defined it:

> *Epistemology is the history of the origins of knowledge;*
> *in other words how you know what you know.*

Beginning with questions about what we can know, and how we come to know what we think we know, epistemology moves to the question, "How do we know anything at all?"*
Bateson continues:

> *Philosophers have recognized and separated two sorts of problem. There are first the problems of how things are, what is a person and what sort of world this is. These are the problems of **ontology**. Second there are the problems of how we know anything, or more specifically, how we know what sort of a world it is and what sort of creatures we are that can know something (or perhaps nothing) of this matter. These are problems of **epistemology**.*

NLP is both a way of being (an "ontology") and a way of knowing (an "epistemology"). At the core of NLP as an ontology is a set of fundamental presuppositions about communication, choice, change, and the intentions behind our behaviors. At the heart of NLP as an epistemology is *modeling*—an ongoing

---

* The fact that epistemology is considered an esoteric, intellectual subject by Westerners is a telling indicator of how little we typically examine the foundation of our own beliefs, values, and perceptions, and the behaviors which flow from them.

process for expanding and enriching our maps of the world through awareness, curiosity and the ability to synthesize multiple perspectives and descriptions.

Both the ontology and epistemology of NLP begin with the presupposition that "the map is not the territory." NLP teaches that no one map is any more true or real than any other, yet your ability to be effective and evolve beyond where you are now is a function of having a map that permits the greatest possible range of choices. Thus, NLP inherently promotes inclusiveness rather than rigidity.

As we have already established, NLP is not about the content of the subjective experiences it is studying. It is the *manner in which* those subjective experiences are studied and represented that is at the essence of the epistemology of NLP

Throughout the years, for example, some NLP practitioners, and even trainers, have argued that subjects like "spirituality," "love," "past lives" or "reincarnation" have no place in NLP. On the other hand, these subjects clearly relate to powerful and shared subjective experiences of many people. As subjective experiences, they all certainly come under the scope of study of NLP.

In the same way that any form of language would be relevant to linguistics (the study of language), any form of subjective experience is relevant to NLP.

Of course, NLP is not going to be interested in the particular content of these subjective experiences or whether or not they are objectively "true." The questions to be explored by NLP will be, "How do people experience these subjective phenomena differently than any other subjective phenomena?" "What consequences do these subjective experiences produce in people?" "Do they produce resourceful or problematic reactions and responses?" "Does the structure of these experiences help or hinder successful performance?" "Does our relationship with such experiences enhance or diminish our sense of personal satisfaction?" "Does the way we experience them empower us with more choices or create a sense of helplessness and dependence?"

In other words, if an NLP practitioner or coach is working with someone who begins speaking about a "past life" experience, the practitioner would not begin to argue with that person about the validity of his or her experience. Rather, the NLP practitioner would become curious about the structure and consequences of that particular subjective experience and how it fits with the rest of the person's subjective model of the world.

Since its beginnings, Bandler and Grinder have argued that NLP is not merely another model of human behavior, but rather a "meta model." That is, NLP is a model of how humans create their models of the world.

What determines whether or not something is part of NLP, then, is not its content but rather the approach to how it is studied and the form in which the resulting structures are organized.

Ultimately, regardless of what area of subjective experience is being studied, NLP breaks down the structure or process behind that experience into specific distinctions and steps involving *sensory representations* (images, sounds, felt sensations, etc.), *language patterns* and *physiology*. All core NLP distinctions and formats are built on a combination of these three aspects of our human make-up.

Clearly, in order for something to be part of "Neuro-Linguistic Programming," it must be perceived and described as something that is fundamentally *neurolinguistic*.

The *neuro* component of Neuro-Linguistics is about the nervous system. A large part of NLP has to do with understanding and using principles and patterns of the nervous system. According to NLP, thinking, remembering, imagining, decision-making, desiring, willing, arguing, and all other cognitive, emotional or behavioral processes are all the result of programs processed within the human nervous system. That is, human "experience" is a product of the information that we receive, synthesize and generate through our nervous system. Experientially, this has to do with sensing the world – seeing, feeling, hearing, smelling, and tasting.

Thus, whether the subjective experience one is studying relates to motivation, memory, the cosmos, religion, art, politics, education, etc., NLP places attention on how that part of human experience is organized in the human nervous system.

In the NLP view, *language* is clearly a product of the human nervous system. Language, however, also arouses and shapes the activity within our nervous systems. Certainly, language is one of the primary ways a person has to activate or stimulate the nervous system, his or her own nervous system or that of others. Subjective experience is both shaped and expressed through the way we use language. For something to be a part of NLP, then, it must be grounded in language patterns that show up naturally and spontaneously in human communication patterns, both verbal and non-verbal.

The *programming* aspect of Neuro-Linguistic Programming is based upon the idea that the influence of our experience on processes such as learning, memory, motivation, creativity, or any other type of performance, is a function of programs - neurolinguistic programs that function more or less effectively to accomplish particular objectives or outcomes. The implication of this is that, as human beings, we interact with our world through the inner programming within our nervous systems. We respond to problems and approach new ideas according to the type of internal programs that we have established - and not all programs are equal. Some programs are more effective than others for accomplishing certain kinds of activities.

In this sense, one of the most important aspects of NLP is its emphasis on the practical applications of the modeling process. NLP concepts and training programs emphasize interactive, experiential learning contexts so that the principles and procedures may be readily perceived and understood. Furthermore, since NLP processes are drawn from effective human models, their value and underlying structures are often intuitively recognized by people with little or no previous experience.

In summary, NLP is—as it has been since its foundation—the study of the structure of subjective experience; the "structure" being inherently *neuro-linguistic* in nature. Thus, we can say that what makes something NLP is that it:

- Emphasizes process and structure, as opposed to content

- Grounds processes and distinctions in the anatomy and functions of the human nervous system

- Ensures that distinctions and processes are able to be easily identified and influenced through natural and spontaneous patterns of verbal and non-verbal communication

- Organizes the results of the study into practical exercises, techniques, tools and practices that can be used to influence or make a difference in people's experience or behavior

Why a "New" Generation of NLP? What Does It Mean?

Why call a particular group of developments a "new generation" and not simply an enrichment of what already exists? A
truly new generation of any field includes, yet significantly
expands upon, its predecessors. A new "generation" can be
said to emerge when an expansion in the discipline:

1. Incorporates new phenomena that were not part of
   earlier generations

2. Makes it possible to address a larger scope of issues and
   experiences

3. Introduces significantly new distinctions, tools and methods

In our view, the evolution of NLP into a new generation
has come about as a result of both external and internal
influences on the field. *External influences* include the fact
that people (clients and students) have needs to be met and
problems to be solved that have not yet been adequately
addressed. In addition, the world has continued to change
and earlier solutions are no longer fully effective or satisfac-
tory. As the world has changed, the needs of the world have
also changed.

NLP has always maintained that "the map is not the
territory." It is also important to keep in mind that in many
ways "the territory is not *the territory*" because the territory
is constantly changing. What the world is calling for from
NLP in the 21st century is different than in the late 1970s
when NLP first emerged. There are new challenges, new
opportunities and a shifting focus from a more individual
orientation to one that encompasses the ecology of the entire
system or "field."

Another external influence comes from the continued evolution in other disciplines. NLP has always integrated useful
knowledge and processes from sources outside of the field. In
the thirty years since NLP began, there has also been
significant cross-fertilization of ideas and processes resulting

from new developments in other fields. Some of the most notable contributions come from:

- Stephen Gilligan – Self-Relations and Generative Self
- Gabrielle Roth – 5Rhythms® Movement Practice
- Richard Moss – Conscious Living and Transformation through Awareness
- Ken Wilber – Integral Studies
- Eugene Gendlin – Focusing
- John Welwood – The Psychology of Awakening
- Bert Hellinger – Family Constellations
- Harville Hendrix – Relational Paradigm and Imago Therapy
- Donald Epstein – Network Spinal Analysis™, Somato-Respiratory Integration™
- Rupert Sheldrake – Morphogenic Fields
- Timothy Gallwey – The Inner Game of Coaching
- Carol Pearson – Archetypal Psychology

Many next generation NLP ideas and processes have also emerged from a deeper re-examination of the contributions of individuals who served as the original models for many of the first generation NLP principles and techniques:

- Milton H. Erickson – Hypnotherapy
- Virgina Satir – Family Therapy
- Fritz Perls – Gestalt Therapy
- Gregory Bateson – Systems Theory and Systemic Therapy

NLP has also transformed as a result of *internal influences* such as the growth and evolution of the developers and practitioners within the field and through innovations introduced by new people entering the practice of NLP from increasingly diverse backgrounds. Early on, for instance,

NLP practitioners were largely psychologists and therapists. Today people from occupations as varied as coaching, management, ministry, arts and entertainment, organizational development, education and law enforcement attend NLP programs and seminars.

Another internal influence on the evolution of NLP has been through the continuing practice of *modeling*—searching for the success factors or *differences that make a difference* between poor versus average performance; average versus good performance; and good performance versus that which is consistently great. The spirit and generative engine of NLP from its beginning has been curiosity and the adventure of creating models of excellence. As NLP co-founder Richard Bandler has said, "NLP is an attitude, not the trail of techniques left in its wake." NLP co-founder John Grinder has maintained, "If you don't know how to model, then you don't really do NLP." In fact, from the inception of NLP, Bandler and Grinder have referred to themselves as "modelers." Thus, the legacy and future of NLP has always been in the process of modeling. It is the primary mechanism through which the field of NLP grows, replenishes and enriches itself.

Due to the ongoing application of the modeling process, NLP developers and practitioners have pushed and expanded the boundaries of NLP applications. NLP has always had a commitment to *the study of the structure of subjective experience.* In the beginning, that commitment was focused primarily on the environmental, behavioral and cognitive factors influencing human performance. Through time, the modeling of new phenomena has created an expansion both in the applications of NLP and in the foundations of the field itself to include other levels of factors such as beliefs, values, identity and larger system dynamics. NLP has continued to be responsive to changes in the world and in people. As long as there are new human phenomena to model, the scope of NLP will increase; and as the scope increases, new tools and models will emerge to create new generations.

What Are First and Second Generation NLP?

We consider *first generation NLP* to be the original model of NLP derived by Bandler and Grinder from their study of effective therapists. These early applications of NLP were all applied one-on-one, with the focus almost entirely on the individual. First generation NLP presupposed a therapeutic relationship in which the therapist knew what was best for his or her client. NLP was generally considered something that one "did to other people."

Most first generation tools and techniques were focused on problem solving at level of behavior and capabilities. It was primarily focused on the cognitive mind. In fact, the book *NLP Volume I* focused almost exclusively on *cognitive strategies*.

Other key distinctions and tools of the first generation of NLP include:

The Meta Model (Precision Model) language patterns
Representational Systems and the 4-Tuple
Submodalities
Eye Accessing Cues
Anchoring
Six-Step Reframing
Changing Personal History
Visual Squash
V-K Dissociation Technique
New Behavior Generator
Metaphor and the "Milton Model" of hypnotic language patterns

These are all useful and powerful distinctions, models and formats, and continue to be the bedrock and foundation for NLP.

In our view, *second generation NLP* began to emerge in the mid to late 1980s, expanding to embrace other issues beyond the therapeutic context. While still focused on individuals, second generation NLP emphasized the relationship between oneself and others and widened its scope to include such areas of application as management, negotiation, sales, education and health.

The tools of NLP also expanded to include higher-level issues, such as those related to beliefs, values and "meta programs." Second generation NLP techniques integrated the use of new distinctions such as Time Lines, Neuro-Logical Levels and Perceptual Positions.

Some of the other key distinctions and techniques that emerged from the second generation of NLP include:

Sleight of Mouth Patterns
Spatial Sorting and Psychogeography
Meta Mirror
Belief Change Procedures
Imagineering Strategy and Strategies for Genius
ReImprinting
Integration of Conflicting Beliefs
Neuro-Logical Level Alignment

Other second generation developments include Michael Hall's Meta States, Richard Bandler's Design Human Engineering, and John Grinder and Judith DeLozier's NLP New Code.

What Makes Third Generation NLP Different?

Third generation NLP has been developing since the 1990s. The applications of third generation NLP are generative, systemic and focused on high level issues such as identity, vision and mission. Third generation NLP emphasizes whole system change and can be applied to organizational and cultural development as well as to individuals, families and teams.

All generations of NLP focus on the structure and functioning of "mind" (this is the essence of "Neuro-Linguistic Programming"). The first two generations of NLP, however, placed attention primarily on the cognitive mind. Third generation NLP expands to include both somatic processes and larger system dynamics (i.e. "field") in the total "unit of mind." Thus, third generation NLP works with the interaction between three different intelligences or "minds":

1. A *cognitive mind* that emerges from the brain

2. A *somatic mind* centered in the body

3. A *"field" mind* that comes from our connection and relationships with larger systems around us

Third generation NLP aspires to develop and sustain an organic relationship of balance and alignment between these three minds* in order to produce a deeper and more multi-dimensional intelligence.

The techniques of third generation NLP have to do with centering in our somatic core, sponsoring the development of greater wholeness within people, and connecting through relationships to the wisdom and guidance within the larger systems (collective intelligence) around us. Third generation

---

* The three minds of third generation NLP correspond directly to the "triurnal mind" of Stephen Gilligan's Self-Relations work—see *Walking in Two Worlds*, 2004 and *The Hero's Journey*, 2009.

NLP techniques incorporate principles of self-organization, archetypes and what is known as "fourth position"—the felt sense of being a part of a larger system.

Some of the practices and processes of third generation NLP include:

Centering
The Inner Game and Finding Your "Inner Zone of Excellence"
Opening to the Field
Generative Change
Holding Difficult Feelings
Integrating Archetypal Energies
The Hero's Journey and Archetypes of Change
Transforming Belief Barriers by Building Belief Bridges
Techniques for Promoting Collective Intelligence and Generative Collaboration

Third generation NLP also adds other frames and values to those applied by earlier generations of NLP and places more focus on issues such as:

- Generativity & Empowerment

- Connection & Relationship

- Aesthetics & Harmony

- Purpose & Transformation

As an example, earlier generations of NLP placed a high emphasis on clarity, technique and pragmatism. Third generation NLP maintains that focus, but expands it to integrate the qualities and principles of "beauty" and "aesthetics". *Aesthetics* is a branch of philosophy that deals with the nature, creation and appreciation of beauty. Third generation NLP places importance on what is organic, pleasing and supportive of new and broader perspectives regarding ourselves, family, work, community and humanity. Beauty and aesthetics are the balance to the technical tools and skills of NLP. Together these two sides of NLP provide the impulse to pursue wisdom through promoting a greater "unit of mind," and a deeper relationship with the diverse parts of "mind." In this expansion from the purely technical aspects of NLP we naturally move to the sphere of the body, metaphor, symbol, ritual and field.

As in the emergence of any new generation, the seeds of its growth and direction are held in the legacy of the existing field or community. The spirit of third generation NLP has been implicit in the field from the beginning. The spirit showed up in the relational wisdom of Milton Erickson, in the family constellations of Virginia Satir, in the focus on the present moment of Fritz Perls, and in the use of metaphor and symbol through the years. It has also been present in the form of the "state of not knowing" at the foundation of modeling.

What Does Third Generation NLP Mean Pragmatically?

Third generation NLP applications are fundamentally *heuristic* in their approach—as NLP has been since its beginnings—in which we find solutions by "leading with experience." In fact, the term comes from the Greek word *heuriskein* meaning "to find." Heuristic methods are those that enable people to discover or learn something for themselves.

In Third Generation NLP, this is done through a sequence of six fundamental processes:

- Increasing Awareness
- Modeling Key Factors
- Calibrating the Ongoing Level of Key Factors
- Scaling Key Factors to a More Appropriate or Optimum Expression
- Anchoring Optimum Values of Key Factors
- Exploring Options Created by Adjustments in Key Factors

With respect to problem-solving, these processes are typically applied in the following sequence:

1. Bringing new *awareness* to the "neuro-linguistic programming" that is creating or contributing to some current problem state or situation. This involves becoming aware not only of the consequence of the program on emotions and behavior, but of its deeper cognitive and somatic structure.

2. Using the new awareness to create distance from both the present state and the programming. This makes it possible to begin *modeling* or identifying the key factors, or "differences that are making a difference," by comparing the programming or structure of the present state or

situation to other reference experiences of both success and failure.

3. Once the key factors that are creating or contributing to the present state or situation have been identified, the next step is *"calibrating"* the ongoing level of intensity or activity of those factors (physical, verbal, cognitive, somatic, etc.). This involves evaluating the relative magnitude of the expression of each factor.

4. *Scaling* or adjusting the ongoing magnitude of intensity or activity of the key factors in order to bring them to a more appropriate or effective level. It is important to keep in mind that the optimum level is not always the maximum level.

5. *Anchoring* a particular degree of intensity or activity of a set of key factors in order to maintain them at an optimum level, especially in changing and challenging situations.

6. *Exploring* the impact that this adjustment makes on the emotions, behavior and situation associated with the problem state in order to discover what new choices are possible.

Throughout this book you will find many examples of how this heuristic process can be applied to empower yourself and others to greatly enrich your repertoire of options in all areas of your life.

The practice of Third Generation NLP begins with a state of "not knowing" or what is known as "beginner's mind" in the tradition of Zen. The state of "not knowing" is the foundation for expanding awareness, modeling effectively and exploring new options and possibilities.

Milton Erickson's approach to problem solving is a classic example of the power of "not knowing." When we would go to Phoenix, Arizona to study with Dr. Erickson in the 1970s, we were, of course, full of questions for him. We would ask questions like, "If you use this particular approach with a person who has that particular type of issue, will it produce a certain result?" Erickson would invariably reply, "I don't know." We would ask, "Will it work to use this process to address that problem?" Again, Erickson would respond, "I don't know." We ended up with pages and pages in our notebooks saying, "He doesn't know. He doesn't know. He doesn't know."

It wasn't that he was trying to be evasive. It was that he did not operate from a lot of beliefs and assumptions. Each situation was unique to him; each person was "one of a kind" and his relationship with them was also unique. So when asked about the probability of a particular outcome, Erickson would always say, "I don't know. I really don't know." And then he would add, *"But I am very curious to discover what is possible."*

The state of not knowing combined with curiosity is the essence of generative change.

At the University of California at Santa Cruz, where NLP was initially developed by Bandler and Grinder, there was a psychology professor named Frank Baron. Baron spent his career studying creative genius. Ultimately, he synthesized what he had learned into three fundamental characteristics. Creative geniuses are:

1) comfortable with uncertainty

2) able to hold seeming opposites or paradoxes

3) persistent

Creative people, like Erickson, do not need to know the answer ahead of time. Not only are they able to tolerate uncertainty, they even enjoy not knowing.

Creative people can also hold differing viewpoints and multiple realities. The great Danish physicist Nils Bohr pointed out that there are two types of truth: superficial truth and deep truth. According to Bohr, "In a superficial truth, the opposite is false. In a deep truth, the opposite is also true." Bohr was referring to the fact that the most fundamental units of physical reality, such as photons and electrons, present a paradox. At times they behave like waves of energy and other times they behave like tiny particles of matter.

Such deep truths are also at the foundation of our subjective experience. The fact that we can experience someone as beautiful does not mean that they cannot also be simultaneously ugly. Joy does not come without sadness. The worst thing that has ever happened to you can also be the best thing that has ever happened to you. Where there is light, there are also shadows.

The capacity to be aware of these seeming opposite realities without one having to be "right" and the other "wrong" is an essential aspect of generativity. Gregory Bateson maintained, "Wisdom comes from sitting together and truthfully confronting our differences, without the intention to change anything." When we can hold different perspectives with curiosity, new and surprising solutions often emerge.

This is where the quality of *persistence* is also important. Creative geniuses don't give up, even in the face of uncertainty and dilemma. They remain curious to discover what is possible and continue searching.

Milton Erickson epitomized this quality in many ways. It was a quality he demonstrated throughout his life. When he was 17 years old, he was stricken with a severe case of polio. The illness reached the point where he was unable to move at all. He overheard the doctors telling his mother that he would never move again. Later on he overheard them telling his mother that he probably wouldn't survive until the morning. According to Erickson, he thought that was a terrible thing for anybody to say to a mother, so he began a journey to discover what was possible. He spent hours trying to see if there was any part of his body that he could move.

He finally discovered that he could slightly control the edge of one of his eyelids. And so, for the next several hours, when his mother would come by, he would try to move his eyelid to get her attention. Once he had managed this, for several more hours he struggled to work out a signal system with her. After much time and effort, he finally succeeded in communicating to her the thing that he was so determined to get across. He wanted her to turn his bed toward the window, so he could watch the sun come up the next day.

This was the same type of persistence that Erickson brought into his work with his clients. He did not give up trying to find what was possible, no matter how challenging a situation seemed. And he did not assume anything was impossible.

This combination of beginner's mind (not knowing), curiosity and persistence is at the core of the practice of Third Generation NLP. In the coming chapters we will explore how all of these abilities can make a significant difference in your own life and help you to make a difference in the lives of others.

The Structure of the Book

We have organized the book into four sections that provide a journey through all three generations of NLP.

Beginning with the *cognitive mind*, we examine the foundations of Neuro-Linguistic Programming and some of the significant developments that have occurred in the past 30 years including: Time Perception and Time Lines, Perceptual Positions, Neuro-Logical Levels and Bateson's Levels of Learning, The S.C.O.R.E. Model, Meta Program Patterns and The Unified Field Theory for NLP (The SOAR Model).

We then turn our attention to the *somatic mind*, reviewing recent research into the functioning of our nervous system beyond the brain including: Neurogastroenterology (the brain in the belly) and Neurocardiology (the brain in the heart). In this section, we present a variety of exercises for gaining access to the wisdom of the body utilizing the breath, the spine and body posture, the feet, biofeedback, somatic syntax and Gabrielle Roth's 5Rhythms®.

In the third chapter we explore the *field mind* and its neurological and physical foundations in mirror neurons and the human energy field. We provide formats and practices for utilizing field phenomena, such as creating a "Second Skin," developing "Generative Fields," encouraging Generative Collaboration and gaining access to what Gregory Bateson referred to as the "Larger Mind."

We conclude by surveying some of the innovative ways of *applying Next Generation NLP*, in particular with respect to the evolving field of coaching. We cover principles and processes relating to the "Inner Game," the Power of Presence and what we call the COACH state—an inner zone of excellence from which we are able to access and be the best of ourselves. Next Generation NLP techniques covered include: Holding Difficult Feelings, working with Belief Barriers and Belief Bridges, exploring the impact of Archetypal Energies, and integrating Archetypes of Transition.

We hope you find that these pages offer you a fertile and stimulating map of the evolving territory of Neuro-Linguistic Programming. NLP has always taught that the map is not the territory and we invite you to keep in mind that this is just one map of the territory of NLP.

Bandler and Grinder used to begin their early seminars by telling their audience that everything they were about to say was "lies." Nothing they said was the truth, because no map can accurately cover the entire territory. Thus, it was a matter of choice. The only question was whether or not they were "useful" lies. If you acted "as if" the principles and methods made a difference, what did they bring positively into your life?

We invite you to approach this book with the same attitude. If you find these maps, models and practices useful, use them! If not, perhaps they will at least point to new directions for your personal journnney and help you to become clearer about what does and does not work for you.

Our sincerest wish is that what we present here will bring you greater awareness of the richness of your experience and a fuller connection with yourself, others around you, your environment and the incredible mystery of life.

Enjoy your exploration!

Chapter 1

The Cognitive Mind

Overview of Chapter 1

- **The Brain**
  - **Hemispheres of the Brain**
  - **Sensory Representational Systems**
  - **Accessing Cues**
- **Language**
- **Five Key Developments in Neuro-Linguistic Programming Since NLP Volume I**
- **Time Perception**
  - **The Origin of the Concept of Time Lines**
  - **Expanding the Concept of "Linear" Time**
  - **William James' "String of Beads"**
  - **Time Lines as a Tool for Change**
  - **"In Time" and "Through Time"**
  - **Time Frames**
  - **Exercise: Integrating Time Frames**

Overview of Chapter 1 (Continued)

The Cognitive Mind

Our *cognitive mind* is essentially the mind within our brains. It is the source of our intellectual abilities and capacity for reason, and is one of the hallmarks of being human. The cognitive mind was the first focus of NLP and has provided the foundations for all successive generations of developments.

Cognition is defined as "the act of knowing." The term comes from the Latin *co + gnoscere*, meaning "to come to know." Cognitive science and cognitive psychology are the study of activities related to knowledge and "knowing." These activities include attention, creativity, memory, perception, problem solving, thinking and the use of language.

The origins of the study of the cognitive mind can be traced all the way back to the Greek philosopher Aristotle (385-322 BC). In his treatise *On the Psyche* (or On the Soul), in which he defines sense perception and mental representation as the distinguishing characteristics of the "psyche." Aristotle's reflections on the psyche covered a variety of cognitive issues, ranging from the definition of the five senses, to time perception, memory, language processing, imagination and problem solving. Aristotle claimed that animals built internal maps of the world by feeding information from the senses into their "common sense," or what we might call "mind." As he put it:

> *(1) No one can learn or understand anything in the absence of sense, and (2) when the mind is actively aware of anything it is necessarily aware of it along with an image . . . . To the thinking soul images serve as if they were contents of perception . . . just as if it were seeing, it calculates and deliberates what is to come by reference to what is present; and when it makes a pronouncement, as in the case of sensation it pronounces the object to be pleasant or painful, in this case it avoids or pursues.*

Aristotle's emphasis on sense perception as the basis of the psyche and his laws of association were revived by several 18th and 19th century philosophers as the basis for the study of the cognitive mind, and were finally codified as the beginnings of modern cognitive psychology in the work of William James. James' book *Principles of Psychology* (1889) covered an astonishing array of topics that are still relevant to cognitive psychologists of today, including the different functions of the brain hemispheres, representational system primacy, mental time lines, and even behavioral accessing cues.

The methods of James and other early cognitive psychologists, however, were primarily introspective and offered few practical applications. Freud's analytical psychology and Behaviorism took over as the focus of most applied psychology and psychotherapy until the late 1960's.

The appearance of psychedelic drugs in the 1960's and the rise of intelligent technologies, such as the personal computer, greatly enhanced practical interest in the influence of higher cognitive functions. The subsequent appearance of cognitively oriented therapies, information-processing analyses of intelligence tests, and cognitive theories of personality are a testament that the influence of cognitive psychology has been increasing.

The analogy between brain and computer has greatly influenced the study of the cognitive mind (and in particular NLP). According to most cognitive theories, information picked up by the senses is analyzed, stored, recoded, and subsequently used in various ways. These activities are called *information processing* and do not necessarily require consciousness to function effectively. Concepts such as "coding," "information storage and retrieval," "programming," etc., frequently appear as part of cognitive models. NLP, for instance, considers the mind to be essentially the product of a system of neurolinguistic programs operating within the brain and nervous system.

The Brain

The brain is generally considered to be the central "bio-computer" within the human nervous system, and the part of the nervous system most associated with our cognitive mind. The human brain has been estimated to contain 50-100 billion neurons. The cortex of the brain is where the higher cognitive functions like language, problem solving and imagination take place, and is regarded as the seat of the "mind" and "consciousness." It is made up of roughly ten billion complexly interconnected neurons. These cells pass signals to each other via as many as 1000 trillion synaptic connections.

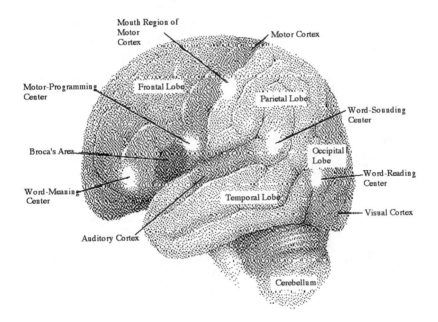

Functions of the Human Brain

The brain monitors and regulates the body's actions and reactions. It continuously receives sensory information, and rapidly analyzes this data and then responds, controlling bodily actions and functions. The brainstem controls breathing, heart rate, and other autonomic processes that are independent of conscious brain functions. The neocortex is the center of higher-order thinking, learning, and memory. The cerebellum is responsible for the body's balance, posture and the coordination of movement.

Hemispheres of the Brain

The cortex is divided into two hemispheres. For right-handed people and some left-handed people, the left hemisphere controls conscious activity in the right hand side of the body and is considered to be primarily responsible for linear kinds of processing such as logic and language. The right hemisphere controls cognitive influence of the left hand side of the body and is regarded as responsible for more simultaneous and spatial kinds of processing such as recognition and synthesis.

Different tasks require different combinations and levels of activity in the right and left hemispheres. Solving a math problem tends to require more activity in the left hemisphere. Visualizing a three-dimensional object rotating in space would probably require more activity in the right hemisphere. Creativity requires a combined contribution from both sides of the brain.

Sensory Representational Systems

The brain interacts with the outside world and the rest of the body through the senses, which function through specialized receptors and sense organs distributed throughout the head and body. The senses provide the basic information upon which we build our cognitive models of ourselves and the world around us.

In *On The Soul*, Aristotle categorized the senses into the five basic classes of sight, hearing, touch, smell and taste. Aristotle's five senses correspond directly with the five "representational systems" employed in all generations of NLP—visual, auditory, kinesthetic, olfactory and gustatory.

According to Aristotle, the five senses provide the mind with information about special features and characteristics of the outside world, such as, "white and black for sight, acute and grave for hearing, bitter and sweet for taste . . . hot cold, dry moist, hard soft, etc., for touch."

These features correspond to what NLP calls "submodalities," since they are sub-components of each of the representational systems. Submodalities are the particular perceptual qualities that may be registered by each of the five primary sensory modalities. Our visual modality, for instance, can perceive such qualities as color, brightness, shape, depth, etc.; our auditory modality is capable of registering volume, pitch, tempo, etc.; our kinesthetic system perceives such qualities as pressure, temperature, texture, etc. Both Aristotle and NLP consider these distinctions to be the fundamental building blocks of the cognitive mind. In a way, they could be considered the fundamental "machine code" of our mental programming.

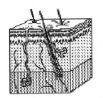

VISUAL	**AUDITORY**	**KINESTHETIC**
BRIGHTNESS	VOLUME	INTENSITY
(dim-bright)	(loud-soft)	(**strong**-weak)
SIZE	TONE	AREA
(large-small)	(**bass**-*treble*)	(large-small)
COLOR	PITCH	TEXTURE
(black & white-*color*)	(high-low)	(rough-smooth)
MOVEMENT	TEMPO	DURATION
(*fast*-slow-still)	(*fast*-slow)	(constant-intermittent)
DISTANCE	DISTANCE	TEMPERATURE
(near-far)	(close-far)	(*hot*-cold)
FOCUS	RHYTHM	WEIGHT
(clear-*fuzzy*)		(**heavy**-light)
LOCATION	LOCATION	LOCATION

Three Primary Human Sensory Modalities and Their "Submodalities"

With respect to the cognitive functions of the human cognitive mind, NLP considers the visual, auditory and kinesthetic senses to form the primary representational systems from which we build our mental models of the world. While olfactory and gustatory senses (smell and taste) play a much more significant role in other animals, they are a much less important aspect of human cognition, especially for more complex cognitive tasks.

As the term implies, a "representational system" is more than simply an information channel. It includes the entire system of processes relating to a particular sensory modality including input, processing, storage, retrieval, and output. Charles Scott Sherrington, the great English physiologist who was awarded a Nobel prize for his work in neurology, pointed out: *"The brain is always the part of the nervous system which is constructed upon and evolved upon the 'distance receptor' organs."*

The sense organ of hearing is the ear, but the vibrations received by the ear need to be relayed to the temporal area of the cerebral cortex (an area at the side of the brain, just above the ears) in order to be processed, stored and "understood" (i.e., represented). In order for words to be recognized and given meaning they need to also be connected with other sensory representations. The output channel of the auditory representational system includes the larynx and mouth.

Similarly, the sense organ of "sight" is the eye, but the visual signals received by the eye are processed and stored (or "represented") in the occipital area at the back of the cerebral cortex. Likewise, the skin and the proprioceptive receptors in the muscles are the sense organs of touch and feeling. In order to be given meaning as "emotions" and internal states, however, the messages from the body must be transmitted to the central and parietal area of the cortex near the top of the brain. The output of the kinesthetic representational system is in the gestures and movements of the body and the responses of the internal organs, such as the heart, stomach, etc.

Accessing Cues

In the same way that we must use a keyboard, mouse or modem to operate our computers, there are physical mechanisms we must use to operate our human bio-computers. In order to register information from the senses, analyze, store and recode it, and then use it in various ways, we must adjust our physiological and neurological machinery to direct our sensory information properly. We do this through subtle behaviors known as "accessing cues" in NLP. Accessing cues both trigger and reflect which representational system a person is using in order to think. Typical types of accessing cues include *eye movements, voice tone and tempo, body posture, gestures and breathing patterns.*

When people are thinking, they cue or trigger certain types of representations in a number of different ways including: breathing rate, non-verbal "grunts and groans," facial expressions, snapping their fingers, scratching their heads, and so on. Some of these are idiosyncratic to the individual and need to be "calibrated" to the particular person. Many of these cues, however, are associated with particular sensory processes.

The notion of microbehavioral "accessing cues" was first proposed by American psychologist William James in his book *Principles of Psychology* (1890). Observing that some forms of micromovement always accompany thought, James wrote:

> *In attending to either an idea or a sensation belonging to a particular sense-sphere, the movement is the adjustment of the sense-organ, felt as it occurs. I cannot think in visual terms, for example, without feeling a fluctuating play of pressures, convergences, divergences, and accommodations in my eyeballs . . . . When I try to remember or reflect, the movements in question . . . feel like a sort of withdrawal from the outer world. As far as I can detect, these feelings are due to an actual rolling outwards and upwards of the eyeballs.*

What James is describing is well known in NLP as a visual eye-accessing cue [eyes moving up and to the left or right for visualization]. James postulated that all mental processes are accompanied and directed by such types of minute physical changes. He noted that, like the processes they reflected, these physiological micro cues would form consistent patterns, independent of the content of a person's consciousness.

> *The peculiarity of the adjustments would be that they are minimal reflexes, few in number, incessantly repeated, constant amid great fluctuations in the rest of the mind's content, and entirely unimportant and uninteresting except through their uses in furthering or inhibiting the presence of various things, and actions before consciousness.*

This is probably one of the most elegant definitions ever written of what NLP means by "accessing cues." By learning to read such "reflexes", one can recognize and influence thought patterns in oneself and others. NLP has developed many techniques for practical application of accessing cues for communication and change. Some common accessing cues in NLP include:

a. **Visual:** *Head and eyes upward, gestures toward the eyes, high shallow breathing, squinting eyes, voice higher pitch and faster tempo.*

b. **Auditory:** *Head and eyes to the side, gestures toward the ears, diaphragmatic breathing, knitted brow, fluctuating voice tone and tempo.*

c. **Kinesthetic:** *Head and eyes downward, gestures toward the body, deep abdominal breathing, deep breathy voice in a slower tempo.*

Language

One of the unique characteristics of the human brain, and a major component of the human cognitive mind, is the capacity for language. In a way, we can say that language is the cement that holds our other sensory representations together.

The English word "language" comes from the Latin *lingua*, meaning "the tongue," hence denoting speech. The term has been expanded through time to include many aspects of coding and communication. Webster's Dictionary defines language as "any means of conveying or communicating ideas; specifically, human speech; the expression of ideas by the voice; sounds, expressive of thought, articulated by the organs of the throat and mouth." According to Webster's:

> *Language consists in the oral utterance of sounds which usage has made the representatives of ideas. When two or more persons customarily annex the same sounds to the same ideas, the expression of these sounds by one person communicates his ideas to another. This is the primary sense of language, the use of which is to communicate the thoughts of one person to another through the organs of hearing. Articulate sounds are represented to the eye by letters, marks, or characters, which form words.*

Thus, language is an essential aspect of both the coding and communication of our sensory experience and ideas. It is both a representation for experience and a means of communicating about it. Language is at the core of Neuro-Linguistic Programming. NLP studies the influence that language has on our cognitive programming and other functions of our nervous systems. It also studies the way in which our mental programming and nervous systems shape and are reflected in our language and language patterns.

Spoken language is a characteristic unique to the human race, and is considered to be one of the key factors that distinguish humans from other creatures. Sigmund Freud, for example, believed that words were the basic instrument of human consciousness and as such had special powers. As he put it:

> *Words and magic were in the beginning one and the same thing, and even today words retain much of their magical power. By words one of us can give another the greatest happiness or bring about utter despair; by words the teacher imparts his knowledge to the student; by words the orator sweeps his audience with him and determines its judgments and decisions. Words call forth emotions and are universally the means by which we influence our fellow-creatures.*

Freud's emphasis on the importance of language resonates with some of the key principles of Neuro-Linguistic Programming. The essence of NLP is that the functioning of our nervous system ("neuro") is intimately tied up with our capability for language ("linguistic"). The strategies ("programs") through which we organize and guide our behavior are made up of neurological and verbal patterns. In their first book, *The Structure of Magic* (1975), NLP co-founders Richard Bandler and John Grinder strove to define some principles behind the seeming "magic" of language to which Freud referred.

> *All the accomplishments of the human race, both positive and negative, have involved the use of language. We as human beings use our language in two ways. We use it first of all to represent our experience—we call this activity reasoning, thinking, fantasying, rehearsing. When we use language as a representational system, we are creating a model of our experience. This*

model of the world which we create by our representational use of language is based upon our perceptions of the world. Our perceptions are also partially determined by our model or representation. . . . Secondly, we use our language to communicate our model or representation of the world to each other. When we use language to communicate, we call it talking, discussing, writing, lecturing, singing.

Thus, according to Bandler and Grinder, language serves as a means to represent or create models of our experience as well as to communicate about it. Aristotle described the relationship between words and mental experience in the following way:

Spoken words are the symbols of mental experience and written words are the symbols of spoken words. Just as all men have not the same writing, so all men have not the same speech sounds, but the mental experiences, which these directly symbolize, are the same for all, as also are those things of which our experiences are the images.

Aristotle's claim that words "symbolize" our "mental experience" echoes the NLP notion that written and spoken words are *surface structures* that are transformations of other mental and linguistic *deep structures*. As a result, words can both reflect and shape mental experiences. This makes them a powerful tool for thought and other conscious or unconscious mental processes. By accessing the deep structure beyond the specific words used by an individual, we can identify and influence the process level mental operations reflected through that person's language patterns.

Considered in this way, language is not just an "epiphenomenon" or a set of arbitrary signs by which we communicate about our mental experience; it is a key *part of* our mental experience. As Bandler and Grinder point out:

The nervous system which is responsible for producing the representational system of language is the same nervous system by which humans produce every other model of the world—visual, kinesthetic, etc. . . . . The same principles of structure are operating in each of these systems.

Thought of in this way, we can view the structure of our language systems as parallel to the structure of our other perceptual systems. Thus, the structure and principles of language would in some way mirror the structure and principles of perception. The strategies for "forming concepts," though, would come more from the "principles of structure" (i.e., syntax or grammar) of the language than from the specific content of the vocabulary or words.

Thus, language can parallel and perhaps even substitute for the experiences and activities in our other representational systems. An important implication of this is that "talking about" something can do more than simply reflect our perceptions; it can actually create or change our perceptions. This implies a potentially deep and special role for language in the process of change and healing.

NLP begins with a conception of language as a "4-tuple." That is, words or "surface structures" (A_d) are symbols or codes for groups of stored sensory representations or "deep structures" derived from the four basic sensory channels: Visual, Auditory tonal, Kinesthetic, and Olfactory. The basic relationship of language to experience is represented as $A_d < A_t, V, K, O>$; where the verbal surface structures (A_d) both trigger and are derived from the sensory deep structure represented by $<A_t, V, K, O>$. Thus, language is an "operator" which organizes and structures other aspects of our experience.

Deep Structure
*Sensory Experience
and Patterns*
<At,V,K,O>

Ad Ad Ad
Language
Surface Structures

**Verbal "Surface Structures" Both Trigger and Are Derived
from the "Deep Structures" of Our Sensory Experiences**

This relationship gives language a special role as a "meta model"—a model of our other mental models; something which other animals do not possess. It is our ability to build meta models that allows us a special degree of choice and flexibility in relationship to our experience of the world.

NLP's focus with respect to language is more on the patterns, processes and form of language than its particular contents. That is, NLP identifies certain classes of words— e.g., nominalizations, sensory based predicates, ambiguity, embedded commands, etc.—which reflect areas of deletion, distortion and generalization in our experience and maps of the world. These types of formal patterns reflect higher level processes, such as beliefs, presuppositions and assumptions, which have a greater influence on our perception of the world than any specific contents.

NLP also stresses non-verbal aspects of language as a key element in forming and communicating our models of the world. Somatic Syntax (see Chapter 2), for example, explores how non-verbal patterns, such as movements and gestures, both shape and reflect our inner experiences and representations.

Five Key Developments in Neuro-Linguistic Programming Since NLP Volume I

To summarize what we have said so far about the cognitive mind, NLP views the human mind as primarily a product of our nervous systems. Our cognitive mind is manifested and expressed through a number of complexly interacting neural systems in the hemispheres of our cerebral cortex and other brain structures, and in the nerve structures that extend throughout our bodies, in particular, those related to the sensory representational systems. NLP views the activity within these structures, in the form of language and different levels of inner *programs,* as the primary source of human experience and intelligence. These programs form the pathway of transformations through which mental deep structures are connected with one another and with behavioral and linguistic surface structures.

Most of the original NLP techniques relied almost exclusively on working with the distinctions of representational systems, submodalities, accessing cues and language patterns, such as:

The Meta Model (and Precision Model) language patterns

Eliciting and utilizing cognitive strategies

Visual Squash

The Swish Pattern

V-K Dissociation Technique

New Behavior Generator Strategy

Metaphor and the "Milton Model" of hypnotic language patterns

Beginning from these fundamental structures and distinctions, NLP has evolved and developed many, many techniques and applications over the years since its inception; too many to review within the limitations of this book.

There have also been a number of significant new distinctions and models that have emerged in NLP over the past three decades: patterns derived from these fundamental patterns. In this chapter we will summarize and review five of these new developments that we believe are most representative and important for the new generations of NLP. They include:

- Time Perception and Time Lines
- Perceptual Positions
- NeuroLogical Levels
- The S.C.O.R.E. Model
- Meta Program Patterns

Time Perception

Time perception is an important component of our sense of reality that influences how we make plans and solve problems. It determines how we approach the constraints with which we must contend.

Our perception of time, however, is largely a cognitive construct. Our physical bodies are always in the present. While our mind can travel into the past and future, our bodies are always in the "here and now" and are primarily wired to perceive the present moment. We must continue to breathe, for example, in the present moment. The breath that we took an hour ago no longer serves to keep us alive.

The ability of our cognitive mind to travel in time can be a source of resourcefulness or suffering, depending upon our relationship with time and the quality of our awareness of that relationship. NLP has made significant explorations into the different ways in which people subjectively represent time and how it influences the way people perceive and give meaning to events (James & Woodsmall, 1987; Andreas & Andreas, 1987; Dilts, 1987, 1990; Bandler, 1988, 1993). The manner in which people represent past and future and how they order events in "time" can greatly affect their thoughts, emotions and plans.

Take a moment, for example, and notice how you subjectively perceive "time." Think of something that happened (a) yesterday, (b) last week, and (c) a year ago. How do you know that one happened a day ago and the other a year ago? How do you represent the "distance" in time between the different events?

Now, look at a clock and mark what time it is. Look away from the clock and look back again when two and a half minutes have elapsed. How do you tell that that much time has elapsed? Do you experience it in a different way than you did when you considered the relationship between the events in the previous questions?

Think of the "now." How do you know that it is "now?" How big is the "now?" When you think of "now," is it large or is it small? When you think about time, which direction is the "past" and which direction is the "future?" For example, is the past behind you, to your left, or somewhere else?

Find another person and ask him or her these same questions. Notice how similar or different his or her answers are from yours. You might be surprised at just how much you differ.

One common method of organizing our perception of time is as a time *line*, made up of points representing past, present and future in a cause-effect relationship. A second, equally important method of perceiving time is as a *frame* of time (long term, medium term, short term) representing the distance, area or relationship of different events along the time line.

The Origin of the Concept of Time Lines

One of the first people to explore the subjective aspects of time was Aristotle. In his book *Physics*, he even somewhat humorously questions the objective reality of time:

> *[T]he following considerations would make one suspect that [time] either does not exist at all or barely, and in an obscure way. One part of it has been and is not, while the other is going to be and is not yet. Yet time — both infinite time and any time you like to take — is made up of these. One would naturally suppose that what is made up of things which do not exist could have no share in reality.*

Yet, although one may question the objective existence of time, the fact remains that we structure much of our lives around time and our perception of it. The way in which one organizes and places events in time can greatly influence the effects they are perceived to have.

In attempting to understand our subjective experience of time, Aristotle maintained:

We apprehend time only when we have marked it by motion, marking it by "before" and "after"; and it is only when we have perceived "before" and "after" in motion that we say that time has elapsed. Now we mark them by judging that A and B are different, and that some third thing is intermediate to them. When we think of the extremes as different from the middle and the mind pronounces that the "nows" are two, one before and one after, it is then that we say there is time. . . . For what is bounded by the "now" is thought to be time. . . . For time is just this — number of motion in respect of "before" and "after". . . . There is a correspondence with the point; for the point also both connects and terminates the length — it is the beginning of one length and the end of another.

This perception of time as "points" on "lengths" of a line for quantifying events, such that the present, or "now," is "after" the past (A) and "before" the future (B), has been picked up and used by scientists and planners ever since. It fact, "time lines" have become the primary mode of thinking about time in Western society.

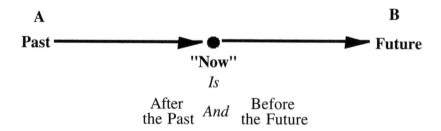

In Aristotle's View, We Perceive Time as a Point in Motion Along a Line

Expanding the Concept of "Linear" Time

Aristotle went on to maintain that linear methods of perceiving and measuring time were only one way of doing it, and were primarily of value with respect to what he called "mechanical causes." He considered the influence of time with respect to biological and mental phenomena in a different way:

> *[There is a] common saying that human affairs form a circle, and that there is a circle in all other things that have a natural movement of coming into being and passing away. This is because all other things are discriminated by time, and end and begin as though conforming to a cycle; for even time itself is thought to be a circle. . . So to say that things that come into being form a circle is to say that there is a circle of time; and to say that it is measured by circular movement.*

Aristotle suggested that time which relates to mechanical processes may be represented by the classical "time line." However, time that relates to more organic processes involving the "natural movement of coming into being and passing away" may be best represented in the form of circles and "cycles."

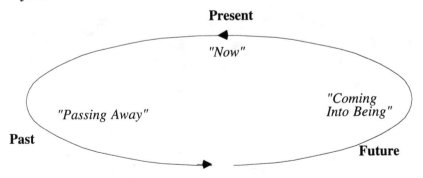

"Circular" or Cyclic Time Line

These different ways of perceiving time will tend to focus our attention in different ways and on different aspects of a situation. Viewing time in terms of cycles, for example, would lead us to perceive and measure the meaning of events in the world around us differently than perceiving it linearly.

There are some cultures, like the Balinese, whose main way of perceiving time is cyclic rather than linear. For them, time runs in overlapping cycles of 2 days, 7 days, 72 days, 72 years, etc. They determine and plan their social interactions, ceremonies, and cultural events based upon their position in one of these cycles, or the intersection of various cycles. As a result, their sense of "reality" is quite different from most Westerners.

Western time presupposes a concept of time that is linear and described in terms of discrete units, i.e., moments, seconds, hours, weeks, etc. The experience of "time" for a culture that does not conceive of the phenomenon of time in a discrete or linear way could involve perceiving "now" and "always" as occurring simultaneously. "Past" and "future" are not segments of a line that become progressively more distant from the present, but rather are frames of time which contain knowledge which informs and influences ongoing experience.

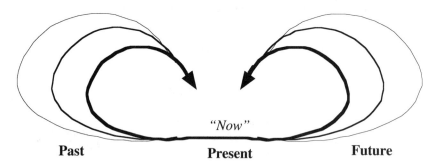

"Now"

Past   **Present**   **Future**

In Cultures Where "Time" Is Not Perceived Linearly, "Past" and "Future" Are Frames of Knowledge which Inform and Influence Ongoing Experience.

William James' "String of Beads"

In the late 1800s, the great psychologist William James tackled the perception of time in his foundational book ***Principles of Psychology*** (1890, pp. 369-420). James related the perception of time to our awareness of what he termed the "stream of consciousness." He likened "the constitution of consciousness" to "a string of bead-like sensations and images, all separate. . . ." From this perspective, our perception of time would be a function of the position of our consciousness amongst the string of beads. According to James:

> *To think a thing as "past" is to think it amongst the objects or in the direction of objects which at the present moment appear affected by this quality.*

An important feature of the analogy of the string of beads is that the string may be manipulated. It could become wrapped up or twisted so that the various beads may take on different relationships with respect to each other. By folding the string in a certain way, beads from the "past" can come in very close contact with the beads representing the "present."

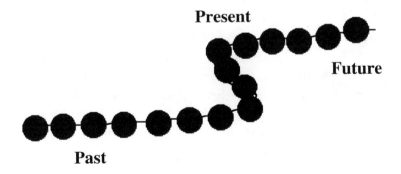

William James' Conception of Time Perception as a String of "Bead-Like" Sensations

James' comment that a key feature of time perception is "direction" is also significant, in that it brings up the issue of our involvement with our own perception of time. James claimed: "The unit of composition of our perception of time is a duration with a bow and a stern, as it were—a rearward- and forward-looking end." Perception of time, then, is like a boat on the stream of consciousness. Whatever is ahead of the "forward-looking end" is the future. What is behind the "rearward-looking end" is the past. The degree to which something fades into the distance is an indication of how far into the past or future it is. As James described it:

> *There is a sort of perspective projection of past objects upon present consciousness, similar to that of wide landscapes upon a camera-screen.*

As the notion of a "landscape" or a "stream" suggests, what James adds to Aristotle's concept of time is the ability to move or reposition oneself with respect to the perception of time. In this way, time does not have a single significance. Rather, our location and perspective with respect to our perception of time determines the relationships and signifi- cance of events.

Time Lines as a Tool for Change

The first therapeutic uses of time perception originated with Sigmund Freud. Freud incorporated people's ability to shift their perception of time as an important part of his psychoana- lytic therapy. He discovered that when people experienced psychological symptoms, they often appeared to "regress" in time and relive earlier experiences in their lives. If the patient was able to put these past events in perspective through analysis, however, and recognize their "temporal relations" to other life events, Freud noticed that the patient would often achieve significant relief from his or her symptoms.

Clearly, our perception of "time" influences the way we give meaning to an experience. Most of us have had experiences in which something seems so important at a particular moment. But when we considered it with respect to a larger time frame, wondered, "Why was I so caught up in that?"

"In Time" and "Through Time"

In the model of NLP, Freud's observations relate to two fundamental perspectives one can have with respect to the perception of time: perceiving something "in time" or "through time." The notion of the "in time" and "through time" time lines first developed in NLP in 1979 with the advent of the so-called "meta program" patterns. Perceiving an event "in time" involves taking a vantage point associated within the event that is unfolding; seeing, hearing and feeling what is happening through one's own eyes, ears and body. From this perceptual position, the "present" is one's current physical position, with the "future" represented as a line extending off in front of oneself and the past trailing behind—such that one is walking into the future and leaving the past behind. One could, however, reverse one's direction and walk back into the past. In order to relive or "regress" to an event, one would be experiencing it "in time" in this way.

Past　　　　　　　Present　　　　　　Future

"In Time" Time Line

When one perceives events "through time", one takes a vantage point that is outside of the sequence of events, disassociated from whatever is being observed. From this perspective, the time line is typically viewed such that the "past" and "future" are lines extending off to the left and right, with the "present" being somewhere in the middle (like Aristotle's point on the segment of a line). In order to describe an event and its accompanying effect and then put them in temporal relationship with one's other experiences, one would need to perceive them "through time" in this way.

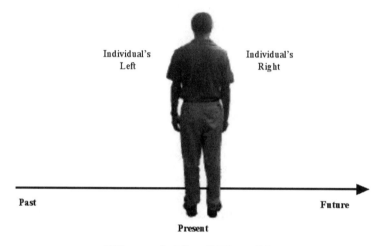

"Through Time" Time Line

The two perspectives (which may be represented either visually or through the use of actual physical space) create different perceptions of the same event. The "through time" perspective is effective for quantitative analysis, but is more passive because it is disassociated. The "in time" perspective is more active and involved but makes it easier to "lose sight of the whole."

Many mental and emotional symptoms are the result of a regression "in time," to past experiences—without having the choice of assuming the more distant "through time" observer perspective. As a result, a person unconsciously reacts in the present as he or she has done at an earlier time in his or her life. As an example, an individual who has a seemingly irrational fear of public speaking in certain circumstances, may find that there was a time when he or she was made fun of or humiliated as a child in front of a class or group of people. Even as an adult, similar circumstances may trigger associations back to the childhood situation that the person feels emotionally but is not conscious of mentally.

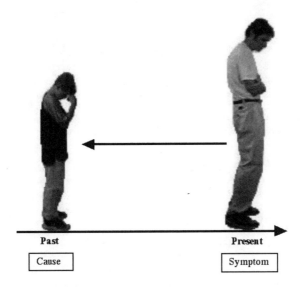

Past   Present

| Cause | | Symptom |

A Symptom in the Present Is Often a Result of a Regression "In Time" to a Past Event

Often, such feelings can be cleared up by shifting from a regressed or associated "in time" perspective to a more disassociated and broader "through time" perspective. This allows the person to understand how and why he or she is having the reaction so that it no longer seems so irrational and frightening. Frequently, this new perspective can often automatically produce a change in the individual's response, leading to what Freud termed "associative correction."

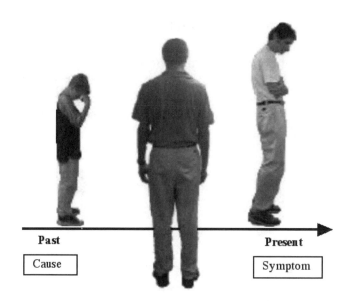

Viewing the "Temporal Relationship" of Past and Present Experiences from a "Through Time" Perspective Changes Its Emotional Effect

Many NLP methods incorporate two ways of perceiving time, using either mental or physical time lines. In Change Personal History, for example, an emotional symptom is first traced "in time" back to its originating circumstances. The experience is then viewed "through time" in order to get a broader perspective of the events. Finally, resources are brought back "in time" to the original event, creating a new perception of the event and altering its emotional effect.

Time Frames

While time lines help us to sequence events into a path, time frames often more strongly determine how events will impact us. Time frames relate more to distance than sequence. Perceiving a particular task or relationship with respect to the distant past, for instance, will give it a different meaning and perspective than perceiving it with respect to the ongoing situation, the immediate future, or the distant future. A person's assessment of the "state" of a particular relationship or task will change depending on the time frame he or she uses to evaluate it.

Setting a time frame of ten minutes for a meeting or exercise, for example, greatly influences what can be accomplished in that meeting. It determines where people will focus their attention, what topics and issues are appropriate for them to include in the interaction, and the type and degree of effort they will exert. A time frame of one hour or three hours for the same meeting or exercise would create quite different dynamics. Shorter time frames tend to focus people on tasks, while longer time frames open up the possibility for people to also focus on developing relationships. If a time limit of 15 minutes has been set for a meeting, it is more likely that the meeting will be interpreted as being task-oriented rather than as an open-ended, exploratory brainstorming session.

Like all cognitive distinctions, time frames have particular verbal, sensory and physical patterns associated with them. Verb tense is the obvious linguistic encoding of time frames. Time frames related to the *past*, for instance, are expressed in the past tense: "saw," "felt," "did," "talked," etc. Cognitively, our past is made up of particular memories, and is physiologically associated with "right brain" processes (typically characterized by eye movements and gestures to the left in right-handed people). Memories are generally "associated" multi-sensory representations of particular events.

The *present* time frame is cognitively anchored in ongoing sensory experience, and is expressed in present tense language: "I see," "feel," "do," "say," etc. Because the present tends to involve immediate sensory experience, the physiology associated with the present time frame is active and responsive to ongoing environmental stimuli (such as ongoing eye contact, adjustment of the eyes and ears in relation to environmental stimuli, etc.).

The *future* time frame is a function of imagination, expectation and fantasy. Linguistically, it is expressed using the future tense: "will see," "will feel," "will do," "will say," etc. Physiologically, fantasized and imagined future scenarios are associated with "left brain" processes (typically characterized by eye movements and gestures to the right-hand side in right-handed people). Mental constructions of the future are more frequently "disassociated" in comparison with representations related to the present or past.

The more distant that an experience is perceived with respect to the past or future, the more disassociated the internal representations and accompanying physiology will be. It is also possible for a person to "associate into" the past and relive it, or into the future and act "as if" it is happening now. In this way, both the past or future can become experienced as the "present," and the physiology and internal representations will become more associated and enriched.

Remembering longer frames of time with respect to the past allows a person to identify long-term patterns of behavior, and consequently make better predictions of actions in the present. Projecting the potential results into a longer-term future allows a person to calculate the consequences of making a particular action in the present. The longer the distance one is able to look into the past and the future, the wiser and more intelligently one is able to act.

NLP has developed an extensive technology for managing and coordinating many issues relating to the perception of time. The following exercise was developed by Robert Dilts and Todd Epstein in the early 1990s as a means to create a personal reference experience for the integration of long term and immediate time perception.

Exercise: Integrating Time Frames

1. Find a partner and stand or sit facing each other, within arms reach.

2. Look at the other person's face and experience yourself in the immediate moment (i.e., be completely aware of what you are seeing, hearing, feeling, tasting and smelling right now— in a state of uptime).

3. When you are able to experience yourself *fully present*, reach out your right hand and hold the right hand of the person in front of you.

4. Release your hand, close your eyes, take a deep breath and turn around.

5. Facing your partner again, extend your perception of time from the immediate moment to the context of this activity, to the time frame of the day, week, month, and year, to the phase of life that you are in, to your whole life, to a time frame larger than your whole life, extending into your past and future into a sense of eternity.

6. When you are able to experience a sense of time approaching *eternity* or timelessness, reach out your left hand and hold the left hand of the person in front of you.

7. Release your hand, close your eyes, take a deep breath and turn around.

8. Face your partner again. Look into each others' eyes and take a breath together at the same time, then reach out and take both of your partner's hands at the same time.

In this process, touching hands is used as a form of anchoring. Anchors for long term and immediate time perception are established and then activated simultaneously to create a neurological state in which both modes of perception may be experienced in an integrated fashion. This often creates a very profound state that many people associate with altered states of consciousness (such as hypnotic trance), and with the level of "spiritual" experience.

Spiritual experiences are very rarely encoded in terms of linear time. In fact, spiritual experiences are typically characterized by a very altered perception of time, such as having a sense of "timelessness," which is frequently the consequence of integrating our sense of "now" and "forever." This process has been adapted by Robert Dilts and Robert McDonald as one of the tools for helping people access a sense of spiritual awareness in their *Tools of the Spirit* program.

Mental and physical "time lines" have become one of the most commonly used tools of NLP in the areas of therapy, business and personal growth. Working with time perception is at the core of such NLP processes as Change Personal History, Reimprinting, Transderivational Search, Future Pacing, strategic planning and practically all of the methods for defining and managing a path from a Present State to a Desired State.

Perceptual Positions

The NLP notion of *perceptual positions* was originally formulated by John Grinder and Judith DeLozier (1987) as extensions of the earlier NLP concepts of "referential index," "meta position" and Gregory Bateson's concepts of "double" and "triple" description.

A "perceptual position" is essentially a particular perspective, or point of view from which one is perceiving a situation or relationship. NLP New Coding defined three basic positions one can take in perceiving a particular experience. *First position* involves experiencing something through our own eyes, associated in a "first person" point of view. *Second position* involves experiencing something as if we were in "another person's shoes." *Third position* involves standing back and perceiving the relationship between ourselves and others from an "observer" perspective. The notion of *fourth position* was added afterwards as a term to describe the sense of the whole system or "relational field" (a sense of a collective "we") derived from a synthesis of the other three positions.

The basis for the various perceptual positions comes from the fact that relational experiences always involve more than one individual in the communication loop. The ability to understand the communication loop, and the ebb and flow of events that occur within the loop, is a powerful tool enabling people to both improve communication and produce ecological outcomes. Even when the participants within the communication loop do not agree, their relationship is enhanced and the possibility of future cooperation is created when they are able to shift perceptual positions in relationship to the interaction. This shifting of perceptual positions is referred to as "triple description" because there are, minimally, three different perceptual positions occurring within a communication loop at any time: those of me/myself (first position), the other individual (second position), and the witnessing of the interaction between these two (third position).

One of the most useful aspects of DeLozier and Grinder's formulation is that it provides an operational process by which people can enter and experience each position, that could be connected with specific language patterns, physiology and internal representations (the three primary operators of NLP). These patterns are summarized in the following descriptions:

First position is you, standing in your own physical space, in your own habitual body posture. When fully associated in first position, you will use words like "me", "I" and "myself" when referring to your own feelings, perceptions and ideas. In first position, you are going through the experience of the communication from your own perspective: seeing, hearing, feeling, tasting and smelling everything that is going on around you and inside of you in that experience from an associated perspective. If you are truly in first position, you will not see yourself, but will be yourself, looking out at the world through your own eyes, ears, etc. You will be fully associated in your own body and map of the world.

Second position is being able to assume another person's perspective within the interaction. (If there is more than one other person in the interaction, there may be multiple "second positions"). This is a temporary, information gathering position in which you shift to another person's perceptual position, taking on his or her physical posture and world view, as though you were that person. You see, hear, feel, taste and smell what the communication loop is like from that person's point of view; i.e., "walk a mile in his or her shoes," "sit on the other side of the desk," etc. In second position, you will be experiencing the world through another person's eyes, thoughts, feelings, beliefs, etc. In this position, you will be disassociated from yourself and associated into another person. You will address your "first position" self as "you" (as opposed to "I" or "me"), using "second person" language. Temporarily assuming another person's position is a wonderful way of evaluating how effective you are on your side of the communication loop. (When you have finished stepping into another person's perspective, it is important to make sure you return to yourself fully, cleanly, and with the information that will aid you in your communication.)

Third position, or "observer" position, puts you temporarily outside of the communication loop in order to gather information, as though you were a witness to, and not a participant in, the interaction. Your posture will be symmetrical and relaxed. In this position, you will see, hear, feel, taste and smell what the communication loop is like from the position of an interested but neutral observer. You will use "third person" language, such as "she" and "he," when referring to the persons you are observing (including the one that looks, sounds and acts like you). You will be disassociated from the interaction, and in a type of "meta" position.* This position gives you valuable information about the balance of behaviors in the loop. The information gathered from this perspective can be taken back to your own first position and used, along with the information gathered in second position, to assist in enhancing the quality of your state, interaction and relationship within the communication loop.

Fourth position is a synthesis of the other three perspectives, creating the sense of "being the whole system." It involves an identification with the system or relationship itself, producing the experience of being part of a collective.

---

*Robert Dilts and Todd Epstein (1990, 1991, 1995 & 1996) suggested that there are subtle but important distinctions between third position, meta position, and observer position. They point out that a "pure" *Third Position* is typically a point of view outside of the communication loop incorporating knowledge of the beliefs and assumptions gathered from being previously associated in both first and second positions. *Meta Position* is a point of view outside of the communication loop with knowledge of the beliefs and assumptions from only one's own first position. *Observer Position* is a point of view outside of the communication loop in which the observer purposefully suspends any beliefs and assumptions about first and second positions. (Third position, of course, should also be distinguished from a "dissociated", feelingless perspective.)

In fourth position you are associated in the whole system or "field" relating to a particular interaction, experiencing the situation with the best interest of the entire system in mind. Fourth position is a "we" position, and is characterized by the use of first person plural language – "We are," "Us," etc. Fourth position is an essential component of wisdom and ecology.

Although it was not included in the original group of perceptual positions (first position – self, second position – other, third position – observer), fourth position is just as fundamental. It is essential for effective leadership, team building and the development of group spirit. As the term implies, fourth position presupposes and encompasses the other three perceptual positions. People who are not able to achieve fourth position have difficulty experiencing themselves as a member of a group or community.

The experience of fourth position comes from finding the deeper common factors and characteristics that unite and connect all of the members of a group or system. It is the foundation of what is known as "group mind." The ability to reach a fourth position perspective greatly facilitates group management and is a key characteristic of visionary leadership. Effective leaders are able to identify with the whole system they are influencing.

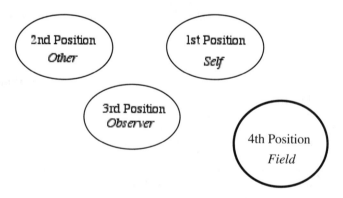

Physical Layout of Different Perceptual Positions

Basic Perceptual Positions Exercise

1. Think about a relationship that you have with someone you consider a mentor or role model.

2. Put yourself fully into your own first position by imagining that the other person is here right now and that you are looking at him or her. Describe the other person and your own personal feelings about the other person using first person language.

3. Now move to second position by putting yourself "in the other person's shoes." Assume the perspective, beliefs and assumptions of the other person as if you were that person for a moment. From the perspective of the other person describe the you that is in first position and your feelings about that person using second person language when you refer to the first position you.

4. Now move to a third location and view the relationship between yourself and the other person as if you were watching a movie of both of you interacting (third position). Keep in mind what you have experienced about the perspective, beliefs, assumptions and feelings of both yourself and the other person.

   Other variations of this perspective involve (a) focusing only on what you know about the beliefs and assumptions of only your first position perspective, or (b) viewing it as if you did not know either of the people in the "movie."

5. Move to a fourth position (either outside of or in-between the other three) and sense the "field" of this relationship as if it were its own entity. If one of you was "hydrogen" and the other "oxygen," what is the "water" that you create together?

Notice how each of these perceptual positions gives you a different appreciation of the relationship.

Practicing "Triple Description"

One way to develop a better sense for perceptual positions is through exploring "characterological adjectives." Characterological adjectives were defined by Gregory Bateson as words which encode fundamental characteristics of a relationship. An important feature of characterological adjectives is that, by defining one part of a relationship, they necessarily imply the other part of that relationship. To be "victimized," for instance, implies a perpetrator. To be "defensive" implies that there is some type of aggression.

For example, think of someone you have a difficult time communicating with, or of a situation that is not a creative or productive interaction, one which doesn't bring out the best in you and where you feel stuck in some way. Now imagine you are in a movie theater. See the person up there on the screen behaving the way they behave, and come up with a word to describe that person's behavior – a characterological adjective, a descriptor. Given all these bits of information of how this person is behaving, this is the way you would describe them. For instance, you might describe the other person as "self-absorbed" or "aggressive."

Now take a big, deep breath and see yourself up there on the movie screen in the loop with this person. Now you are in third position, watching and listening as a neutral observer. Observe the way you behave. What are the words you would use to describe your behavior? For example, when the other person is "self-absorbed," you may become "withdrawn." Or, if the other person is "aggressive," you may become "defensive."

You begin to see your part in the dance. They wouldn't have any fun doing it by themselves, and neither would you. This is what systems are about: getting a big enough piece of the interaction so that you can step back and say, "Oh, now I understand how I'm dancing with this person," and realize what choices you have of changing the dance. From this position you can ask, "When I step back into the relationship with this new perspective, how can that information make a difference to the quality of that interaction?" If one part of the system begins to move, the whole system is going to move.

Another way of experiencing multiple perceptual positions, or "triple description," that can be both fun and interesting, is in terms of creativity. Think of a piece of art that has really moved you in your life. It isn't just something you look at and say, "Oh, that's nice." Rather it is a piece of art that you feel deep inside your soul. This is being in the position of appreciating that art from the perceptual position of the viewer. You can also do this with respect to hearing a piece of music, or watching a dance.

Now take the position of the artist who created it. Going to second position is a way in which we can start to stimulate that neurology within ourselves. When you occupy that perceptual position, begin to use the implicit muscle movements of the painter, the sculptor, or the composer in order to access similar kinds of neurology in yourself. It is there, it is just that you haven't activated it in yourself in a long time. Then you can stand back an ask, "What are the differences between being a perceiver of this art and being the creator?" Do you have different beliefs when you are in each of the two positions? Do you have different beliefs about your ability to be creative when you are in the artist position versus the viewer position?

A third perceptual position would be to become the art itself. Most people report that, when they become the artwork, they have a deep sense of just "being."

Perceptual positions trigger a whole set of other possibilities. The idea of triple description is that out of this dance of multiple perspectives, wisdom may begin to unfold. To really consider the movement from my personal map to an understanding of your personal map, and then to an objective position of the relationship, gives us a basis of wisdom. The ability to move to each of these positions cleanly and quickly can be a powerful tool.

Meta Mapping with Perceptual Positions

The purpose of Meta Mapping is to assist a person to identify and then alter characteristics of the communication loops that are producing or maintaining a problematic interaction. Often, when we experience difficulties in communicating with others, we become entrenched in our own point of view. The Meta Map begins by acknowledging that perspective, but then provides us with the opportunity to see the interaction from other points of view. In addition to identifying "invisible" (i.e., internal and non-physical) influences on the situation, the Meta Map allows us to see and modify some of the ways in which we may be contributing to our own difficulties.

The basic steps of the Meta Map include: (a) identifying a difficult or challenging communication situation; (b) mapping the dynamics occurring between oneself, the other person in the interaction, and one's inner observer; (c) taking the perspective of the other person, and viewing the situation from his or her point of view; (d) establishing a "meta position" from which to examine both mental and physical patterns occurring within the interaction that may be contributing to the problem; and (e) exploring possible changes in communication, attitude or assumptions that could make the interaction more comfortable and productive.

In addition to providing a useful strategy for reflecting on or preparing for a difficult meeting or interaction, the Meta Map can be used as a coaching or consulting technique. A number of the specific steps of the Meta Map were derived from the modeling of effective leaders in companies and organizations. As part of the modeling process, leaders would be placed in challenging, and largely unpredictable, interactive situations. Leaders were then questioned about how they prepared themselves mentally to meet the challenges. A common response was:

> *I would think about the people involved in the situation, and imagine the possible actions they could take that would create problems. I would then look at myself*

and try to see what I could do in response, and whether I felt comfortable with that. I also tried to see the situation from the other person's perspective, and get a sense of what motives might be behind their actions. I would then view the situation from the company's perspective to see what was going to be the best way to handle the situation for all concerned. Having done my "homework," I would finally think about what internal state I wanted to be in, and what state would help me respond most creatively and appropriately. I figured that if I was in the wrong state, I wouldn't be able to respond well no matter what happened; but if I was in the right state, the inspiration would be there, even if something happened that I hadn't prepared for.

Meta Map Exercise

The following is a variation of the Meta Map, based on the strategies of effective leaders, that can be applied as a strategy for reflecting on, or planning for, a challenging leadership situation.

1. Think about a challenging situation you have been in, or are expecting to be in, involving a particular collaborator.

2. Put yourself fully into first position by imagining that your collaborator is here right now and that you are looking at him or her through your own eyes.

3. Now imagine you are "in the shoes" of your collaborator looking at yourself through his or her eyes. Assume the perspective, beliefs and assumptions of the collaborator as if you were that person for a moment.

4. Now view the relationship between yourself and your collaborator as if you were an observer watching a video of some other leader interacting with a collaborator. Notice

the types of messages and meta messages the individuals are sending back and forth to one another (either intentionally or unintentionally).

5. As a final experiment, take the perspective of the whole system and consider what would be in the best interest of the system.

6. Return to your own first position perspective. Notice how taking the different perceptual positions changes your experience of the interaction. What new awareness did you get about yourself, your collaborator or the situation? Which leadership actions and qualities would be most appropriate for you to take on in this situation? What internal state and attitude would best help you to express these leadership actions and qualities?

Since their development, Perceptual Positions have been incorporated as a major part of many NLP techniques. The ability to take multiple perspectives is an essential skill for leadership, teaching, therapy and wisdom. Reimprinting, Meta Mirror, Meta Map, Aligning Perceptual Positions (from Connirae Andreas' Core Transformation work), and the various NLP techniques used for Conflict Integration, Mediation and Negotiation, all use Perceptual Positions as a primary modality of producing change and achieving desired outcomes.

Levels of Change and Interaction

Another very important development in NLP in the past 30 years has been that of different *levels* of change and interaction. The notion of *levels of change and interaction* in NLP refers to the fact that some processes and phenomena are created by the *relationships* and interactions between other processes and phenomena. Any system of activity is a subsystem embedded inside of another system, which is embedded inside of another system, and so on. This kind of relationship between systems produces different levels of processes. Our brain structure, language, and social systems form natural hierarchies or levels of processes.

For example, the "profitability" of a company is at a different level than the machinery used by that company or the services it delivers. The rules governing profitability are different than those for running the machinery or delivering the services, yet they all function together to make up a single system of the business.

As another example, an idea is at a different level than the neurons in the brain that produce that idea. Similarly, the language used to express an idea is a different level of process than the idea itself. The rules governing how ideas interact are of a different order than those that determine how neurons fire or the rules governing how words fit together to express ideas. They are all, however, key parts of the system of the human mind, which would not exist without their being together.

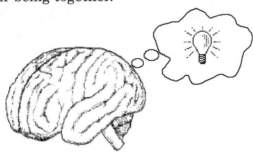

An Idea Is at a Different Level than the Particular Neurons in the Brain that Produce that Idea

The NLP idea of levels of change and interaction, known as Neuro-Logical Levels, refers to a hierarchy of levels of processes influencing the actions and interactions of an individual or group. These levels include (in order from highest to lowest): (1) identity, (2) beliefs and values, (3) capabilities, (4) behavior and (5) environment. A sixth level, referred to as "spiritual," can be defined as a type of "relational field" which encompasses multiple identities, forming a sense of being a member of a larger system beyond one's individual identity.

Bateson's Hierarchy of Logical Types and Levels of Learning

The NLP model of Neuro-Logical Levels was inspired by Gregory Bateson's ideas of hierarchies of logical types and levels of learning. Bateson pointed out that in the processes of learning, change and communication there are natural *hierarchies* of classification of information and knowledge. The function of each level in the hierarchy was to organize the information on the level below it, and the rules for changing something on one level of the hierarchy were different from those for changing at a different level. Changing something on a lower level could, but would not necessarily, affect the upper levels; but changing something in the upper levels would necessarily impact things on the lower levels in order to support the higher level change.

The notion of "hierarchy" originally entered the English language in 14th century as a religious term essentially meaning "a rank or order of holy beings," such as the "division of angels." It later became used to describe "a ruling body of clergy organized into orders or ranks, each subordinate to the one above it." The term comes from the Greek *hieros*, meaning "powerful, supernatural, or sacred," and *arche*, which means "beginning." The implication is that the levels of a hierarchy get closer and closer to the source or beginning of that which is sacred or powerful. This implication has also led to the use of the term "hierarchy" to refer to any graded or ranked series, such as a person's "hierarchy of values," or a machine's "hierarchy of responses." The connotation of this is that those elements at the top of the hierarchy "come first," or are "more important" than those at the lower levels.

The modern use of "hierarchy" involves more than an arbitrary rank ordering of elements. In science and mathematics, for instance, *hierarchy* is used to denote "a series of ordered groupings of people or things within a system." Usually these groupings have "few things, or one thing, at the top and with several things below each other thing," like an inverted tree structure. Examples from computer science include a directory hierarchy, where each directory may contain files or other directories, a hierarchical network, or a class hierarchy in object-oriented programming.

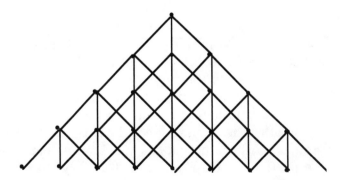

Hierarchies Are Often Represented as "Tree Structures"

Russell's Logical Types

Bateson derived the notion of different hierarchies of *classification* of communication and learning from Bertrand Russell's mathematical theory of logical types—which he called the "most important" criterion of "mind" in his book *Mind and Nature* (1979). The theory of *logical types* states that a class of things cannot be a member of itself. According to Bateson (*Steps to an Ecology of Mind*, p.202):

> *Our approach is based on that part of communications theory which [Bertrand] Russell has called the Theory of Logical Types. The central thesis of this theory is that there is a discontinuity between a class and its members. The class cannot be a member of itself nor can one of the members be the class, since the term used for the class is of a different level of abstraction — a different Logical Type — from terms used for members.*

As an example, the *class* of even numbers cannot itself also be an *even number*. Similarly, the *class* of cats is not a particular cat. Likewise the physical object "cat" cannot be treated the same as the class of cats. (The class of cats does not require milk and kitty litter, but the members of the class frequently do.) Even the name "The class of all words," while it is made up of words, is clearly not the class of all words. To put it another way, the notion of logical types distinguishes between a particular "map" and the "territory" to which the map relates; i.e., between a mental "form" and its "content."

Bateson first formally introduced the concept of "logical types" in his article *A Theory of Play and Fantasy* (1954). In it, Bateson argued that "play" involved distinguishing between different *logical types* of behavior and messages. Bateson noted that when animals and humans engage in "play" they often display the same behaviors that are also associated with aggression, sexuality, and other more "serious" aspects of life (such as when animals "play fight," or children play "doctor"). Yet, somehow, animals and humans are able to recognize, for the most part, that the play behavior is a different type or class of behavior and "not the real thing." According to Bateson, distinguishing between classes of behavior also required different types of messages. Bateson referred to these messages as "meta messages"— messages *about* other messages—claiming that they, too, were of a different "logical type" than the content of a particular communication. He believed that these "higher level" messages (which were usually communicated non-verbally) were crucial for people, and animals, to be able to communicate and interact effectively.

Animals at play, for instance, may signal the message "This is play" by wagging their tails, relaxing their bodies, jumping up and down, or doing some other thing to indicate that what they are about to do is not to be taken for real. Their bite is a playful bite, not a real bite. Studies of humans also reveal the use of special messages that let others know they are playing, in much the same way animals do. They may actually verbally "meta-communicate" by announcing that "This is only a game," or they laugh, wink, nudge, use a different tone of voice, or do something odd to show their intent.

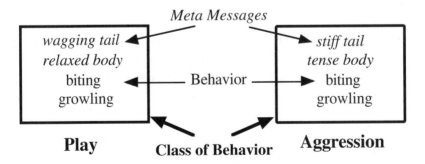

The same behavior (growling) may be a member of two different classifications (play or aggression). Other behaviors serve as meta messages to show to which category a particular behavioral expression belongs.

Bateson claimed that many problems and conflicts were a result of the confusion or misinterpretation of these meta messages. A good example is the difficulties that people from different cultures experience in interpreting the non-verbal subtleties of each other's communications.

In fact, Bateson next applied the concept of logical types as an explanation for some of the symptoms of serious psychological problems and mental illness. In *Epidemiology of Schizophrenia* (1955), Bateson maintained that the inability to correctly recognize and interpret meta messages, and to distinguish between different classes, or logical types, of behavior, was at the root of many seemingly psychotic or "crazy" behaviors. Bateson cited the example of a young mental patient who went into the pharmacy of the hospital. The nurse behind the counter asked, "Can I help you?" The patient was unable to distinguish whether the communication was a threat, a sexual advance, an admonishment for being in the wrong place, a genuine inquiry, etc.

When one is unable to make such distinctions, Bateson contended, that individual will end up, more often than not, acting in a way that is inappropriate for the situation. He likened it to a telephone switching system that was unable to distinguish the "country code" from the "area code" and the local telephone number. As a result, the switching system would inappropriately assign numbers belonging to the country code as part of the phone number, or parts of the phone number as the city code, etc. The consequence of this would be that, again more often than not, the dialer would get the "wrong number." Even though all of the numbers (the content) are correct, the classification of the numbers (the form) is confused, creating problems.

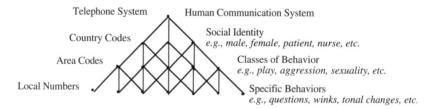

Bateson likened hierarchies of logical typing in human communication to different classifications of numbers in a telephone switching system.

Korzybski's Order of Abstractions

Bateson's classification of logical types was also partially influenced by General Semantics founder Alfred Korzybski who emphasized the importance of differentiating between various "orders of abstraction." These include differences between what we see (our internal representations) and the external stimuli themselves, and between verbal maps and the inner representations they intend to depict. Inner representations are more abstract, but more encompassing, than the external reality they represent. Similarly, verbal descriptions are more abstract, and potentially more encompassing, than the inner representations they stand for.

According to Korzybski, differentiating orders of abstraction also included distinguishing between (a) descriptions of experiences and (b) inferences (conclusions drawn from our experiences and our descriptions of those experiences); and between descriptions *about* descriptions, inferences based upon other inferences, affect about affect (feelings about other feelings), and between one person's abstractions and another person's abstractions, etc.

Bateson combined the notion of "orders of abstraction" with that of hierarchy of classification to identify several different levels of learning and change in animals and humans—each level synthesizing and integrating processes on the level below it, and consequently having a greater degree of impact on the individual. In *The Logical Categories of Learning and Communication* (1964) he extended the notion of logical typing to explain different types and phenomena of learning as well as communication. He defined two fundamental types, or levels, of learning which must be considered in all processes of change: "Learning I" (stimulus-response type conditioning) and "Learning II", or *deutero learning* (learning to recognize the larger context in which the stimulus is occurring so that its meaning may be correctly interpreted). The most basic example of Learning II phenomena is set learning, or when an animal becomes "test-wise"—that is, laboratory animals will get faster and faster at learning new tasks that fall into the same class of activity. This has to do with learning *classes* of behavior rather than single isolated behaviors.

An animal trained in avoidance conditioning, for instance, will be able to learn different types of avoidance behavior more and more rapidly. It will, however, be slower at learning some "respondently" conditioned behavior (e.g., salivating at the sound of a bell) than some animal that has been conditioned in that class of behavior earlier. That is, it will learn quickly how to identify and stay away from objects that might have an electric shock associated with them but will be slower at learning to salivate when a bell rings. On the other hand, an animal trained in Pavlovian type conditioning will rapidly learn to salivate to new sounds and colors, etc., but will be slower to learn to avoid electrified objects.

Bateson pointed out that this ability to learn patterns or rules of a class of conditioning procedures was a different "logical type" of learning and did not function according to the same simple stimulus-response-reinforcement sequences used to learn specific isolated behaviors. It was a different "order of abstraction." Bateson noted, for instance, that the reinforcement for "exploration" (a means of learning-to-learn) in rats is of a different nature than that for the "testing" of a particular object (the learning content of exploration). He reports (*Steps to an Ecology of Mind* p. 282):

> . . . *you can reinforce a rat (positively or negatively) when he investigates a particular strange object, and he will appropriately learn to approach it or avoid it. But the very purpose of exploration is to get information about which objects should be approached or avoided. The discovery that a given object is dangerous is therefore a success in the business of getting information. The success will not discourage the rat from future exploration of other strange objects.*

The whole purpose of exploring strange objects is to discover whether or not they are dangerous. So, getting punished for approaching a particular strange object does not stop the rat from exploring other strange objects to discover if they are safe to approach.

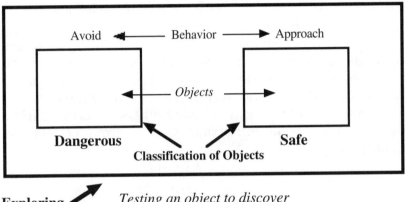

Exploring ➔ *Testing an object to discover if it is dangerous or safe*

According to Bateson, exploring an object to discover whether or not it is safe is a different level of learning than avoiding objects that have been discovered to be dangerous or approaching those that have been discovered to be safe.

"Exploring" an object to discover if it is dangerous or safe and to be avoided or approached, then, is a different order of abstraction and at a different hierarchy of classification of learning than avoiding an object that has been discovered to be unsafe. The ability to explore, learn a discrimination task, or be creative is a higher level of learning than the specific behaviors that make up these abilities—and the dynamics and rules of change are different on this higher level.

As another example, our ability to generalize what we have learned functions in a different way than primary learning. Consider the experience of learning to write. Most readers probably learned to write using one of their hands to laboriously master the specific finger, hand and arm movements necessary to form the individual letters on a piece of paper. Once mastered, however, this basic pattern can be transferred much more quickly to other parts of the body and different environmental contexts. For instance, each of us could probably easily make a recognizable letter "A" by tracing it in sand with our big toe. We can probably even use one of our elbows to outline the same letter on a wall or take a pencil in our teeth and create a recognizable facsimile of the letter on a piece of canvas.

What is impressive is that the particular groups and relationships of bones and muscles we use to move our feet, toes, elbows and neck are quite different than those in our hands and fingers, yet we can transfer what we have learned using one part of the body to many others. This is clearly a different level of learning than that of stimulus-response conditioning.

Levels of Learning

Applying the theory of logical types and the notion of different orders of abstraction, Bateson (*Steps to an Ecology of Mind* p. 293) identified a number of levels of learning—each responsible for making corrective changes and refinements in the lower level of learning upon which it operated.

Zero learning is characterized by specificity of response [i.e., having a specific behavior in a specific environment— RD] which—right or wrong—is not subject to correction.

Learning I is change in specificity of response by correction of errors of choice within a set of alternatives.

Learning II is a change in the process of Learning I, e.g., a corrective change in the set of alternatives from which choice is made, or it is a change in how the sequence is punctuated.

Learning III is change in the process of Learning II, e.g., a corrective change in the system of sets of alternatives from which choice is made.

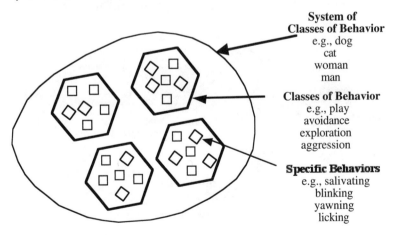

Different Levels of Learning Relate to Changes in Different Classifications of Behavior

Using Bateson's earlier analogy of a telephone system, *learning 0* would be like an autodial that always dials the same number whether it successfully reaches the right person or not. *Learning I* would be a corrective change in the local number (altering the expression of specific behaviors). *Learning II* would be a corrective change in the area code (shifting the classification of objects or behaviors—from "safe" and "playful" to "dangerous" and "protective," for example). *Learning III* would be a corrective change in the country code (the larger system of classification).

Beyond these three levels, Bateson also hinted at the possibility of a *Learning IV*—a level of learning that he believed was not possible to achieve by any individual member of a species, but only collectively as a group or species as a whole. Learning IV would involve the establishment of completely new behaviors that do not fit <u>any</u> current system of classes of behavior. Learning IV would be a truly revolutionary type of learning that would involve the creation of whole new archetypes or systems of behavior.

When our ancestors stood up on two feet and spoke the first words, they were not selecting from some existing set of alternatives, nor were they modeling some other species or creature that already existed. They began something completely new that revolutionized our role on the planet.

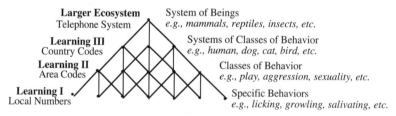

Learning 0 - No adjustment
Learning I - Appropriately adjust local number
Learning II - Appropriately adjust area code
Learning III - Appropriately adjust country code
Learning IV - Creating a new system of telephone numbers

An analogy for Bateson's levels of learning would be making adjustments to different parts of a telephone number in order to successfully reach the desired person.

As an example of how these different levels might work, consider the situation of Pavlov and his dogs. Pavlov discovered that he could condition his dogs to salivate at the sound of a bell by repeatedly ringing the bell when he fed them. The dogs learned to associate the sound of the bell with receiving food. Pretty soon, all Pavlov needed to do was ring the bell and, even if he had no food, the dogs would begin to salivate, triggered by the sound alone.

According to Bateson's levels of learning model, the dogs' initial act of salivating when given food is a case of *Learning Zero*. It is a preprogrammed, instinctual response that is inherited and which would be difficult, if not impossible, to extinguish.

Learning to extend the reaction of salivation from the sight and smell of the food to the sound of the bell is an example of *Learning I*. Through repetition and reinforcement, the dog is learning to associate the specific response of salivating (as opposed to other responses, such as yawning, licking, blinking, etc.) with the specific stimulus of a particular bell.

Learning II would involve a "change in the *set* of alternatives from which choice is made." This would mean that, once a dog had learned to salivate at the sound of a bell, it would have to change that response to something completely different (like barking or running away) when it heard the bell (as opposed to simply increasing or decreasing the amount of salivation). Salivating is a member of a set of "eating" behaviors. Other "sets" of alternatives would be "play," "avoidance," "exploration," "aggression," etc. Making a shift at this level would obviously be more complex than Learning I.

Learning III would be an even bigger change. Bateson says it would be a "change in the system of sets of alternatives from which choice is made." A dog, for instance, is one "system" of sets of alternatives. Other animals (cats, birds, humans, wolves, etc.) would constitute different systems. To accomplish Learning III, Pavlov's dogs would have to suddenly shift from "dog-like" behaviors to "cat-like" behaviors (meowing, climbing trees, etc.) when the bell rang. This would clearly be quite challenging and, as Bateson pointed out, is practically impossible for adults of most species (although imitating other animals like dogs, cats and birds is a natural and normal pastime for human children).

Learning IV would involve the development of a new species, or a significant evolution within an existing species (like growing wings, evolving a bigger brain, etc.). Such a change would make completely new and unprecedented behaviors suddenly possible.

Thus, in Bateson's framework, a simple, mechanical reflex would be a case of "zero learning." *Learning Zero* processes could also include habits, addictions and other patterns that seem fixed and unchangeable. Learning Zero is a common state of affairs for many people and organizations. Many of our behaviors become unconscious and embedded habits that make it difficult to adapt and adjust effectively to changes in the world around us. This frequently leads to stuckness, resistance, complacency and inefficiency.

Behavioral conditioning, psychomotor learning, process reengineering or incremental quality improvement would be operations relating to "corrective changes" with respect to particular behaviors and actions in people and organizations—*Learning I*. Learning I is essentially about behavioral flexibility; updating and improving the procedures and patterns of behavior that are already in place. Learning I is best facilitated by helping people to develop better "metacognition," the awareness of one's actions, internal experience and thinking processes. This is done by providing basic coaching and teaching techniques such as contrastive analysis and providing feedback.

Changing higher level processes like policies, values and priorities would relate to operations that address entire sets of alternatives—*Learning II*. If a company, for instance, decides to shift to being more "service oriented" than "product oriented," it will require large-scale changes across whole areas of procedures and behaviors, and this will probably imply the establishment of new sets of behaviors and procedures modeled from others.

Another example of change at the level of Learning II in an individual would be an abrupt switch from exploratory behavior to avoidance, or from aggression to exploration or play. To accomplish such an immediate and dramatic turnaround requires shifts in beliefs and values. If one believes that a certain context is "dangerous," for instance, he or she will more than likely select "avoidance" behaviors rather than those in the class of "play." On the other hand, if a person believes that a context is "safe," he or she is not likely to choose behaviors from the classes of "fight" or "flight."

A good illustration of this is the rapid drop off in the number of people choosing to travel in airplanes after the September 11, 2001 hijackings. It was not a gradual change brought about by higher airfares or poorer service (which would have been an instance of Learning I). Rather, it was an immediate and intense shift brought on by the belief that it was not longer "safe" to fly. Clearly, the effects of Learning II are more immediate and far reaching than Learning I.

With respect to humans, Learning II shifts are supported by the ability to take "meta position"— that is, to disassociate from oneself and consider one's actions in context, and in comparison to other "sets of alternatives." This is one of the main goals of mentoring.

"Imprinting" and personality development would relate more to the establishment of change in whole "systems" of alternative behaviors—*Learning III*. Shifting such "systems" essentially involves a change at the level of identity. It involves expanding our range of behavior to include possibilities outside of our current role or collection of "sets" of alternatives. The Internet and the "new economy," for instance, forced many companies to stretch into completely new management and marketing approaches, sometimes far beyond what they were used to or comfortable with.

Modeling, benchmarking and taking "second position" with others are ways to support the process of Learning III. They facilitate us to reach beyond the threshold and limits of our current sense of self and identity. As Bateson

maintained, "To the degree that man achieves Learning III
. . . his 'self' will take on a sort of irrelevance." Bateson
asserted that change at the level of Learning III was quite
difficult, and that "to demand this level of performance in
some men and some mammals is sometimes pathogenic."

Acts of genius frequently have the characteristics of *Learning IV*—unprecedented and transformative—leading to revolutions in the way we understand and interact with the
world around us. In the Silicon Valley world of technology
entrepreneurs, people often distinguish between "evolutionary" and "revolutionary" technologies. Evolutionary technologies are those which make a significant improvement on
what already exists, extending its functionality or characteristics in some important way or integrating it with other
technologies. Revolutionary technologies are those which
change or create a new industry and transform the way that
people work or communicate. Things like the printing press,
automobile, airplane, radio, television, personal computer,
the Internet could be considered revolutionary technologies.

As Bateson suggests, the insights and awakenings that
constitute Learning IV most likely come in the form of some
type of inspiration or revelation that has its source beyond
the individual and in the larger system or "field" surrounding
us—what Bateson referred to as the "larger Mind" or "pattern which connects."

Access to Learning IV requires a strong connection with
our unconscious mind and derives from states of "not knowing," "uptime," "active dreaming," which involve being centered and open to all possibilities, without making any
judgments or interpretations. These special states give us
the experience of being able to unconsciously tap into the
possibilities present in the larger "field" or "Mind" around us.
(See the chapter on Field Mind.)

We can summarize Bateson's levels of learning in the
following manner:

- **Learning 0** is *no change*. It involves repetitive behaviors in which the individual, group or organization is stuck in a rut or trapped "inside the box"—e.g., habits, resistance, inertia.

- **Learning I** is gradual, *incremental change*. It involves making corrections and adaptations through behavioral flexibility and stretching. While these modifications may help to extend the capabilities of the individual group or organization, they are still "within the box"—e.g., establishing and refining new procedures and capabilities.

- **Learning II** is rapid, *discontinuous change*. It involves the instantaneous shift of a response to an entirely different category or class of behavior. It is essentially the switch from one type of "box" to another—e.g., change in policies, values or priorities.

- **Learning III** is *evolutionary change*. It is characterized by significant alterations that stretch beyond the boundaries of the current identity of the individual, group or organization. We could say that not only are they outside the "box," they are outside of the "building"—e.g., transition of role, brand or identity.

- **Learning IV** is *revolutionary change*. It involves awakening to something completely new, unique and transformative. At the level of Leaning IV, the individual, group or organization is out of the box, out of the building and in a new world—e.g., completely new responses, technologies or capabilities that open the door to previously unknown and uncharted possibilities.

To use a computer analogy, data stored in a computer is like Learning 0. It just sits there, unchanging, to be used over and over again, whatever programs are running on the computer. Running a spell check program on that data would be like Learning I. A spell check program makes corrective changes in a particular set of data.

If the data being checked, however, is not text but numbers and financial figures that need to be updated, no amount of running the spell checker will be able to make the proper corrections. Instead, the user would have to switch to a spreadsheet or some type of accounting software. Getting "out of the box" of one program and switching to another is like Learning II.

Sometimes the computer one is using is incapable of running the needed program and it is necessary to switch computers altogether, or change operating systems. This would be like Learning III.

To develop a completely new device, such as a programmable molecular computing machine composed of enzymes and DNA molecules instead of silicon microchips, would be like Learning IV.

The Neuro-Logical Levels Model of NLP

The NLP *Neuro-Logical Levels* model (Dilts, 1989, 1990, 1993, 2000, 2003), is an adaptation of Bateson's theory. According to the model, there are a number of different levels, paralleling those defined by Bateson, that influence and shape our relationships and interactions in the world:

Spiritual   Vision & Purpose   *For Whom? For What?*

A. Who I **A**m - *Identity*   Mission   *Who?*

B. My **B**elief system - *Values and Meanings*
           Permission & Motivation   *Why?*

C. My **C**apabilities - *Strategies and States*
           Maps & Plans   *How?*

D. What I **D**o or have **D**one - *Specific Behaviors*
           Actions & Reactions   *What?*

E. My **E**nvironment - *External Context*
           Constraints & Opportunities   *Where? When?*

The most fundamental level of influence on our relationships and interactions is the shared *environment* —i.e., *when* and *where* the operations and relationships within a system or organization take place. Environmental factors determine the context and constraints under which people operate. An organization's environment, for instance, is made up of such things as the geographical locations of its operations, the buildings and facilities which define the "work place," office and factory design, etc. In addition to the influence these environmental factors may have on people within the organization, one can also examine the influence and impact that people within an organization have upon their environment, and what products or creations they bring to the environment.

At another level, we can examine the specific *behaviors* and actions of a group or individual—i.e., *what* the person or organization does within the environment. What are the particular patterns of work, interaction or communication? On an organizational level, behaviors may be defined in terms of general procedures. On the individual level, behaviors take the form of specific work routines, working habits or job related activities.

Another level of process involves the strategies, skills and *capabilities* by which the organization or individual selects and directs actions within their environment—i.e., *how* they generate and guide their behaviors within a particular context. For an individual, capabilities include cognitive strategies and skills such as learning, memory, decision-making and creativity, which facilitate the performance of a particular behavior or task. On an organizational level, capabilities relate to the infrastructures available to support communication, innovation, planning and decision-making between members of the organization.

These other levels of process are shaped by *values and beliefs,* which provide the motivation and guidelines behind the strategies and capabilities used to accomplish behavioral outcomes in the environment—i.e., *why* people do things the way they do them in a particular time and place. Our values and beliefs provide the reinforcement (*motivation* and *permission*) that supports or inhibits particular capabilities and behaviors. Values and beliefs determine how events are given meaning, and are at the core of judgment and culture.

Values and beliefs support the individual's or organization's sense of *identity*—i.e., the *who* behind the why, how, what, where and when. Identity level processes involve people's sense of role and mission with respect to their vision and the larger systems of which they are members. Identity can be viewed as being composed of two complementary aspects: the ego and the soul. The *ego* is oriented toward survival, recognition and ambition. The *soul* is oriented toward purpose, contribution and mission. Charisma, passion and presence emerge naturally when these two forces are aligned.

Typically, a mission is defined in terms of the service performed by people in a particular role with respect to others within a larger system. A particular identity or role is expressed in terms of several key values and beliefs, which determine the priorities to be followed by individuals within the role. These, in turn, are supported by a larger range of skills and capabilities that are required to manifest particular values and beliefs. Effective capabilities produce an even wider set of specific behaviors and actions, which express and adapt values with respect to many particular environmental contexts and conditions.

There is another level that can best be referred to as a *spiritual* level. This level has to do with people's perceptions of the larger systems to which they belong and within which they participate—we could call this level one of "trans-mission." These perceptions relate to a person's sense of *for whom* or *for what* their actions are directed, providing a sense of vision, meaning and purpose for their actions, capabilities, beliefs and role identity.

The way in which these levels interact with each other is directly parallel to Bateson's levels of learning:

- A particular behavioral reaction to a particular environmental stimulus is essentially a reflex or habit—Learning 0.
- Corrective change in behaviors in order to reach a particular outcome involves connecting that behavior to something beyond the environmental stimuli—some internal mental map, plan or strategy. This involves the exercise of a particular capability or the development of a new one—Learning I.
- Developments in capabilities are stimulated and shaped by beliefs and values which function to classify and categorize aspects of our mental maps, behaviors and environment and connect them to emotions and other motivational structures—Learning II.
- Changes in beliefs and values would involve linking to a system beyond those beliefs and values (an identity) that they have been established to serve—Learning III.
- Getting outside that system and connecting to a larger "system of systems" (i.e., the "field" or "spirit") would be necessary to achieve a change within a particular system or identity itself—Learning IV.

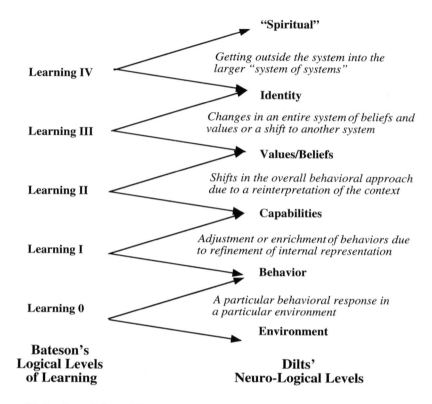

Relationship of Bateson's Levels of Learning to Neuro-Logical Levels

Each level in the hierarchy is related to groupings of phenomena or experiences from the level below it. A single identity is shaped by, and reflected in, a particular group of beliefs and values. Each belief and value, in turn, is related to a particular group of capabilities. The capabilities relate to specific groupings of behaviors, and the behaviors ultimately relate to particular clusters of environmental conditions.

Thus, the system of levels can be represented as an inverted tree structure.

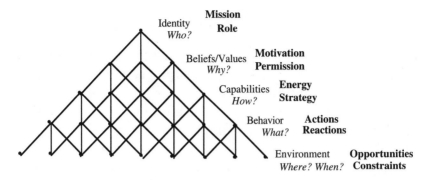

Neuro-Logical Levels can be Represented as a Series of Ordered Groupings in the Form of an Inverted "Tree Structure"

When we reach the level of "spirit" and field, we can flip the tree structure so that it extends upward like the branches of a tree. This illustrates the successively larger systems and "fields" of which we are a part.

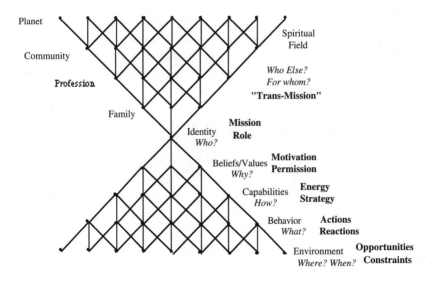

Total System of Neuro-Logical Levels

Set Theory

This perspective of Neuro-Logical Levels, as a hierarchy formed from a series of ordered groupings, brings us back to set theory and Bertrand Russell's original notion of the theory of logical types. *Set theory* is a branch of mathematics, which is based on the assumption that any collection of objects or phenomena can be described as some sort of "set." For example, one could talk about a "set" of even numbers, automobiles, people with brown hair, colors, behaviors, NLP practitioners, ideas, other "sets," etc. Set theory is the study of the relationships existing among such sets. Set theory began with the work of Georg Cantor in the 19th century, but its roots in logic go back all the way to Aristotle and Plato. In addition to its applications to logic, computer science, and other branches of mathematics, set theory has important implications for the study of psychological and behavioral processes.

According to set theory, any phenomenon, or group of phenomena, can ultimately be described as some sort of set, or collection of sets, and as belonging to some larger set. A set may be specified in one of two basic ways. The roster method, or tabulation method, simply lists all the elements in the set. The descriptive method, or set-builder notation, gives a rule for determining which things are in the desired set and which are not (similar to the logical syllogisms established by Aristotle).

One of the key principles of set theory is that a particular set can be made up of numerous "subsets." Stated formally, the principle maintains, "if every element of a set A is also an element of the set B, set A is a subset of B." So, if all of the members of set A (the set of potatoes) are also in set B (the set of vegetables), then set A (the potatoes) are a subset of B (vegetables).

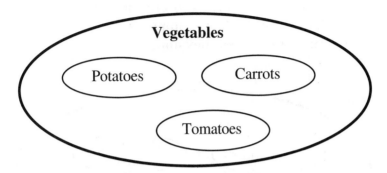

Sets May be Composed of Other "Sub-Sets"

Similarly, if set A is made up of all of the behaviors associated with mixing oil paints, and set B is made up of the behaviors associated with using a brush to apply paint to a canvas, and all of the behaviors of both set A and set B are included within set C (painting), then A and B are subsets of C.

One result of this principle is that sets can be organized into a series of ordered groupings of sets and sub-sets. This is one of the key notions behind the Neuro-Logical Levels model. According to the model, each level of process incorporates elements from the level below it into successive groupings of subsets. For instance:

a. Particular behaviors apply to a certain set of objects in the environment.

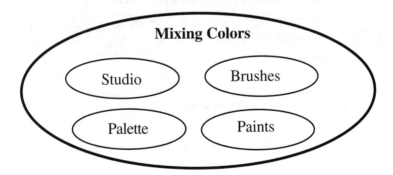

Behaviors Relate to Subsets of Environmental Elements

b. Capabilities involve the coordination of specific sets of behaviors (and the environments or portions of the environment to which they apply).

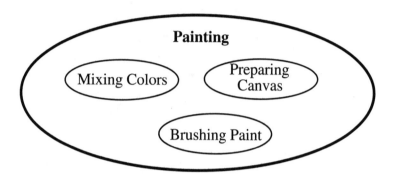

Capabilities are Made Up of Subsets of Specific Behaviors

c. Beliefs and values relate to sets of capabilities (and the behaviors those capabilities include).

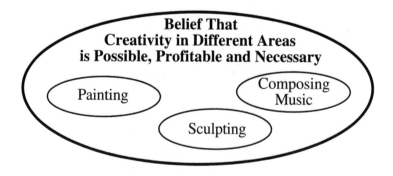

Beliefs and Values Relate to Certain Subsets of Capabilities

d. Identity encompasses a set of beliefs and values (and the capabilities, behaviors and environments included within them).

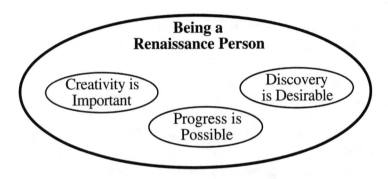

A Particular Identity is Made Up of Subsets of Beliefs and Values and Their Corresponding Capabilities and Behaviors

e. Spiritual experience in the form of vision and purpose unites sets of identities.

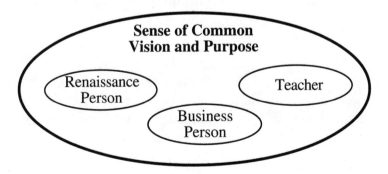

Vision and Purpose Integrate Subsets of Identities

Neuro-Logical Levels as an Operational Hierarchy

Of course, Bateson's levels of learning and the NLP Neuro-Logical Levels are more than a simple "chunking up" of sets based upon logical inclusion. Each level functions by integrating and operating upon relationships and activities at the level beneath it. Clusters of change or activity at any particular level will also influence the level above it.

In a paper written in November 1976 (published in *Roots of NLP*, 1983) co-author Robert Dilts attempted to distinguish between logical types and logical levels. Dilts asserts that *logical types* are hierarchies related to classification based on the class-member hierarchy of sets. *Logical levels* are hierarchies related to functions in which operations on one level select and organize elements on the level below it.

Consider the following examples:

- The speed of a car is a function of the change in distance it makes in relationship to time (*environment*).

- Pushing the gas peddle or brake of a car with one's foot is a *behavior* which alters its speed.

- The *capability* of maintaining the speed limit is a function of integrating a mental map with one's perceptions in order to regulate the way in which one uses one's foot.

- Respecting the speed limit is a result of *valuing* laws and *believing* that there are consequences if they are not kept. If one does not value the speed limit, one will not maintain it, even if one is capable.

- Being a "good driver" (*identity*) is a function of aligning all of the previous levels.

- Creating a new type of vehicle (airplane, helicopter, space shuttle, etc.) would result from the collective actions and shared vision and purpose of a larger system of drivers and engineers (*field*).

- The keys of a piano, the sound it makes and notes on a page of sheet music are in the *environment*.

- Pushing down a piano key with one's finger is a *behavior*.

- Playing music (sight reading the notes and coordinating one's finger to produce sounds in the right order) or creating music is a *capability*.

- Appreciating, judging and selecting music, and sustaining the motivation necessary to learn to read and play music are a function of *beliefs and values*.

- Taking on the *identity* of "a musician" is a combination of all of the levels.

- Developing a new style of music (classical jazz, rock and roll, etc.) would emerge from a collective generative collaboration among many musicians (*field*).

This illustrates a fundamentally different type of organization than simple logical inclusion, although the two share some properties. In this type of hierarchy, activity at one level is organizing activity at a lower level. This is most easily described formally.

For instance, we can describe a particular *behavior* as a process similar to a mathematical function; i.e., $f(x)$—in which x is some portion of the environment and f is some action, algorithm or program that operates upon it. As a specific example, x could be a key on a piano keyboard. The function f could be something like "pressing the key with your finger." All of our behaviors require interaction with our environment in some way. The behaviors of playing a piano, driving a car, skiing down a mountain slope, riding a bicycle, speaking with another person, etc., all require an interaction with particular parts of the environment.

Capabilities are processes that operate upon and coordinate behaviors. It is one thing to be able to press the keys of a piano or a computer keyboard, it is another altogether to play Mozart or write Shakespeare. This relationship would be shown mathematically as $f'(f(x))$, in which f' is a function that operates upon the process defined by $f(x)$. To express it more directly we could show the relationship as (capability (behavior (environment))), meaning capabilities are functions that *operate upon* behaviors that *operate upon* parts of the environment.

Another way to formally notate the level of capabilities would be $f(y,x)$, where y represents a behavior, x represents some part of the environment, and f is a function or program that coordinates them together.

Extending this description, we can say that *beliefs and values* are functions that operate upon capabilities: $f''(f'(f(x)))$, identity operates upon beliefs and values, and so on. The entire operational hierarchy could be represented as:

field (identity (values/beliefs (capabilities (behavior (environment))))).

Updating Patterns of Behavior through Bateson's Levels of Learning

The following format applies Gregory Bateson's Logical Levels of Learning and some aspects of Neuro-Logical Levels to help identify and update patterns of behavior that may have become outdated and ineffective. It involves systematically moving from Learning 0 all the way to Learning IV.

Learning I, II and III are like the rungs of a ladder that help us to achieve the possibility of Learning IV. This process demonstrates the various types of approaches and support that help people to make the types of adjustments and changes in perspective necessary to successfully accomplish each level of learning, building upon the insights and knowledge generated by each level to support the capacity of Learning IV.

The process involves the following steps:

1. Think of a problem situation or relationship in which you continue to fall back into an old pattern of behavior, even though it is ineffective (Learning 0). Associate into an example of the experience and internally "relive" what it is like. Demonstrate or role play the behavioral response that you have in that situation, and identify the structure of the pattern or habit (i.e., blaming, giving in, freezing up, shrinking, making yourself invisible, etc.). Be aware of how you do this behaviorally. Pay particular attention to your posture, movements, body tension, breathing, etc.

2. Take a step back from the situation and reflect upon this pattern of behavior. Notice how you are responding both mentally and physically in that situation. Explore how you could adjust or adapt your behavior (Learning I). Role play some possibilities exploring how you could vary the current behavior you are engaging in; i.e., exaggerate it, dampen it, shift it, etc.

3. Take a further step back from the situation and go to an "observer" position, such that you are "watching yourself" in the problem situation.

   a. Notice how you have been categorizing or classifying this situation up until now (i.e., dangerous, serious, urgent, threatening, etc.). What is the belief you have been holding about the situation?

   b. Think of some other time and situation in which you were able to act or respond in a completely different and more resourceful way (Learning II)—e.g., calm, accepting, open, centered, etc. Associate into a situation in which you were able to enact this other class of behavior.

   c. Create a "belief bridge" to the problem situation: What is the belief that you have that allows you to act resourcefully in this other situation? What belief would you need to have in order to support the new class of behavior in the problem situation?

   d. Revisit the problem situation and act "as if" you had this belief and the different class of behavior associated with it in the problem situation. What would be different?

4. Step back again so that you are outside of yourself, reflecting on yourself and the range of behaviors that you have had available to you in your life. Consider the possibility of a completely different system with a completely different range of behavior (identity) that is not your own (Learning III).

   a. Find a person, animal or being that would have a completely different strategy than you in that situation. Identify a role model for that system of behavior and put yourself fully "into his or her shoes" (second position). [If you need to, create a "belief bridge" to get into the perceptual position of the model (i.e., What belief would you need in order to be able to put yourself fully into the other?)]

b. From the perspective of the role model, what is your metaphor for yourself as that model? What is your "calling" as that model? Think of a sponsor in your life who helped you to expand your perception of who you are and imagine putting yourself back into the problem situation and responding "as if" you were this other person, applying the calling and the metaphor you have created.

5. Step back beyond the Learning III location. Enter a state of "not knowing" in which you feel centered and open to all possibilities, without making any judgments or interpretations. Open yourself up to what Gregory Bateson called the "pattern which connects" and the "larger Mind," and what Einstein referred to as "God's thoughts" and "universe." Think of an awakener in your life who helped you widen your view of what was possible. Create an anchor or symbol for this state. Using the anchor or symbol to hold the state, step back through each of the other levels of learning and back into the problem situation and act spontaneously. What is a behavior you could do that would not fit <u>any</u> current system of classes of behavior? (Learning IV)

Learning 4	State of Openness and Connection to a "Larger Mind" (Unconscious/Field Mind)
Learning 3	Modeling a Completely New Pattern from Someone Else
Learning 2	Different Pattern Coming from a Different Situation
Learning 1	Variation within the Pattern
Learning 0	Recurring Pattern of Behavior

Koestler's Holarchies

Throughout his life, Bateson continued to apply the theory of logical types more generally to many aspects of behavior and to biology. To him, logical typing was a "law of nature," not simply a mathematical theory. He contended that a tissue that is made up of a group of cells, for instance, is a different logical type than the individual cells—the characteristics of a brain are not the same as a brain cell. The two can affect each other through indirect feedback—i.e., the functioning and connections of the overall brain can influence the behavior of a single brain cell and the activity of a single brain cell contributes to the overall functioning of the brain. Indeed, a cell may be said to affect itself through the rest of the brain structure.

In addition to being "hierarchical," these levels of classification could be said to be "holarchical." Arthur Koestler used the term *holarchy* to describe what he considered to be fundamental levels of integration within physical and social systems. In *The Act of Creation* (1964, p. 287) Koestler explained:

> *A living organism or social body is not an aggregation of elementary particles or elementary processes; it is an integrated hierarchy of semiautonomous sub-wholes, consisting of sub-sub-wholes, and so on. Thus the functional units on every level of the hierarchy are double-faced as it were: they act as whole when facing downwards, as parts when facing upwards.*

So something that integrates parts on the level below into a larger whole becomes a part itself for the level above it. Water, for instance, is a unique entity that emerges from the integration of hydrogen and oxygen. Water itself, however, can become a part of many other larger entities from orange juice to oceans to the human body. Thus, water is both a whole and a part of other larger wholes.

In *A Brief History of Everything* (1996), transformational teacher and author Ken Wilber described this relationship in the following way:

> *Arthur Koestler coined the term "holon" to refer to an entity that is itself a whole and simultaneously a part of some other whole. And if you start to look closely at the things and processes that actually exist, it soon becomes obvious that they are not merely wholes, they are also parts of something else. They are whole/ parts, they are holons.*
>
> *For instance, a whole atom is part of a whole molecule, and the whole molecule is part of the whole cell, and the whole cell is part of a whole organism, and so on. Each of these entities is neither a whole nor a part, but a whole/part, a holon.*

According to Wilber, each new whole *includes yet transcends* the parts on the level below it. It is important to point out that, in a holarchy, if a lower level of such a system is not present the levels above it will not be able to be fully expressed. The lower levels are the necessary components of all higher levels.

The human heart, for example, is itself a whole system of valves, vessels and muscles, and is also a part of the larger system of the human body. The heart affects, and is affected by, all of the other sub-systems of the body (eyes, stomach, kidney, autonomic nervous system, etc.), either directly or indirectly. Similarly, the human body is also itself a sub-system of the larger systems of family, community, environment, and so on.

Sub-systems themselves are also made up of other sub-systems, going all the way down to the systems of molecules, atoms, and sub-atomic particles that form the basis of our physical world.

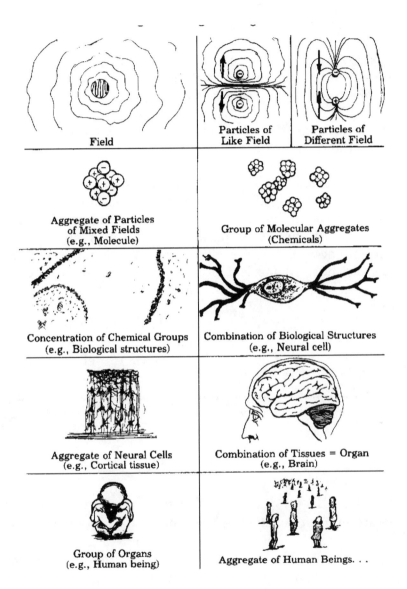

| Field | Particles of Like Field | Particles of Different Field |

Aggregate of Particles of Mixed Fields (e.g., Molecule)

Group of Molecular Aggregates (Chemicals)

Concentration of Chemical Groups (e.g., Biological structures)

Combination of Biological Structures (e.g., Neural cell)

Aggregate of Neural Cells (e.g., Cortical tissue)

Combination of Tissues = Organ (e.g., Brain)

Group of Organs (e.g., Human being)

Aggregate of Human Beings. . .

Our Universe Is Made Up of an Ecology of Systems That Are Themselves Sub-Systems in Successively Larger Systems

One of the fundamental presuppositions of NLP is that our minds, our bodies, our societies and our universe form an ecology of complex systems and sub-systems all of which interact with and mutually influence each other. It is not possible to completely isolate any part of the system from the rest of the system.

As an analogy, the 26 letters of the English alphabet can exist without the word "home," but the word "home" cannot exist without the alphabet. The word "home," however, is at a higher level than the letters of the alphabet because "home" organizes the letters of the alphabet and signifies or points to more than the alphabet itself. Similarly, sentences are at a higher level than words; paragraphs are at a higher level than sentences; chapters are a higher level than paragraphs; and so on. Each higher level forms a greater whole because it embraces, yet is more than the previous structures from which it is formed.

Bateson's levels, and consequently the NLP Neuro-Logical Levels, share this property. Each level is made up of relationships between parts of the level below it, yet transcends those parts to make a more encompassing structure (similar to the way that hydrogen and oxygen atoms form a water molecule). In this way they are both "hierarchic" and "holarchic."

Neuro-Logical Levels and the Nervous System

From the NLP perspective, each level of learning, change or interaction must be a function of some form of "neurolinguistic programming." One of the purposes of the NLP Neuro-Logical Levels model is to relate Bateson's levels of classification and learning to the nervous system. The concept of "neuro-logical levels" proposes that different levels of process are a function of different types of neurological organization, and mobilize successively deeper commitments of neurological "circuitry."

Bateson himself (*Steps to an Ecology of Mind* pp, 249-250) contended that the hierarchy formed by the various levels of learning would correspond to "hierarchies of circuit structure which we may—indeed, must—expect to find in the telencephalized brain," claiming that "we should look forward to a classification or hierarchy of neurophysiological structures which will be isomorphic with [the various levels of learning]." The concept of "Neuro-Logical Levels" proposes that different "logical levels" are a function of different types of neurological organization, and mobilize successively deeper commitments of neurological "circuitry."

The level of neurology that is mobilized when a person is challenged at the level of mission and identity, for instance, is much deeper than the level of neurology that is required to move his or her hand. To experience the environment, a person can passively adjust his or her sense organs. To take action in a particular environment, a person needs to mobilize more of his or her nervous system. In order to coordinate those actions in a complex sequence, such as dancing or driving an automobile, a person has to utilize even more of the nervous system. Forming and manifesting beliefs and values about capabilities, behaviors and the environment, requires an even deeper commitment of neurology (including those related to the "heart" and "guts"). A sense of self arises from a total mobilization of the nervous system at all of the other levels. In general, then, higher levels of process mobilize a deeper commitment of the nervous system.

A particular *environment* is made up of factors such as the type of external setting, weather conditions, food, noise level, etc., that surround an individual or group. Neurologically, our perceptions of the environment relate to information coming from our sense organs and peripheral nervous system. To perceive a particular environment, for instance, an individual views it with his or her eyes to see any relevant objects, listens with his or her ears to hear significant sounds, smells odors through his or her nose, and feels the temperature of the air on his or her skin. The person also makes many subtle and unconscious adjustments to maintain balance, respond to changes in the intensity of light and sound, acclimate to temperature changes, etc. Thus, the peripheral nervous system essentially relays information related to the environment to and from the brain. It is responsible for producing sensations and purely reflex reactions.

Behavior relates to the specific physical actions and reactions through which we interact with the people and environment around us. Neurologically, our external behavior is a result of activity in our motor systems (the pyramidal system and cerebellum). Non-reflexive behaviors involve the psychomotor system, a deeper level of neurology than the sense organs. The psychomotor system coordinates our physical actions and conscious movements.

Capabilities have to do with the mental strategies and maps people develop to guide their specific behaviors. While some behaviors are simply reflexive responses to environmental stimuli, most of our actions are not. Many of our behaviors come from "mental maps" and other internal processes whose source is within our minds. This is a level of experience that goes beyond our perceptions of the immediate environment. You can make pictures of things that do not relate to the particular room you are in, for instance. You can remember conversations and events that took place years ago. You can imagine events that may happen years from now. Behaviors without any inner map, plan or strategy to guide them are like knee jerk reactions, habits or rituals. At the level of capability we are able to select, alter and adapt a class of behaviors to a wider set of external situations. Thus, "capability" involves mastery over an entire class of behavior—i.e., knowing *how to* do something within a variety of conditions.

This occurs in our brain structure as a result of the relationship between our sensory nerves, motor system and the cerebral cortex. It is in the cortex (or gray matter) of the brain that sensory information is represented in the form of mental maps, associated with other mental representations, or pieced together in imagination, and then connected to appropriate actions and responses. Studies of the brains of monkeys, for instance, show that if the motor cortex is damaged or removed, the monkeys can still execute any particular behavior. What is lost is their ability to integrate behaviors together into larger more coordinated activities.

Developing capabilities is the most cognitively intensive of the Neuro-Logical Levels. This type of processing is usually accompanied by semi-conscious micro movements, or "accessing cues" (eye movements, breathing rate changes, slight postural adjustment, voice tone shifts, etc.).

Values and beliefs relate to fundamental judgments and evaluations about ourselves, others and the world around us. They determine how events are given meaning, and are at the core of motivation and culture. Our beliefs and values provide the reinforcement (*motivation* and *permission*) that supports or inhibits particular capabilities and behaviors. Beliefs and values relate to the question, *"Why?"*

Neurologically, beliefs are associated with the limbic system and hypothalamus in the midbrain. The limbic system has been linked to both emotion and long-term memory. While the limbic system is a more "primitive" structure than the cortex of the brain in many ways, it serves to integrate information from the cortex and to regulate the *autonomic nervous system* (which controls basic body functions such as heart rate, body temperature, pupil dilation, etc.). Because they are produced by deeper structures of the brain, beliefs produce changes in the fundamental physiological functions in the body that are responsible for many of our unconscious responses. In fact, one of the ways that we know that we really believe something is because it triggers physiological reactions; it makes our "heart pound," our "blood boil," or our "skin tingle" (all effects that we cannot typically produce voluntarily). This is how a polygraph functions to detect whether or not a person is "lying." People show a different physical reaction when they believe what they are saying than when they are being untruthful or incongruent.

It is the intimate connection between beliefs and deeper physiological functions that also creates the possibility for them to have such a powerful influence in the area of health and healing (as in the case of the placebo effect). Because expectations generated by our beliefs affect our deeper neurology, they can also produce dramatic physiological effects. This is illustrated by the example of the woman who adopted a baby, and because she believed that "mothers" were supposed to provide milk for their babies, actually began to lactate and produced enough milk to breast feed her adopted child!

The level of *identity* relates to our sense of *who* we are. It is our perception of our identity that organizes our beliefs, capabilities and behaviors into a single system. Our sense of identity also relates to our perception of ourselves in relation to the larger systems of which we are a part, determining our sense of "role," "purpose" and "mission." In our neurology, our identity can be associated with our nervous system as a whole, and probably involves deep brain structures such as the reticular formation. The reticular formation is a large group of cells deep within the brain stem. Fibers from this area project via thalamic nuclei to large association areas in the cortex. The reticular formation is a regulator of the state of alertness; its destruction at the midbrain level results in a state of coma. (In contrast, large areas of the cortex may be destroyed without a loss of consciousness.)

Identity is also physiologically related to the immune system, endocrine system, and other deep life sustaining functions. Thus, change or transformation of identity can have a tremendous and almost instantaneous effect on one's physiology. Medical research on individuals with multiple personalities (Putnam 1984) shows that remarkable and dramatic changes can occur when an individual switches from one identity to another. For instance, the brain wave patterns for the different personalities are usually completely different. Some people with multiple personalities carry several different pairs of eyeglasses because their vision changes with each identity. Other individuals will have allergies in one personality and not in another. One of the most interesting examples of physiological change with different identities is that of a woman, admitted to a hospital for diabetes, who "baffled her physicians by showing no symptoms of the disorder at times when one personality, who was not diabetic, was dominant . . ." (Goleman, 1985).

Spiritual level experience has to do with our sense of being part of something, on a very deep level, that is beyond ourselves. It is the awareness of what Gregory Bateson called "the pattern which connects" all things together into a larger whole. We, as individuals, are a subsystem of this larger system. Our experience of this level is related to our sense of purpose and mission in life. It comes from asking the questions: "For whom?" and

"For what?" This is the level that Bateson was most likely indicating when he referred to Learning IV.

Neurologically, spiritual level processes have to do with a type of "relational field" between our own nervous systems and those of other people, forming a type of larger, collective nervous system. The results of this field of interaction are sometimes referred to as a group "mind," a group "spirit," or a "collective consciousness." This field also includes the "nervous systems," or information processing networks, of other creatures and beings, and even our environment.

In summary, Neuro-Logical Levels are made of the following "hierarchy" of neurophysological circuitry:

Spiritual: *Field*—Individual nervous systems combining to form a larger system

A. Identity: *Nervous system as a whole*—deep life-sustaining functions (e.g., immune system, endocrine system and reticular system)

B. Beliefs & Values: *Limbic and autonomic control system* (e.g., heart rate, pupil dilation, etc.)—Unconscious responses

C. Capabilities: *Cortical systems*—Semi-conscious actions (eye movements, posture, etc.)

D. Behaviors: *Motor system (pyramidal & cerebellum)*—Conscious actions

E. Environment: *Peripheral nervous system*—Sensations and reflex reactions

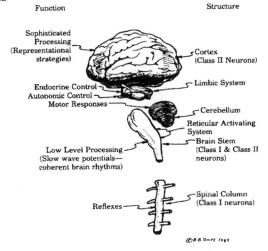

Hierarchy of Neural Systems

Neuro-Logical Levels and Language

As with all key NLP models and distinctions, Neuro-Logical Levels are not only neurological. They also have a linguistic component that shows up in our intuitive use of language. For example, compare the following statements:

That object in your environment is dangerous.

Your actions in that particular context are dangerous.

Your inability to make effective judgments is dangerous.

Your beliefs and values are dangerous.

You're a dangerous person.

The judgment being made in each case is about something being "dangerous." Intuitively, however, most people sense that the "space" or "territory" implied by each statement becomes progressively larger, and feel an increasing sense of emotional affect with each statement. For someone to tell you that some specific behavioral response you made was dangerous is quite different than telling you that you are a "dangerous person."

Try it for yourself. Imagine someone was saying each of the following statements to you:

Your *surroundings* are (stupid/ugly/exceptional/beautiful).

The way you *behave* in that particular situation is (stupid/ugly/exceptional/beautiful).

You really have/don't have the *capability* to be (stupid/ugly/exceptional/beautiful).

What you *believe and value* is (stupid/ugly/exceptional/beautiful).

You are (stupid/ugly/exceptional/beautiful).

Again, notice that the evaluations asserted by each statement are the same. What changes is the level to which the statement is referring.

Examples of Statements at Different Logical Levels

The following groups of statements provide other examples of verbal expressions directed toward different Neuro-Logical Levels.

Statements indicating different levels of response to a student who has done poorly on a spelling test:

A. Identity – *You are a stupid / learning-disabled person.*
B. Belief – *If you cannot spell well you cannot do well in school.*
C. Capability – *You are not very good at spelling.*
D. Specific Behavior – *You did poorly on this particular test.*
E. Environment – *The noise in the room makes it difficult to take tests.*

Statements indicating different levels of response in someone with a drinking problem.

A. Identity – *I am an alcoholic and will always be an alcoholic.*
B. Belief – *I have to drink in order stay calm and be normal.*
C. Capability – *I can't seem to control my drinking.*
D. Specific Behavior – *I had too much to drink at the party.*
E. Environment – *When I get around my friends I like a drink or two.*

Statements indicating different levels of response from a person who has discovered that he or she has cancer.

A. Identity – *I am a cancer victim.*
B. Belief – *It is false hope not to accept the inevitable.*
C. Capability – *I am not capable of keeping well.*
D. Specific Behavior – *I have a tumor.*
E. Environment – *The cancer is attacking me.*

Statements indicating different levels of response in someone who is working toward a health goal.

A. Identity – *I am a healthy person.*
B. Belief – *If I am healthy I can help others.*
C. Capability – *I know how to influence my health.*
D. Specific Behavior – *I can act healthy sometimes.*
E. Environment – *The medicine healed me.*

Language Patterns Associated with Different Neuro-Logical Levels

There are several verbal patterns associated with different Neuro-Logical Levels of experience summarized below:

- Language at the *environmental level* refers to specific observable features or details in one's external context, e.g. white paper, high walls, large room, etc. Environmental level experiences are characterized by impersonal but detailed sensory-based descriptions:

  e.g., I tasted a juicy red apple; I saw a beige automobile moving at a high speed; I heard a high pitched tone coming from the receiver; The sponge was cold, wet and soft; etc.

- *Behavioral level* language refers to specific behaviors and observable actions, e.g. "do," "act," "walk," "say," etc. Behavioral level experience is expressed by relatively specific, sensory-based active verbs and adverbs (specified verbs):

  e.g., He was walking down the street; She winked at me; They all stood up; He pushed his sister; etc.

- The *level of capabilities* is indicated by word such as "know," "how," "I am able," "think," etc. Capability level processes are best expressed through what are typically known as unspecified verbs in the Meta Model (creating, communicating, thinking, etc.):

e.g., I see what you are saying; I am able to grasp the meaning; She has the capability to fly a plane, drive a car, play a musical instrument, build a chair; etc.

- *Belief and value level* language is often in the form of statements of judgments, rules and cause effect, e.g. "if ... then ...," "one should ...," "we have to ...." Beliefs and values language includes broader generalizations than capability level language, and are reflected in judgment words of "lost performatives" (good, bad, ethical, positive, unfriendly, etc.), "nominalizations" (success, love, acceptance, achievement, power, etc.), "cause-and-effect" statements (makes, forces, causes, etc.), "modal operators" (should, have to, must, ought, etc.) and "universal quantifiers" (always, never, ever, nobody, everybody, etc.):

e.g., Nothing will ever be as good as it was; Well-behaved children should be seen and not heard; Practice makes perfect; We tried everything and nothing worked; etc.

- *Identity level* expressions are associated with language like: "I am a ..." or "He is a ..." or "You are a ...." Identity level descriptions are characterized by broad generalizations. They are necessarily highly encoded and, in a certain way, are very abstract. Representations reflecting identity are often expressed in symbolic and metaphoric language. Paradoxically, people actually reveal less of themselves by giving sensory-based descriptions than they do by speaking in symbols and analogies. For example, if I describe myself as a "Caucasian male who is wearing a pair of black jeans, sitting in a wooden chair, typing at a laptop computer, drinking a cup of tea, etc.," I have really revealed very little about "me." If, on the other hand, I describe myself as, "A pioneer that likes to explore new territory, but gets bored if he stays in one place too long," I have made a description that is not literally accurate at all, but has said a lot more about who I am and what "makes me tick."

e.g., I am like a lighthouse, He is a bitter person; They are animals; She is like the sunshine; etc.

- *Spiritual level* language is also largely in the form of symbols and metaphors, as in the parables of Jesus. According to Gregory Bateson, the language of the sacred is necessarily a non-literal language. That which is "sacred" and "meaningful" is usually not in the literal interpretation of the events, but is in their deeper structure.

Bateson used to give the example of a particular British hymn about Mary and Joseph on their way to Bethlehem for the census. Mary was "great with child" and tired of traveling. She begins complaining to her husband about being very tired and hungry. So they pull the donkey over and stop by the side of the road. Mary, who had become a bit irritable from their long journey, says to Joseph, "I'm hungry. Get me something to eat." Joseph, who was also a little tired and irritable, and not too happy about having to stop, responds, "Let the one who got you pregnant get you something to eat." Just then, a nearby cherry tree bends over and offers Mary a cherry from its branches.

Bateson points out that if you say, "Wait a minute, there were no cherry trees in Palestine in the first century," you have missed the purpose of the story. To take the story literally will rob it of its deeper meaning. The literal interpretation obscures the intention of the story. In other words, when Jesus talked about a sower planting seeds, he wasn't really intending to give a lecture on gardening. Rather there was a symbolic nature to the story.

Levels of Questions

Another place where the natural hierarchy of Neuro-Logical Levels shows up intuitively in language is in our most fundamental questions. Consider the six fundamental "W" questions that we use to organize our lives: where, when, what, how (the backward "w" question), why and who.

Environment: *Where? When?*
Behavior: *What?*
Capability: *How?*
Beliefs and Values: *Why?*
Identity: *Who?*

The level of spirit and purpose shows up in the questions *"For whom?"* and *"For what?"*

We often intuitively move up the various Neuro-Logical Levels as we go more deeply in a conversation. If I give a young child a list of spelling words (the *what*) and tell the child that there will be a test on those words in class at the end of the week (the *where* and *when*), he or she might legitimately ask, *"How* am I supposed to remember how to spell all these words?" If I tell the child to position his or her eyes up and to the left and form a mental picture of each word in his or her mind's eye (answering the how question), the child might then ask, *"Why* will that help me to remember the words?" I could answer the question by explaining my belief that the ability to spell is a result of remembering how the words look and that this process will help to get the image of the word to stick in the mind. The child might then move to the level of identity, asking, "Will that make me a good speller?"

The same intuitive pattern is illustrated in the following interactions:

Doctor: I'd like to schedule an appointment with you at my office next Wednesday afternoon for about 45 minutes.

Patient: OK. What is it about?

Doctor: I'd like to conduct a glucose tolerance test.

Patient: How is this procedure done?

Doctor: We have you drink some very sweet liquid, like a cola, wait a while, take a blood sample and see how well your body is metabolizing the sugar.

Patient: Why do I need to go through all this?

Doctor: Your last blood test showed a higher than normal blood sugar level, and we believe it could be an indicator of gestational diabetes.

Patient: Does that mean you think I am a diabetic?

Doctor: Not necessarily. Many women develop higher than normal blood sugar levels during pregnancy.

Manager: Do you have Tuesday afternoon free to meet with me in my office?

Collaborator: Yes. What do you want to meet about?

Manager: I'd like to get together with you to prepare for our presentation next week.

Collaborator: How specifically do you want to "prepare"?

Manager: I thought we might go over the sequence of information we're planning to present and see if we will need to make any visual aids.

Collaborator: Why? Do you think it is going to be difficult for people to understand our point?

Manager: Well, I believe it is good to have key ideas represented in several different ways.

Collaborator: All right. Do you want me to be mostly in the role of a co-developer, or should I be ready to play "devil's advocate"?

Manager: It might be a good idea for you to put yourself into the shoes of our audience, and perceive the presentation as if you were one of them.

Discussions about topics that go more deeply will eventually reach "spiritual" level questions such as whom and what our lives serve. This level of language becomes essential in matters of life and death. In his famous Gettysburg address, for example, Abraham Lincoln's language was almost entirely directed to these questions. He asserted, "We have come to dedicate a portion of that field, as a final resting place for those who here gave their lives that a nation might live." Lincoln is clearly stating "for whom" and "for what" the group had gathered. The emphasis on this deep Neuro-Logical Level becomes even more clear when Lincoln concludes, "It is rather for us to be here dedicated to the great task remaining before us – that from these honored dead we take increased devotion to that cause for which they gave the last full measure of their devotion – that we here highly resolve that these dead shall not have died in vain – and the government of the people, by the people, for the people, shall not perish from the earth."

Levels and Non-Verbal Meta Messages

The level to which a particular message is being directed can also be communicated by different non-verbal meta messages. For example, consider the difference in the implications of the following messages in which the words in italics indicate a shift in voice stress:

"You should not be doing *that* here."

"You *should not* be doing that here."

"*You* should not be doing that here."

Based on the placement of voice inflection, the message takes on different implications relating to a particular level of emphasis: You (identity) should not (beliefs/values) be doing (capability) that (behavior) here (environment). It is the presence or lack of such meta messages that often determines how a message is interpreted and whether or not a message will be interpreted appropriately.

For example, if an authority figure says, "YOU weren't respecting the rules," this is much more likely to be taken as an identity message. If the person says, "You weren't respecting the RULES," then he or she is not emphasizing the individual identity so much as the level of behavior.

Verbally Reframing Experiences by Using Language to Shift Logical Levels

One powerful way to use language associated with different Neuro-Logical Levels to help people get out of stuck states and reframe their experience involves re-categorizing a characteristic or experience from one logical level to another (e.g., separating a person's *identity* from his or her *capabilities* or *behavior*). Negative identity judgments are often the result of interpreting particular behaviors, or the lack of ability to produce certain behavioral results, as statements about one's identity. Shifting a negative identity judgment back to a statement about a person's behavior or capabilities greatly reduces the impact it has on the person mentally and emotionally.

As an example, a person might be depressed about having cancer, and refer to himself or herself as a "cancer victim." This could be verbally "reframed" with the response, "You are not a *cancer victim* (**A** = identity), you are a normal person who has not yet developed the *capability to take full advantage of the mind-body connection* (**B** = capability)." This can help the person to shift his or her relationship to the illness, open up to other possibilities, and to view himself or herself as a participant in the healing process.

The same type of reframe could be done with a belief like "I am a failure." One could point out, "It is not that you are a 'failure,' it is just that you have not yet mastered all of the elements necessary for success." Again, this puts the limiting identity level judgment back into a more proactive and solvable framework.

Categorizing something into a different logical level changes its meaning and impact.

These types of reframes can be designed using the following steps:

a) Identify the negative identity judgment (**A-**):

I am _____ (e.g., "I am <u>a burden to others</u>.")

b) Identify a specific capability or behavior that is related to either the present state or desired state implied by the identity judgment (**B**):

Ability to _____ (e.g., "Ability to <u>resolve problems on one's own</u>").

c) Substitute the capability or behavior for the negative identity judgment:

*Perhaps it is not that **you** are a* _____
(negative identity: e.g., "burden to others"), *it is just that you don't yet have the **ability to*** _____
(specific capability or behavior: e.g., "resolve problems on your own").

Voice stress or other non-verbal meta messages (indicated by the bolded words in the example above) may be used to add emphasis to the logical level shift.

S.C.O.R.E. Model

The S.C.O.R.E. Model was developed by Robert Dilts and Todd Epstein in 1987 to describe the process that they were intuitively using to define problems and design interventions. It arose as a result of a series of supervision seminars that they were leading on the applications of NLP. Dilts and Epstein realized that they were systematically organizing the way they approached a problem differently from their advanced NLP students, in a way that allowed them to more efficiently and effectively get to the root of a problem. The two men noticed that what they were doing intuitively but systematically was not precisely described by any of the existing NLP techniques or models.

The traditional NLP approach to problem solving up to that point was oriented around defining (1) a present state or "problem state," (2) establishing a desired state or goal, and then (3) identifying and implementing the steps of the solution or procedure that would hopefully help someone resolve the problem state and get to their desired state. Dilts and Epstein found that they were consistently breaking these various elements of problem solving down into smaller pieces during the information gathering process. In defining "problem states," for example, they were constantly distinguishing between the "symptoms" that characterized the problem and the "causes" of those symptoms. To establish desired states and goals, they found it important to distinguish between the specific behavioral "outcome" which represented the desired state and the longer term "effects" (which were often not at the level of behavior) that were the anticipated consequences of that outcome. Dilts and Epstein further noticed that it was important to separate techniques from the deeper "resources" that those techniques were attempting to mobilize and activate as the means to reach the solution that would transform problems and achieve desired goals.

The letters "S.C.O.R.E." stand for these additional distinctions made by Dilts and Epstein: Symptoms, Causes, Outcomes, Resources and Effects. According to the model, these elements represent the minimum amount of information that needs to be addressed by any process of change or healing.

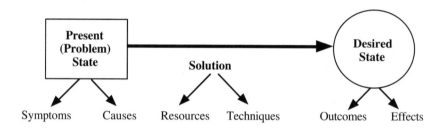

The S.C.O.R.E. Model Makes Additional Distinctions with Respect to the Traditional NLP "Present State—Desired State" Model of Problem Solving

It is interesting to note that the term *score* has several relevant connotations in English. The word derives from the Old Norse word *skor*, which means "notch" or "cut." Merriam-Webster's Dictionary defines a "score" as "a mark used as a starting point or goal" or "a mark used for keeping account." When a score is kept in a game or athletic competition, for instance, its purpose is to track the current status of the interaction (i.e., "Present State Pirates"—0, "Desired State Daredevils"—4).

Thus, a "score" is a means of keeping track of the progress of some event or interaction. A "musical score," for instance, refers to the description of the music for a movie or theatrical production. The "score" of a dance is a description of the dance composition, made in special choreographic notation. The term is even used to mean "the stark inescapable facts of a situation." It is said, for instance, that a person "knows the score" when he or she understands all of the relevant issues involved in a particular situation.

Another use of "score" is as the expression of accomplishment (as in a game or test), or excellence (as in quality), either absolutely in points gained or by comparison to a standard. "Score" can even be used to refer to the act of accomplishment itself. A "score," for example, is the term used for a goal, run, or touchdown, in any of various games or contests that gains points. It can even be used to indicate general success in obtaining something desirable.

The NLP S.C.O.R.E. Model incorporates all of these implications to some degree. In fact, the ultimate purpose of gathering information and forming it into a S.C.O.R.E. is to "tell the story" of the path from present state to desired state. Similar to the score of a theatrical production, each part of the S.C.O.R.E. for a problem must "hang together" in some type of meaningful whole. Thus, the S.C.O.R.E. model is more than a list of analytical categories. It defines the minimum information necessary to get a sense of the "story of change" necessary to resolve a particular problem.

"Knowing the S.C.O.R.E."

To better understand the S.C.O.R.E. distinctions, consider the following questions: What is a problem? What makes something a problem? What are the important elements to define about a problem in order to be able to successfully resolve it?

First, it is important to realize that if you have no **outcome**, you have no problem. If you don't want to be anywhere other than where you are, you have no problem. In fact, often the process of establishing a goal actually creates a problem. A "problem" is the difference between your present state and your desired state, and the issues that have to be dealt with in order to get to the desired state.

Questions to elicit outcomes include: *What, specifically is your goal? What do you want more of? If you were able to get what you wanted, what would it be?*

In the process of moving toward a desired state, **symptoms** come up in the form of constraints, resistances and interferences to reaching the outcome. Symptoms are typically the most obvious aspect of a problem. Physical symptoms often emerge as pain, weakness, or lack of mobility. Psychological symptoms occur in the form of inner conflicts and emotional struggles. A typical kind of symptom in a company or business might be a drop in profits, motivation or productivity.

Symptoms may be elicited by asking questions such as: *What is the problem? What is going wrong or giving you trouble? What do you want to change? What stops you from getting what you want, or being the way you want to be?*

Of course, effective problem solving involves finding and resolving the deeper *causes* of a particular symptom or set of symptoms. Treating the symptom alone will only bring temporary relief. Causes are often less obvious, broader and more systemic in nature than the particular symptom that is being manifested at the moment. Physical pain, for instance, may be caused by unseen factors such as lack of appropriate circulation, viral infections or internal wounds. Emotional struggles may be a consequence of limiting beliefs (thought viruses), suppressed memories, or a distortion of mental maps and representations. A drop in profit or productivity may be the result of something related to competition, organization, leadership, change in the market, change in technology, communications channels, or something else. What you identify as the cause determines where you will seek to create the solution.

Aristotle maintained there were four different types of causes. *Antecedent* (historical) causes relate to chains of events, whose roots are in the past. *Constraining* causes are a function of boundaries or opportunities arising in the "here and now." *Final* causes relate to anticipated future consequences and goals of present actions. *Formal* causes relate to the way we perceive, chunk and filter ongoing events. In seeking the causes of a symptom, it is important to check several of these areas in order to make a thorough investigation.

Another important type of "cause" for a particular symptom relates to the potential positive purposes or secondary gains served by the symptom. The "cause" for an emotional symptom like anger, for example, might be self-protection or establishing boundaries. Physical symptoms sometimes produce "secondary gains" such as care and attention, or serve as a good "excuse." Lack of motivation may serve as a way to avoid possible stress and failure. This is an important area of potential causes that is often overlooked by problem solvers.

In summary, causes may be explored and discovered by asking questions such as: *Where is the symptom coming from? What is triggering or creating the symptom? What was going on just before, or at the time that the symptom started? What is holding the symptom in place? What prevents you from changing the symptom? What is the positive intention behind the symptom—what purpose does it serve? Are there any positive consequences that result or have resulted because of this symptom?*

The desired ***effects*** of achieving a particular goal or outcome can also be significant factors in defining a problem space. A specific outcome is generally a step along a path to longer-range effects (what are sometimes referred to as "meta outcomes" in NLP). It is important that the solution to a problem is congruent to the longer-range desired effects. Sometimes the way in which an outcome is reached can actually interfere with reaching the longer-term target; i.e., it is possible to "win the battle but lose the war."

Questions related to effects include: *What would happen if you reached your outcome? What will it do for you to attain your goal? After you have reached your outcome, what will you do, or what will happen next?*

Thus, an overall "problem space" is defined by the relationship between the goal or outcome, the kind of symptoms that are getting in the way of achieving the outcome, the causes of those symptoms and the longer-range desired effects of reaching the outcome. In order to find the ***resources*** that will produce an effective solution for a particular symptom, it is necessary to know the causes of the symptom, the outcome, and the ultimate desired effect to be reached. Sometimes the resources needed to address the problem state are different from those necessary to reach the outcome (e.g., an aspirin for "aches and pains," and bed rest for "more energy"). Other times, a single resource will effectively address the entire problem situation. It is useful, however, to explore resources that would both (a) help to address the symptom and its causes and (b) help to achieve the desired outcome and effects.

Identifying resources involves asking questions such as: *What* (behavior, state, ability, belief, support, etc.) *do you have that will help you to reach your outcome* (solve your problem)? *Have you ever been able to achieve an outcome* (or solve a problem) *like this before? What did you do? Do you know anyone else who has been able to achieve an outcome* (or solve a problem) *like this before? What did that person do? If you had already achieved your outcome* (solved your problem), *and were looking back, what would you see that you had done in order to accomplish it? What other choices do you have that could maintain the positive intent or consequences of the problem yet allow you to reach your desired state?*

Techniques are sequential structures for identifying, accessing and applying particular resources to a particular set of symptoms, causes and outcomes. A technique is not in and of itself a resource. A technique is only effective to the extent that it accesses and applies the resources that are appropriate to address the whole system defined by the other S.C.O.R.E. elements.

Depending upon how specific or general a problem situation is, particular techniques and resources might produce an immediate result or they might only be intermediate steps on the way to reaching a result. Some solutions may require a number of different resources applied over a space of months or years. The process of defining symptoms, outcomes, causes and potential effects is an ongoing process.

In summary, according to the S.C.O.R.E. Model, effective problem solving ability involves defining the "problem space" and identifying potential areas of "solution space" by establishing the relationship between the following elements:

1. **Symptoms**—typically the most noticeable and conscious aspects of a present problem or problem state.

2. **Causes**—the underlying elements responsible for creating and maintaining the symptoms. They are usually less obvious than the symptoms they produce.

3. **Outcomes**—the particular state or behaviors that will take the place of the symptoms.

4. **Resources**—the underlying elements (skills, tools, beliefs, etc.) responsible for removing the causes of the symptoms and for reaching and maintaining the desired outcomes. Techniques, such as Six-Step Reframing, Change History, Anchoring, etc., are structures for applying particular resources.

5. **Effects**—the longer-term results of achieving a particular outcome. Specific outcomes are generally stepping stones to get to a longer-term effect.

   a. Positive effects are often the reason or motivation for establishing a particular outcome to begin with.

   b. Negative effects can create resistance or ecological problems.

Basic S.C.O.R.E. Questions

The basic questions used to define the S.C.O.R.E. related to a particular problem include the following:

1. What is the *"symptom"* in this problem?
2. What is the *"cause"* of the symptom in this problem?
3. What is the desired *"outcome"* or goal?
4. What would be the longer-term *"effect"* of reaching that goal?
5. What *"resource"* would help address the cause?
6. What *"resource"* would help achieve the outcome?

Applying the S.C.O.R.E. Model

One effective way to conceptualize and use the S.C.O.R.E. Model distinctions is to organize these elements on a time line. Typically, the symptoms are something you are experiencing now, in the present, or have experienced in the recent past. The causes of those symptoms tend to precede the symptoms. That is, the cause of a symptom comes before the symptom in time— either immediately before the symptom, or potentially much earlier. Outcomes occur in the same time frame as the symptom, since the outcome is what you want to replace the symptom with. So, if the symptom is in the present, the outcome will also be in the present or in the very near future. Effects are the longer-term results of the outcome. They are usually in the short term to long-term future. Resources can come from anywhere in time. A resource can be something that just happened to you, happened to you a long time ago, or it could be something you are imagining that could happen in the future. In creative problem solving, a majority of resources come from asking "what if?" and acting "as if."

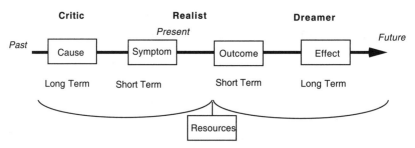

Placing the S.C.O.R.E. Distinctions on a Time Line

Effects are the macro goals that shape specific outcomes. We are not always going to know what the effect of some outcome will be, could be, or even should be. Sometimes you have to apply a resource and reach an outcome first, before you can explore its effects.*

*In terms of the Disney Imagineering strategy, the short and long-term future is the arena of the "Dreamer"; the ongoing expression of symptoms and outcomes is the field of the "Realist"; past causes and problems is the space of the "Critic."

"Meta Program" Patterns

Meta Programs emerged as a part of NLP in the late 1970s. They are one of the key developments associated with the second generation of NLP. A number of the patterns were initially proposed by Richard Bandler as ways in which people kept "coherency" in their mental programming (like the reference beam in an optical hologram). Further research into these and other patterns was spearheaded by Leslie Cameron-Bandler (together with David Gordon, Robert Dilts and Maribeth Meyers-Anderson). As the name implies, *"meta"* programs are *about* other programs. They are the programs which guide and direct other thought processes. Specifically, they define common or typical patterns in the strategies or thinking styles of a particular individual, group or culture.

Both Meta Program patterns and much of the current NLP submodality technology came from the attempt to better understand the functioning of cognitive strategies. In particular, they developed as a way to explain how individuals with the same cognitive structure to their strategies could sometimes end up with widely divergent results. For instance, two people might share a decision strategy with the structure: V^c—>K^i (deriving feelings from constructed images as a way to make a decision). One person, however, might report, "I picture several options, and choose the one that feels right to me." The other person, on the other hand, might complain, "I picture several options, and then feel overwhelmed and confused by them." The notion of Meta Programs arose from attempting to discover what made the difference between such diverse responses. Because the general representational structure of the strategies was essentially the same, it was postulated that the differences came from patterns outside of, or "meta to," the strategy (or internal program); i.e., a "Meta Program."

Meta Program patterns and submodalities determine the qualities of, and relationships between, the experiences and information that is being represented in a particular cognitive strategy. They address characteristics relating to the experiential substance of a particular image, set of words or feeling state. They influence how experiences are represented, sorted and punctuated. They also direct where we place our attention, operating as another set of filters on our experience.

Meta Programs (in contrast with submodalities) are more abstract than our specific strategies for thinking, and define our general approach to a particular issue rather than the details of our thinking process. Meta Program patterns are descriptions of the different ways in which a "problem space," or elements of a problem space, may be approached.

As with other NLP distinctions, a person can apply the same Meta Program pattern regardless of the content and context of a situation. Also, they are not "all or nothing" distinctions and may occur together in varying proportions.

Overview of Meta Program Patterns

In approaching a problem or goal, one can emphasize moving *toward* something *positive*, *away* from something *negative*, or some combination of both. Approaching positives involves seeking to achieve desired visions, outcomes and dreams, and tends to foster entrepreneurship and *"proactivity."* Avoiding negatives involves attempting to circumvent potential mistakes and problems, and accompanies a more careful, conservative and *"reactive"* approach to planning, decision-making and problem solving. Those who exclusively "move toward," however, can make decisions that are naive and potentially risky. Those who only "move away" can seem overly pessimistic or "paranoid." Good decisions and plans generally involve some combination of both.

The Meta Program pattern of *chunk-size* relates to the level of specificity or generality with which a person or group is analyzing a problem or problem space. Situations may be analyzed in terms of varying degrees of *detail* (micro chunks of information) and *generalities* (macro chunks of information). Again, too much focus on details leads people to lose sight of the "big picture." Similarly, an overemphasis on generalities can compromise and weaken the ability to "follow through," because you can't see the discrete steps.

Goals or problem situations may be examined with reference to different *time frames,* i.e., long term, medium term or short-term consequences. The time frame within which a problem or outcome is considered can greatly influence the way in which it is interpreted and approached. Placing too much emphasis on *short-term* success, for instance, may lead to problems in *long-term* ecology (i.e., one can "win the battle, but lose the war"). On the other hand, blindness to short-term and medium-term needs and challenges can threaten the success of long-term goals ("the chain is no stronger than its weakest link").

Outcomes and problems can also be defined with reference to the *past, present* or *future.* Sometimes people attempt to repeat successes or avoid problems that have recently occurred and are fresh in their minds. Other times people may seek to achieve or avoid more distant future outcomes or problems. Some people tend to look at history for solutions more so than the future. A good example is the difference between former Soviet leader Mikhail Gorbachev and the people who attempted to overthrow him before the dissolution of the Soviet Union in the early 1990s. One was trying to prepare for the future, while the others were trying to preserve the past.

Locus of control is another important Meta Program pattern. *Internal reference* is an NLP term used to describe the process by which a person uses his or her own inner feelings, representations and criteria as the primary source of his or her actions, and for evaluating the success of those actions. Internal reference may be contrasted with *external reference*, in which the locus of control, or the evidence of success, with respect to a particular action or decision, is placed *outside* of the individual. Picking a job based on internal reference, for example, would involve determining one's own personal needs and desires, and selecting a position based on how well it matched those needs and interests. Choosing a job based on external reference would involve selecting one that pleased another person, or because it is the only position available. Thus, doing what one "wants" to do is more internally referenced. Doing what one "has to" do, or has been told one "should" do, is more externally referenced. Successful evidence and evidence procedures typically involve some combination of both internal and external references.

Success with respect to achieving a goal, or avoiding a problem, may be evaluated by either *matching* (sorting for similarities), or *mismatching* (seeking differences) between the current state and the goal state. Matching focuses attention on what has been achieved. Mismatching emphasizes what is missing. Matching tends to support the perception of unity and consensus, while mismatching can encourage diversity and innovation. Too much matching, however, can make a person seem insincere and easily swayed by the opinions of others. Too much mismatching makes a person seem disagreeable and overly critical.

Problems and outcomes may be considered in relation to the achievement of a *task*, or with respect to issues involving *relationship*, such as "power" and "affiliation." Emphasis on task or relationship can be an important distinction for understanding differences in culture and gender. Men, for instance, are often considered to be more task-oriented, while women are frequently seen as more attentive to relationships. The question of balance of focus with respect to task and relationship is often a key one with respect to working with groups and teams. In the achievement of a task, either goals, procedures or options may be emphasized. (This in and of itself can lead to significant differences in approach to problem solving or planning; a procedure-oriented strategy will emphasize "doing it by the book," for instance, while an options-oriented approach would involve finding as many variations as possible.) Issues involving relationship may be approached with an emphasis on the point of view of oneself, others or the larger system (the company, the market, etc.) to varying degrees.

Strategies for approaching problems may emphasize various combinations of *vision, action, logic* or *emotion*. A particular emphasis on one of these cognitive strategies can produce a general *thinking style* at the level of a group or culture. Vision, action, logic and emotion are more general expressions of the elements of a particular cognitive strategy: i.e., visualization, movement, verbalization and feeling. Thinking style is akin to the NLP notion of "primary" or "most valued" representational system.

Summary of Key Meta Program Patterns

1. Approach to Problems
    a. Towards the Positive
    b. Away From the Negative

2. Time Frame
    a. Short Term – Long Term
    b. Past – Present – Future

3. Chunk Size
    a. Large Chunks – Generalities
    b. Small Chunks – Details

4. Locus of Control
    a. Internal or "Self" Reference – Proactive
    b. External or "Other" Reference – Reactive

5. Mode of Comparison
    a. Match (*Similarities*) – Consensus
    b. Mismatch (*Differences*) – Confrontation

6. Approach to Problem Solving
    a. Task (Achievement)
       1) Choices – Goals
       2) Procedures – Operations

    b. Relationship (Power; Affiliation)
       1) Self – *My, I, Me*
       2) Other – *You, His, Their*
       3) Context – *We, The Company, The Market*

7. Thinking Style
    a. Vision
    b. Action
    c. Logic
    d. Emotion

A person's Hierarchy of Criteria and Logical Level of focus can also be considered as Meta Program features. A *Hierarchy of Criteria* is essentially the order of priorities that a person applies to an outcome or problem. Hierarchies of criteria relate to the degree of importance or meaning that people attach to various actions and experiences. Criteria are essentially values that provide the motives for action, such as: achievement, power, survival, efficiency, consensus, profit, growth, productivity, affiliation, quality, ecology, etc. Criteria such as these can determine and reveal a lot about other Meta Program patterns. A person who has "achievement" at the top of his or her Hierarchy of Criteria, for instance, is much more likely to be task oriented than a person who most highly values "affiliation." Likewise, a person who focuses on "power" is more likely to be proactive and internally referenced than a person who emphasizes "consensus", and so on.

Logical Level of focus relates to where a person or group typically tends to place their attention while problem solving or planning a path to a desired state. Emphasis may be placed on either: environment - *Where, When;* behaviors - *What;* capabilities - *How;* beliefs and values - *Why*; identity - *Who*; or the system - *Who Else* and *For Whom*. The Logical Level of focus determines the scope of activity to which other Meta Program patterns apply. Avoiding something in the environment is different than attempting to avoid being something at the identity level. Mismatching behaviors is different than mismatching beliefs and values, and so on. It is also possible to avoid, mismatch or have an internal reference, at one level, but to approach, match or have an external reference at another level. In fact, factoring in the Logical Levels of focus often helps to sort out seeming discrepancies or paradoxes related to identifying the basic Meta Program patterns (one can be "approaching" something at one level, and "avoiding" something at another level, for instance).

Meta Program Clusters and Group Process

Different problem solving styles and approaches are characterized by different clusters and sequences of Meta Program patterns in various ratios. One person's approach might involve an 80% focus on relationship and 20% focus on task, and 70% emphasis on long-term versus 30% short-term considerations. Someone else may emphasize the task as 90% of the focus and think mostly in terms of short term consequences.

The different clusters of Meta Program patterns clearly cover different areas of a problem space. In this respect, there are no "right" or "wrong" Meta Programs. Rather, their effectiveness in connection with problem solving relates to the ability to apply them to cover the space necessary to adequately deal with a problem or reach a goal. The different phases of the Disney Imagineering Strategy (Dreamer, Realist and Critic), for example, may be characterized by particular clusters of Meta Program patterns:

Thinking Style	Dreamer	Realist	Critic
Level of Focus	What	How	Why
Representational Preference	Vision	Action	Logic
Approach	Toward	Toward	Away
Time Frame	Long Term	Short Term	Long/Short Term
Time Orientation	Future	Present	Past/Future
Reference	Internal - Self	External - Environment	External - Others
Mode of Comparison	Match	Match	Mismatch

Different Clusters of Meta Program Patterns Combine to Form Different Thinking Styles

Different kinds of activities require different sorts of attitudes and approaches. Some activities require or emphasize the ability to focus on the micro chunks and details.

Others require the ability to see the big picture. Different phases in the planning or problem solving cycle of a group or team may call upon different thinking styles. Therefore, particular attitudes or clusters of meta program patterns might be more or less beneficial at different stages in a group's process. An emphasis on results more than procedures might be either a help or a constraint to a group's functioning at different times. Some phases might require achieving consensus, and during other phases, it is important to encourage differences in perspectives.

Different thinking styles and approaches will have different values for different types of tasks. In brainstorming, for example, it may be beneficial to direct thinking in terms of the big picture and a longer time frame. For developing plans and procedures it may be more useful to be focused on short term actions. For analytical tasks it may be more appropriate to logically consider details with respect to the task, etc.

In this view, managing the process of a group essentially involves the pacing and leading of the different Meta Program patterns of the group members to fill in "missing links" and widen the perception of the problem or solution space.

Identifying Meta Program Patterns

Meta Programs may be identified through linguistic cues in the form of key words and phrases. As an example, consider the following: while attending a class on a particular subject, a student complains, "I don't feel like putting so much effort into learning this material because it will be obsolete soon and I don't want to waste my time." Such a comment reveals a great deal about the learner's operating Meta Program patterns. The student's statement indicates that he or she is oriented toward "feelings," for instance, and is focused on avoiding perceived negatives (i.e., "so much effort" and "wasting time"). The use of the word "I" also indicates a strong self-reference ("I don't feel," "I don't want"). The student's comment also implies an emphasis on the short-term future ("it will be obsolete soon") and generalities (the student refers to "this material" rather than referring to any particular aspect of the material).

Meta Program patterns may be stimulated through questions and cognitive instructions. Meta Program patterns are often determined as a result of self-assessment, using multiple-choice questions that draw out a person's preferences in relationship to a particular context or situation.

One of the simplest and most profound ways of finding relevant cognitive patterns and behavioral cues is through what is called "contrastive analysis." Contrastive analysis refers to the process of comparing different states, representations, maps, performances or descriptions, for the purpose of discovering the "differences that make a difference." By comparing and contrasting, a person can discover information that allows that person to have a better understanding of the structure of the experience. For example, if a person has an experience of creativity in one context, and an experience of being uncreative in another, these two experiences can be analytically contrasted with respect to the differences involved. The person can notice how the feelings, body language, focus of attention, beliefs and values, thinking strategies, and environmental cues differ. From gaining knowledge of these cues and areas of difference, strategies of learning can be applied for changing portions of the experiences. Contrastive analysis is at the basis of most NLP "utilization" processes.

Mapping Across Meta Program Patterns

One of the values of being able to elicit Meta Programs is that you can better perceive their influence on a particular communication or interaction. As with other cognitive capabilities, people will sometimes prefer certain Meta Program patterns to others. And, as with other patterns, this can be a source of both strengths and problems.

Sometimes Meta Programs are treated as if they were a type of NLP "personality theory." The fact is, however, that they are distinctions relating to patterns and trends in cognitive strategies, and are not rigid and unchangeable features of identity. Clusters of Meta Program patterns can be a powerful means for understanding and describing individual and cultural differences in a non-judgmental way. They are also useful tools for building models of individual thinking styles or cultures. The purpose of Meta Program patterns is to describe a general trend in a particular context. These patterns, however, are always flexible and evolving.

Meta Program patterns are often contextually based, and can shift, depending on the situation. Like other NLP distinctions, Meta Program patterns can be transferred, or "mapped across," from one situation to another in order to create change or improvement. The following exercise involves the use of a simple Contrastive Analysis to identify and utilize Meta Program patterns elicited from a resourceful state or situation in order to address a challenging situation.

1. Identify a situation involving decision-making, problem solving or motivation that you find personally difficult to manage effectively. Identify another challenging situation that is similar to the first one, but that you have been able to manage resourcefully.

2. Create two physical locations for the different situations, and a third location for a "meta position."

3. One at a time, associate into the challenging and resourceful situations, in order to get a good sense of how you experience them differently inside of you.

4. From meta position, contrast the Meta Program patterns that are operating in each of the situations. How are the Meta Program patterns you are using in the resourceful situation different from those of the challenging situation?

5. Step into the resource situation location and focus on the most important Meta Program patterns that you are using in that experience. Create an anchor so that you can easily feel and remember what it is like to be acting from those Meta Program characteristics.

6. Step over into the challenging situation and use your anchor to transfer the Meta Program patterns associated with the resourceful experience into that situation. Notice how your experience of the challenging situation is changed and enriched.

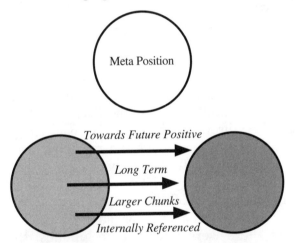

Resourceful Situation or State | Problem Situation or State

Meta Program Patterns

Towards Future Positive
Long Term
Large and Small Chunks
Internally Referenced
Matching and Mismatching
Vision and Logic Oriented

Meta Program Patterns

Avoid Present Negatives
Short Term
Focused on Details
Externally Referenced
Mismatching
Logic and Emotion Oriented

Meta Program Patterns Can Be Transferred from One Situation to Another in Order to Help Create Balance

The Unified Field Theory for NLP:
An Overview of 30 Years of NLP Development

One way to summarize the key developments of the previous generations of NLP and their contributions to our understanding of the cognitive mind is through what we call the Unified Field Theory for NLP.

Albert Einstein sought a "unified field theory" for physics that would tie together all physical theories into a single model of how the universe operated. Einstein believed that it was possible to establish a fundamental framework and identify basic principles that could unite the many different models and theories of physics. Similarly, in psychology there are a wealth of theories, each providing different perspectives and techniques that can be extremely effective and rewarding, but have yet to be brought together into a single unified structure.

As its name implies, Neuro-Linguistic Programming itself began as a type of unified field theory — an operational framework that synthesized the fields of neurology, linguistics and artificial intelligence. With NLP, John Grinder and Richard Bandler brought these fields together to form a "meta model" — a model about the modeling process. The mission of NLP was to find the "neurolinguistic" patterns that were effective in many different fields of human activity. Before there were any NLP distinctions such as representational systems, accessing cues or submodalities, and certainly before there were any NLP techniques, the field of NLP existed as a set of core presuppositions about the structure of subjective experience and its implications on human interaction. These presuppositions defined the philosophy and "epistemology" of NLP. NLP techniques and distinctions emerged as expressions and manifestations of these underlying principles. In fact, the initial role models from whom many of these expressions and manifestations were derived were founders of the systemic movement in psychology and therapy: Gregory Bateson, Virginia Satir and Milton Erickson.

As the basic principles of NLP were developed into specific applications and reduced to smaller "chunks" for training purposes, the teaching of NLP moved away from the systemic model and more towards a linear step-by-step capability level approach. While this has facilitated a rapid transfer of skills and techniques, much of the ecology and "wisdom" of the "bigger picture" has for the most part been left behind. Today, many students of NLP find themselves struggling to see how all of the numerous tools and techniques they've learned fit together.

In the mid 1980s, co-author Robert Dilts began developing a Unified Field for NLP, which he has continued to expand and evolve. On one level, the Unified Field Theory for NLP is about how all the techniques of NLP fit together. On another level, the Unified Field Theory addresses the relationship between NLP and other systems of thought. For example, how using NLP in education relates to using NLP in managing organizations, or to the process of scientific discovery, computer programming or therapy.

The SOAR Model

In the same way that Chomsky's model of transformational grammar was the framework for the original models and techniques of NLP, the SOAR Model is the underlying framework for the Unified Field Theory for NLP.

The SOAR Model is an AI (Artificial Intelligence) programming model for general problem solving. SOAR stands for **S**tate-**O**perator-**A**nd-**R**esult, which defines the basic process for navigating a path from a present state to a desired state. The application of an operator changes the present state in a direction that is either toward or away from the desired state. The results of applying operators becomes stored as "condition-action" rules (or what could also be referred to as T.O.T.E.s), which are composed of (a) evidences for identifying key *states*, and (b) *operations* with which to change those states in the desired direction.

SOAR was developed by Allen Newell, Herbert Simon and Clifford Shaw in the 1950s. It was used to create the computer chess playing programs by teaching the computer how to become a chess expert by learning from its experience through remembering how it solved problems. These expert chess programs have been the most successful application of AI to date.

According to the model, all the mental activity being devoted to a given task takes place within a cognitive arena called the problem space. A problem space in turn consists of a set of states, which describe the situation at any given moment, and a set of operators, which describe how the problem solver can change the situation from one state to another. In chess, for example, the problem space would be [the set of parameters which define] "a chess game" [such as the two opponents, the chessboard, etc.], a state would consist of a specific configuration of pieces on the chessboard, and an operator would consist of a legal move, such as "Knight to King-4." The task of the problem solver is to search for the sequence of operators

that will take it from a given initial state (say, with the
pieces lined up for the start of the chess game) to a
given solution state (the opponent's king in a
checkmate). (Waldrop, 1988)

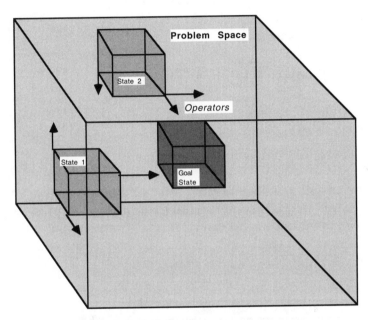

States Within a Problem Space

Once these parameters have been defined, the problem solver
must formulate a guidance strategy in order to find the sequence of operators that will lead from the starting state to the
goal state. This takes place through a set of prioritized condition-action rules in the form of "IF you perceive a certain state,
THEN apply a certain sequence of operators."

If an impasse is reached, sub-goals and sub-operations (i.e.,
sub-T.O.T.E.s) are triggered, which are then remembered as
new condition-action rules. Following this course, the problem
solver moves from a *Trial-and-Error* guidance strategy (novice),
through *Hill Climbing* (doing what seems best at the time) to
one involving *Means-Ends Analysis* (expert).

Combining NLP and the SOAR Model

By combining the SOAR Model with the distinctions of NLP, we may begin to build a practical and effective expert systems model of human behavior that provides a unifying framework for all other NLP techniques and procedures. From the perspective of Next Generation NLP, the general "problem space" of human experience and interaction can be defined according to three key dimensions:

1. Time Perception
2. Perceptual Positions
3. Levels of Change and Interaction

The two dimensions of time lines and perceptual positions can be laid in a two dimensional grid, with past, present and future extending in one direction and first, second and third position in another. This makes a type of life chessboard upon which we can map our experiences.

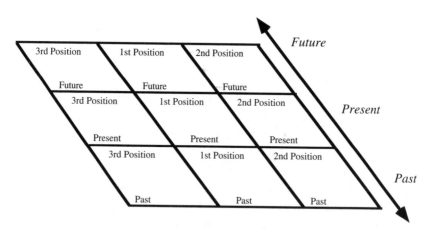

Time perception and perceptual positions can be laid out into a grid that makes a type of "life chessboard" upon which we can map our experiences.

These three "state" dimensions of (1) time frame, (2) perceptual position, and (3) level of change and interaction, can be represented as a three-dimensional matrix or "workspace," illustrated by the following diagram, in which practically any NLP intervention can be viewed and considered.

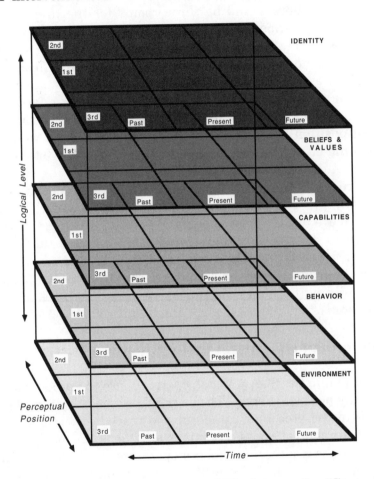

The "Jungle Gym": A Conceptual Workspace for "States" and NLP Interventions Based on the SOAR Model

This "workspace" is sometimes referred to as the NLP "Jungle Gym" because, if one experiences it kinesthetically, it resembles a child's play structure. It is as if one can move or climb around onto various platforms representing different time frames, perceptual positions and levels of experience.

Another good analogy for this space would be an apartment building. The apartments could be considered to be the spaces created by past, present and future. Within each apartment there would be three rooms for the first, second and third position perspectives. The floors of the building would be a created by the different levels. The environment is the bottom floor; behaviors would be the next floor, then capabilities, beliefs and values, and identity would be the penthouse. On each floor, of course, are three apartments (past, present and future) with three rooms (first, second and third position). We can say that the spiritual level would be standing on the roof of the building looking out over the rest of the buildings in the city.

To move through this apartment building, we need to have the keys to the various apartments and know where the entries are to the various rooms. We would also need to know where to go to get to the elevator that will take us to the higher level floors. Once we have this know-how, we can begin to move particular resources from the various parts of the building to others. At times, we may also have to clean out some of the rooms, replace the furniture, etc.

Neurolinguistic Operators for Changing States

According to the SOAR Model, operators are the processes that actually produce change. They are "where the rubber meets the road" in the process of attempting to reach a desired state. In the metaphor of chess, operators are the legal moves of the various chess pieces. It is these operators that determine and change the state of the pieces of the two opponents on the chessboard. According to NLP, "neurolinguistic" processes relating to cognitive strategies, physiology and language patterns are the primary *operators* with which we change our mental and behavioral states. In order to be effective, all plans and techniques must be finalized in specific, observable cognitive, verbal or physical cues and patterns.

Representations such as "goal," "level of change," "perceptual position" and "time" are cognitive concepts and abstractions that we create mentally. Human beings are not equipped to directly perceive or change "self," "other," "time," etc. Rather, we perceive and affect them through "real time" operators within our nervous system—our senses, our language and our physical behavior. In fact, the name "Neuro-Linguistic Programming" implies these three fundamental operators for change:

"Neuro"—Specific Sensory Representations (and Submodalities)

"Linguistic"—Language Patterns

"Programming"—Physiological Cues and Responses

People operate in real time to change perceived states by using their senses, language and physical behavior. These are the only processes that we can directly observe and influence. In the end, it is these cognitive, linguistic and behavioral skills that will separate effective from ineffective behavior, and determine the states we are in.

In order to implement the steps of a particular change process, people need to make specific alterations in their cognitive experience and physical behavior. For example, in order to shift a problem state in the direction of a resourceful state, a person might "operate" by forming a mental image of himself or herself at a time when he or she felt centered and flexible. The person may then verbally label this desired state as "confident" and physically shift his or her posture to more closely match the posture of the internal image. These "micro" operations will stimulate neurological changes that will alter the state of the individual to some degree. Specific "neurolinguistic" processes such as these are defined or presupposed by the steps of any psychological technique.

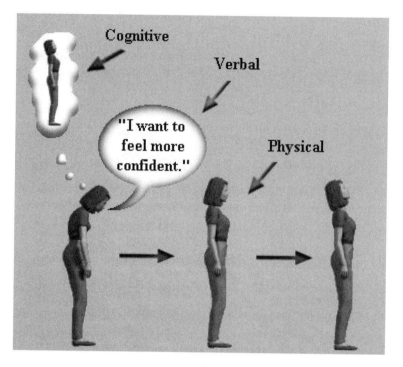

Specific cognitive processes, linguistic patterns, and physical cues are the "neurolinguistic" operators through which the steps of change are enacted.

Thus, each location within the NLP-SOAR workspace is defined by a specific set of a) sensory representations and submodalities, b) linguistic cues and patterns, and c) behavioral manifestations and expressions.

The following is a summary of the key neurolinguistic operators for influencing the three basic dimensions of the NLP-SOAR workspace that we have presented thus far in this chapter.

Neurolinguistic Operators for Shifting Time Perception

Shifting our experience of time and different time frames (past, present and future) involves a shift in the particular verbal, sensory and physical patterns associated with them.

Past: Neurologically, our past is made up of particular memories, and is physiologically associated with "right brain" processes (typically characterized by eye movements and gestures to the left in right-handed people). Memories are generally "associated" multi-sensory representations of particular events.Linguistically, the past is expressed in words using the past tense; i.e., "saw," "felt," "did," "talked," etc.

Present: Neurologically, our experience of the present is anchored in ongoing sensory experience. Because the present tends to involve immediate sensory experience, the physiology associated with the present time frame is active and responsive to ongoing environmental stimuli.Linguistically it is expressed in present tense language; "I see," "feel," "do," "say," etc.

Future: Neurologically, our perception of the *future* is a function of imagination, expectation and fantasy. These are associated with "left brain" processes (typically characterized by eye movements and gestures to the right-hand side in right-handed people). Cognitive constructions of the future are more frequently "disassociated" in comparison with representations related to the present or past. Linguistically, it is expressed using the future tense: "will see," "will feel," "will do," "will say," etc.

Experiences that are perceived as more distant with respect to the past or future will be accompanied by more disassociated internal representations and physiological cues. Associating into the past and reliving it, or into the future and acting "as if" it is happening now, will bring them more into the "present," and the physiology and internal representations will become more associated and enriched.

Neurolinguistic Operators for Shifting Perceptual Positions

First position is characterized by "associated" sensory representations; seeing, hearing, feeling, tasting and smelling
what is going on around you and inside of you from your own
perspective. If you are in first position, you do not see
yourself, but are inside yourself, perceiving the world through
your own eyes, ears, nose, skin, etc. The physiology of first
position is generally active, and involves gestures toward
oneself, with the hands often touching the chest or midline of
the body. Linguistically, first position is characterized by first
person pronouns such as "me," "I" and "myself" when referring to your own feelings, perceptions and ideas.

In *second position* you take on another person's perspective, shifting to his or her physical posture, standing, sitting
or moving as that person would. You experience the world
through the other person's senses, taking on his or her
thoughts, feelings, beliefs, etc. In this position, you are
disassociated from yourself and associated into the other
person, seeing yourself from that person's perspective. You
address your "first position self" as "you" (as opposed to "I" or
"me"), using second person language.

Third position involves a physical posture that is symmetrical and relaxed, with very little movement – as if one
were a distant observer. All of your representations of the
experience are disassociated; and you use third person pronouns, such as "she" and "he" when referring to the persons you
are observing (including the one that looks, sounds and acts like
you).

Fourth position is an identification with the system or
relationship itself, producing the experience of being part of a
collective. Fourth position is a "we" position, and is characterized by the use of first person plural language – "We are,"
"Us," etc. Physically, in fourth position the body expresses
the energetic characteristics experienced as being produced
by the interactions within the system or relationship.

Neurolinguistic Operators for Shifting Levels of Change

Language at the *environment* level refers to specific observable features or details in one's external context: e.g., "white paper," "high walls," "large room," etc. Perceptions of the environment are related to the verbal questions "where" and "when?" The cognitive focus is on one's ongoing sensory experience of the external world. Body movements tend to be limited, and gestures are directed away from the body (such as pointing at objects or stimuli around you).

Behavioral level language refers to specific behaviors and observable actions, e.g. "do," "act," "walk," "touch," "say," etc. This type of language typically arises in response to the question "what?" The representational focus is very sensory based, emphasizing particular perceptions or mental movies of actions and reactions. There is also a heavily kinesthetic orientation, involving the awareness of muscles and motions. The physiological patterns of this level also tend to be very action-oriented, with the legs, arms and hands acting on objects, or in response to stimuli in the world around you (or reproducing such motions with imaginary objects or situations).

The level of *capabilities* is indicated by word such as "know," "understand," "am able," "think," etc. Capabilities are associated with the question "how?" The cognitive focus is on mental representations involving imagination and memory. Capabilities are developed and represented in the form of inner pictures, sounds, feelings, self-talk, etc. The physiological patterns associated with capability level processes tend to center around the head. A person may make gestures toward the eyes and ears, or touch his or her mouth. Mental capabilities and strategies are also characterized by a variety of micro behavioral cues known as "accessing cues" in NLP (eye movements, voice tone shifts, etc.).

Language patterns associated with *beliefs and values* are typically in the form of statements of judgments, rules and cause-effect relationships, e.g. "if ... then ...," "one should ...," "we must not ...," "...causes...," etc. These patterns are most associated with the verbal question "why?" Because beliefs and values refer to judgments and evaluations made about entire classes of

behavior, the inner representations associated with them generally lack detail. Cognitively, then, beliefs and values tend to be
derived much more from the basis of the formal characteristics
of internal representations (i.e., submodalities) rather than
their contents. Neurologically, beliefs and values also are connected with autonomic processes (heart rate, blood pressure,
breathing rate, etc.) which makes them much more emotionally
based. In fact, when talking about beliefs, a person will often
gesture toward organs such as the heart and stomach.

Identity level processes and evaluations are associated with
language like: "I am a ...," "He is a ...," or "You are a ...," etc. These
are generally responses to the question "who?" Both the verbal
descriptions and cognitive representations used to express
identity are frequently symbolic or metaphorical (e.g., "I am like
a lighthouse," "He is a bitter person," "They are animals," "She
is like the sunshine," etc.). The physiology associated with
identity level processing is very deep and pervasive. When a
person is in touch with and expressing his or her identity, that
person will typically use symmetrical gestures that involve the
whole body in some way.

Spiritual level processes involve accessing and connecting with a
larger field. This generally involves the ability to think with a
complete absence of muscular tension. Perceiving in this way often
produces a trancelike state of reverie in which a person is:

- Using only peripheral (as opposed to foveal) vision.
- Focusing his or her hearing on external sounds (turn off
  any internal dialog).
- Maintaining a relaxed physiology (no excess emotional
  or physical tension).

Spiritual level language is also largely in the form of
symbols and metaphors, as in the parables of Jesus. It is
necessarily a non-literal language. Meaning at this level is
not in the surface expressions of objects and events, but is in
their deeper structure.

Modeling and Mapping with the NLP Unified Field Theory Framework

The distinctions of the NLP Unified Field Theory provide a powerful framework for both elicitation and modeling. They can be used to track and relate different "chunk sizes" of practically any cognitive activity. Let's say, for example, a person is modeling the process used by a trainer or consultant to plan a training intervention. The elicitation process often begins with the identification of the "big chunks" which make up the process or skill to be modeled. To do so, it is useful to physically lay out the timeline and perceptual position dimensions NLP-SOAR space. To explore the structure of the process, you can step into the relevant area of that space as you are defining and tracking each stage of the skill or strategy being modeled.

Tracing a Path of Change

1. Think of an important life change that you have made in your past that you feel you were able to manage successfully.

2. Trace the path you took through the NLP-SOAR workspace. It is best to do this by physically laying out a grid work of locations for Past, Present and Future, and First, Second and Third positions. Then, as you recall the strategy by which you managed the past change, physically walk through the various areas of NLP-SOAR space that you covered.

For example, perhaps you (1) reached a point in which your current situation had become intolerable; (2) considered what you wanted to achieve in the Future from an Observer Position; then (3) you planned what steps you would need to take by looking at your Present situation; then (4) sought advice from a friend or mentor; (5) recalled resources from your Past; and (6) finally began to take the ongoing steps needed in order to reach your goal.

You could map this path of change in the following way:

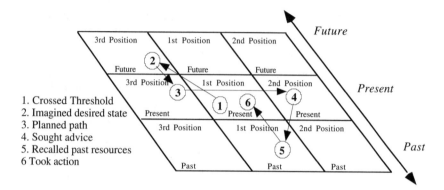

Mapping a Path of Change Using the NLP-SOAR Space

The specific T.O.T.E.s and patterns of neurolinguistic operators may then be detailed for each of these key "chunks" or steps. Again, the SOAR space can be physically laid out and used to help elicit the details of the strategy, and to assist others in following and learning the steps of the process. In this way, learners can walk through relevant squares of the SOAR space and try out each step of the procedure as it is being described.

SOARing Through Change

Another way to apply the distinctions of the NLP Unified Field Theory and SOAR space is to plan and map the path from a present state to a desired state. Instead of looking to the past to model a path that we have already successfully taken, we look to where we want to move in the future and create models of possible trajectories that will take us there.

1. Identify a present or problem state, and a desired future state.

2. Locate the present state and desired state within the "problem space" distinctions defined by the "workspace" created by combining NLP and the SOAR Model (e.g., Problem State: stuck in an old identity conflict with a significant other in the past; Desired State: feeling of freedom and independence in the future).

3. Create a path of 7 ± 2 steps through the SOAR space leading from the present state to the desired state (or from the desired state to the present state). Each step can only be to an adjacent space. That is, you change only one distinction (past, present, future; 1st, 2nd, 3rd position; environment, behavior, capability, beliefs and values, identity, etc.) at a time. For example, you cannot move directly from past to future, skipping the present. Similarly you cannot move immediately from the level of behavior to identity. You would have to first go to the level of capabilities, and then beliefs and values, before reaching the identity level.

The S.C.O.R.E. Model—Defining a Path Within a Problem Space

According to the SOAR Model, the most effective sequence for planning or problem solving involves a series of successive approximations in which:

1. The problem space is thoroughly defined in terms of the relevant and meaningful elements of the system related to the problem or project.

2. The present state, desired state and available resources within the problem space are identified.

3. The preferred sequence of concrete operators is selected and applied in order to access available resources and move towards the desired state.

From the Next Generation NLP perspective, all effective techniques and interventions have this structure. To effectively reach desired states, individuals must be able to (a) conceptualize the overall problem space of the significant issues, (b) assess the relevant states to be achieved and avoided within the context that they are working, and (c) apply the sequence of operators necessary to move from the perceived present state to the most ecological and appropriate desired state, given the purpose and overall problem space of the intervention.

According to the S.C.O.R.E. model, a path through a particular "problem space" is defined by the relationship between the goal or *outcome*, the kind of *symptoms* that are getting in the way of achieving the outcome, the *causes* of those symptoms and the longer range desired *effects* of reaching the outcome. In order to find the *resources* that will produce an effective solution for a particular symptom, it is necessary to know the causes of the symptom, the outcome, and the ultimate desired effect to be reached.

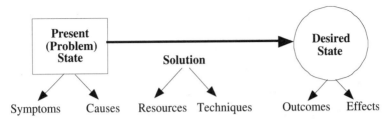

The S.C.O.R.E. model defines the distinctions necessary to define a path from a Present State to a Desired State within a particular problem space.

Placed in the context of the SOAR Model, each S.C.O.R.E. element will be defined in terms of the levels of change, perceptual positions and time frames that determine the relation of self, others and goals which make up that state. A particular symptom, cause, outcome, effect or resource can be defined in terms of a) the relevant persons, perspectives and roles involved, b) the relevant time frame(s) and c) the relevant levels of interaction and change (environment, behavior, capabilities, beliefs, values and identity).

The following diagram, for instance, shows how the various S.C.O.R.E. distinctions might be mapped with respect to those defined by the SOAR Model.

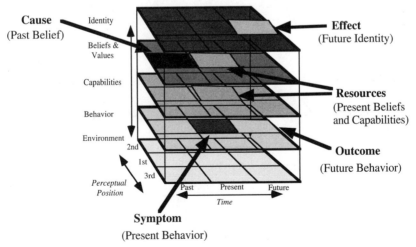

The various elements of a S.C.O.R.E. may be defined with respect to the SOAR space.

According to the Unified Field Theory of NLP, all techniques are essentially paths that cover some aspects of this overall work space, and leave others untouched. The key to the effectiveness of a technique is whether or not it addresses all of the aspects of the "problem space" that need to be addressed. The interface of the SOAR and S.C.O.R.E. models offers important guidance for the development of new and more effective techniques by providing an overview of areas of possible "problem space" and potential "solution spaces." Very few NLP techniques, for instance, formally utilize Second Position, Future.

The following worksheet can be used to help track which parts of the NLP-SOAR space are involved in making a particular intervention. (You can use colored pens or markers to indicate which areas of the SOAR space are relevant to each S.C.O.R.E. distinction.)

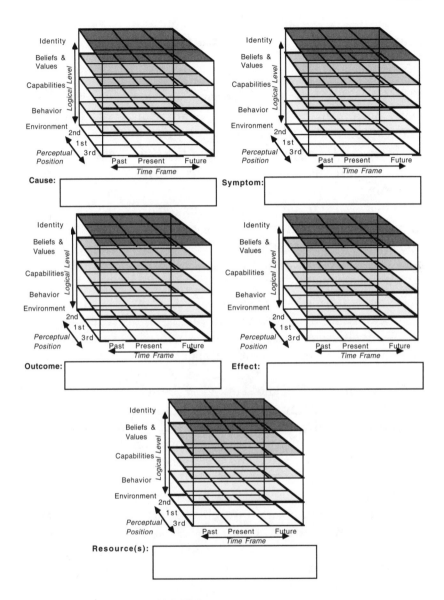

Using the NLP-SOAR Distinctions to Track the Key Aspects of an Intervention

Meta Program Patterns and the NLP Unified Field Theory

The NLP Unified Field Theory distinctions and SOAR workspace provide a powerful framework with which to understand and influence Meta Program patterns and sorting styles. Where you stand within the SOAR workspace will actually shift the Meta Program from which you are operating. For instance, you can easily influence a person to be *in time* or *through time*; *away from* or *toward*; sort by *"present to past"*, *"past to future"*, or *"present to future"*; sort by *self*, *others*, or *context*; and so on. These Meta Program patterns essentially have to do with a person's orientation within the SOAR workspace.

Being *"in time,"* for example, would involve associating onto a particular time line and facing the future. *"Through time"* involves viewing the time line from Third Position, seeing it in a left-to-right perspective instead of back-to-front.

Going *"toward"* some behavior, belief, or event would simply involve facing that event from whatever point you are currently standing in within the SOAR space. Going *"away from"* it would involve turning your back on it.

Sorting by *"self"* would involve associating into First Position and considering other areas of the workspace. Sorting by *"other"* would involve stepping to the Second Position area. An "external" reference, in which you sort by *"context,"* would involve moving to Third Position.

A *"task"* orientation would come from looking at your Future behaviors. Alternately, a *"relationship"* orientation would involve turning to face a significant other.

The *"chunk size"* to which you are attending is essentially a function of the Logical Level you are focusing on. Environment and behavior level information is more sensory based and specific. Beliefs, values, identity and spiritual perceptions are necessarily larger chunks.

From the perspective of Next Generation NLP and the Unified Field Theory, every change technique can be described in terms of a series of Meta Program shifts, which, when successful, pace and lead the Meta Program of the client, bringing him or her closer to a desired state. The New Behavior Generator strategy, for example, involves going "toward" a new future behavior. It is also primarily "self" referenced. People whose operating Meta Program is externally referenced and oriented "away from" problems will struggle to find the relevance of such a technique, and may experience difficulties in following the steps of the procedure.

Change Personal History, in contrast to the New Behavior Generator, starts by going "toward" the past cause of a problem. This can be frightening and difficult for people who are attempting to go "away from" the problem altogether. They may resist the technique and experience difficulties remembering anything about their past. Change Personal History is also primarily a "self" referenced activity. Reimprinting, on the other hand, shifts the reference from "self" to significant "others."

People will feel more comfortable with techniques that pace their natural Meta Program constellation. This is why certain techniques appeal to some people more than others, regardless of the effectiveness of the technique. It is useful for advanced level NLP practitioners to recognize the Meta Program patterns and SOAR space that is presupposed by the steps of the various NLP techniques.

Generative NLP Format

The Generative NLP Format is a process developed by Robert Dilts in 1990 as an application of the "Unified Field Theory for NLP." The Generative NLP Format is a method for applying NLP and the SOAR Model in order to take something that is already a resource and make more of it. Rather than being "problem" oriented, it is resource oriented. One of the beliefs behind the Generative NLP Format, however, is that problems which are ready to be solved by a particular resource will be spontaneously drawn to it and resolved gently and easily, if the resource has been expanded and enriched fully enough. You don't have to start by identifying a problem and then struggle to find a resource that you hope will produce an adequate solution. The Generative NLP Format is designed to "widen" and "deepen" the basin associated with the resource, which changes the internal landscape and leads to the self-organization of a solution to the problem.

Generative change is essentially about the discovery, creation, enrichment, strengthening and elaboration of resources. It is about finding the "deep structure" of a resource and facilitating the transformation of that resource into many other contexts where it has yet to be applied. Metaphorically, it is about finding dormant resources and activating them, making them more available and "holographic." Generative change involves developing higher level forms and processes that can function in an evolutionary way towards new possibilities.

The generative applications of NLP help people to solve problems and achieve goals in a more systemic and organic way. When new resources are discovered, released and developed, problems that are ready to be solved by those resources emerge and resolve naturally and without effort.

Steps of the Generative NLP Format

1. Establish a grid of spaces representing a matrix of time frames and perceptual positions:

1st position future - 2nd position future - 3rd position future.

1st position present - 2nd position present - 3rd position present

1st position past - 2nd position past - 3rd position past.

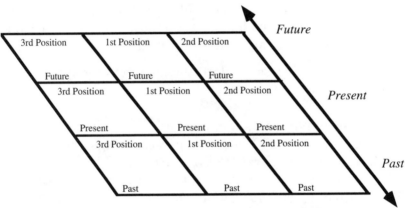

Spatial Layout for the Generative NLP Format

2. Associate into the location representing first position present. Identify a recent resource you have developed or discovered.

3. Fully experience the resource in the 1st position, present location.

4. One by one associate into each of the surrounding positions bringing the resource with you:

1st position future - 2nd position future - 3rd position future.

2nd position present - 3rd position present.

1st position past - 2nd position past - 3rd position past.

a. Notice how bringing the resource into each space strengthens and enriches the experience of the resource.

b. From each location, look at the you in the 1st person present location who is the focal point of the resource and offer a message or belief that would help strengthen the resource even more.

c. Associate back into the you in first position present and receive the message from the other perceptual position. From first position present, experience and describe how the resource has been strengthened and enriched with respect to achieving your goals.

5. Repeat this process until all the surrounding spaces have been entered.

As an example, let's say a person has chosen the resource "practical optimism." When the person brings the resource into the location of **First Position Future**, his or her future self may face the present self and give the message, *"Cherish this. It is what your life is all about."*

The person would bring the resource to **Second Position Future** by stepping into the shoes of a significant other in his or her future. From the perspective of this future other, the person may turn back to his or her present self and say, *"I'm grateful. Thank you for teaching me to have faith."*

Taking the resource to **Third Position Future** would involve bringing it into the perspective of a kind and wise observer of his or her future. From this perspective the message to the present self may be, *"Keep going. You are succeeding in your mission."*

Bringing the resource into **Second Position Present** would involve taking the point of view of a significant other who is currently in the person's life. The message that comes from being in this person's shoes might be, *"We're proud of you and we will make you proud."*

Third Position Present would involve observing oneself in one's ongoing reality. Bringing the resource to this location may stimulate the person to say to his or her first position self, *"Stay focused. All will be well."*

To bring the resource to **First Position Past** the person would step back into a location representing an earlier time in his or her life. Upon receiving the resource, the person's younger self might respond, *"Your commitment pays off. It always pays off."*

Taking the resource to **Second Position Past** would involve stepping into the shoes of a significant other from his or her personal history. Possessing the resource (even though he or she did not have it in reality at that time), the past other might send the message, *"You can do anything you want. You have my blessing and support."*

Going to **Third Position Past** would involve taking the standpoint of an observer of one's personal history. Having the resource in this perspective might prompt the past observer to say, *"What you have is sacred. Share it with as many others as you can."*

Receiving all of these messages can be a deep and enriching experience, leaving the person's sense of the resource much richer and stronger than it began.

The following worksheet can be used to keep track of the messages that arise from the different locations during the Generative NLP Format.

Generative NLP Worksheet

Message from **1st Position Future**:

_____

Message from **2nd Position Future**:

_____

Message from **3rd Position Future**:

_____

Message from **2nd Position Present**:

_____

Message from **3rd Position Present**:

_____

Message from **1st Position Past**:

Message from **2nd Position Past**: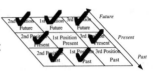

Message from **3rd Position Past**: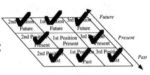

Conclusion

Explicit knowledge of the models, distinctions and relationships defined by the Unified Field Theory for NLP is not necessary in order for people to effectively use NLP techniques and principles. However, the ability to recognize, understand and apply them will vastly increase a person's mastery with NLP.

The Unified Field Theory is also a potential source of great freedom, flexibility and creativity with respect to applying NLP, because it allows practitioners to operate from the "deeper structure" of the various NLP techniques.

The exercises we have explored in this chapter are only a few of the many possible applications of the NLP-SOAR space. Becoming more familiar with the SOAR Model and the NLP-SOAR distinctions can greatly increase and enrich your understanding and mastery of NLP and many other areas of your professional and personal life. [See the entries on the SOAR Model and the Unified Field Theory in the *Encyclopedia of Systemic NLP and NLP New Coding*.]

Recent developments in cognitive sciences, such as Information Theory, Cognitive Psychology, Psychoneuroimmunology, Neuroscience and NLP, are just beginning to unlock some of the mysteries of "mind." A major part of the mission of Next Generation NLP is to extend the frontiers of our understanding of these mysteries and bring them into practical applications. This is what we will begin to explore in the coming chapters.

Chapter 2

The Somatic Mind

Overview of Chapter 2

- **Felt Sense: Our Subjective Experience of Our Somatic Mind**
- **Neurogastroenterology and the Brain in the Belly**
- **Neurocardiology and the Brain in the Heart**
  - **HeartMath**
- **The Breath**
  - **Somato Respiratory Integration™**
- **The Spine**
  - **Body Posture**
  - **Network Spinal Analysis™ (NSA)**
- **The Feet**
  - **Foot Pad Release Practice**
- **The Cortical Homunculus – The Body In The Brain**
  - **Exploring Your Subjective Homunculus**
  - **Steps of the Somatic Foreground-Background Process**

Overview of Chapter 2 (Continued)

The Somatic Mind

Soma is the Greek word for "body." The *somatic mind* is the mind within your body. Our somatic intelligence is our foundational intelligence. Not all creatures possess a cognitive mind, but all living organisms depend on the somatic mind for survival and effective interaction with their environment. The somatic mind is our mammal mind and the primary form of intelligence for young children.

There is a whole pattern of intelligence and wisdom within the body to which a person may or may not be attuned. When we are in contact with our somatic mind, we inhabit our bodies. This means that part of our awareness rests in the body. Since the body only lives and breathes in the present moment, when we are connected to our somatic knowledge, part of our awareness is also anchored in the present moment. While our attention can be directed toward a task at hand, an interaction, an intellectual activity, or any other place we choose to give our attention, when our awareness is simultaneously rooted in our body with its ever-changing universe of physical sensations and feelings, we have access to a vastly rich and resource-filled wealth of information that enriches our experience of whatever we are attending to.

When we say that someone is "all in their head" or "cut off from their body," this indicates a lack of access to the rich world of somatic experience and intelligence. When we are "in our head," it usually means that our attention has taken us away from the present moment awareness of our body. This is often accompanied by certain types of physical and emotional manifestations: shallow or rapid breathing, talking quickly, tension in the shoulders, neck and face, emotions that tend toward anxiety, a sense of stress or contraction.

Inversely, when we are well grounded in the body and in the present moment, we tend to be physically relaxed, to breathe more slowly and deeply, to experience emotions that tend toward peacefulness and resourceful states of being like relaxed alertness and heightened vitality. As transformational teacher Richard Moss has pointed out, when the body is happy, the emotions tend to be positive and the mind quiet.

The subjective experience of a somatic intelligence has appeared in all cultures and throughout history and is reflected linguistically through a class of words known as "organ language" in NLP. *Organ language* relates to seemingly metaphorical statements or idiomatic statements that people make which refer to parts of the body or body functions.

Sayings like, "I had a gut intuition," "I followed my heart," or "I knew it in my heart," indicate parts of the body other than the brain as having some type of capacity for intelligence. We can also talk about something being "gut wrenching," "difficult to stomach," "heart breaking," or "spine tingling." In addition to its metaphorical significance, however, NLP considers organ language to often be more than the simple use of idioms. Like sensory based predicates ("I see what you are saying," "It is not clear," "That speaks to me," "It clicked," "I got in touch with," "It feels right," etc.), organ language often reflects deeper underlying "neuro-linguistic" patterns and processes that can give us insight into some of the deeper structures of these subjective experiences—structures that we will be exploring in this chapter.

Felt Sense:
Our Subjective Experience of Our Somatic Mind

Subjectively, we know our somatic mind through what philosopher and psychotherapist Eugene Gendlin calls a "felt sense" that forms the basis of his treatment method called *focusing*. Gendlin asserts that an organism's living interaction with its environment necessarily comes prior to more abstract cognitive knowledge about its environment. According to Gendlin, living is an intricate, ordered interaction with the environment, and as such, living itself is a kind of knowing. Abstract cognitive knowledge is a development emerging from this more basic knowing that is the deeper structure of our conscious thinking process.

In other words, the somatic mind is the first mind—it is the base for the rest of our mental functioning. The quality and effectiveness of our cognitive consciousness depends to a large degree on the quality of the somatic mind.

Gendlin says that our somatic knowing asserts itself in the form of a subjective *felt sense*, which he claims is quite different from "feeling" in the sense of emotions. The felt sense is one's bodily awareness of the ongoing life process. Because a felt sense comes from our living interaction in the world, it is not as disassociated or abstract as are cognitive concepts, and thus contains fewer deletions, distortions and generalizations. A felt sense is actually more ordered than cognitive thinking and has its own properties, different from those of logic. It is a type of somatic thinking that can be quite precise and more intricate than cognitive knowing. This perspective is very similar to Milton Erickson's notion of a wise and intelligent "unconscious mind."

Gendlin arrived at his conclusions through a method similar to NLP modeling. He and a number of colleagues studied thousands of hours of recordings of psychotherapy sessions in order to explore what was "the difference that made a difference" when the sessions were successful.

He observed that successful clients were not highly verbal or analytical. Instead, they allowed themselves to experience and tolerate feelings that were vague, blurry and unclear— even when they were uncomfortable or painful—and they allowed these feelings to unfold in their own time and way. They attended to their inward, bodily-felt sensations beneath their problems or issues (their "deeper structure"). Rather than going around in circles mentally, they stayed in contact with the ever-changing flow of their experience without being overwhelmed by their emotions. They slowed down, took time to sense their feelings, and listened to whatever message these feelings were trying to convey.

Gendlin called this process "focusing" and developed teachable steps so that others could learn how to productively attend to their inner sensations in a similar fashion. By placing attention within the body, Gendlin was clearly attempting to guide people to gain access to what we are calling the somatic mind, which he referred to as "trusting the wisdom of the body." Rather than seeking solutions only with our cognitive mind, it is a process of inviting other parts of the nervous system to reveal what they know and finding resolutions by holding feelings and issues in the body. Effectively resolving challenging and complex issues thus involves contacting, working with, and speaking from our subtle, underlying felt sense of life held within our greater nervous system.

Gendlin's work parallels the view of Third Generation NLP that the body is not just a machine that is controlled by the brain in your head. There is also a brain in your body. In fact, there are multiple brains in your body. This is an important extension of the "neuro" part of NeuroLinguistic Programming.

Neurogastroenterology and the Brain in the Belly

One of the brains in the body is called the *enteric brain*, or *enteric nervous system* (*enteric* literally means "inside the intestines," from the Greek *enteron* for "intestine"). This system contains 100 million neurons - more than the spinal cord. Modern neuroscience calculates that the system of nerves surrounding the large intestine and the other digestive organs in the belly has a sophistication and complexity roughly equivalent to the brain of a cat. In fact, it is frequently called the "second brain" of the human body.

Many of the key details of how the enteric nervous system mirrors the central nervous system have been emerging in recent years. Dr. Michael Gershon, professor of anatomy and cell biology at Columbia-Presbyterian Medical Center in New York is one of the founders of a new field of medicine called "neurogastroenterology." In his book, *The Second Brain: The Scientific Basis of Gut Instinct and a Groundbreaking New Understanding of Nervous Disorders of the Stomach and Intestines,* Gershon claims that the enteric brain plays a major role in human health and happiness as well as discomfort and distress. Many gastrointestinal disorders, like colitis and irritable bowel syndrome, originate from problems within the enteric nervous system.

The role of the enteric nervous system is to manage every aspect of digestion from the esophagus to the stomach, small intestine and colon. Neurogastroenterologists also believe that there is a complex interplay between the enteric nervous system and the immune system.

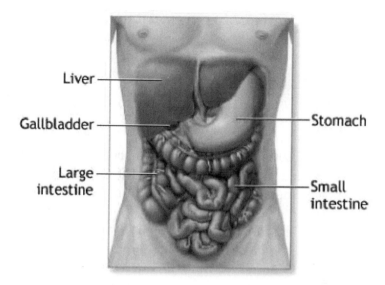

**The Enteric Nervous System
Manages the Process of Digestion**

Due to its significance, biologists believe that, as mammals evolved, the enteric nervous system was too important to reside inside the head of a newborn with long connections going down to the belly. Babies need to eat and digest food from birth. Therefore, the process of evolution seems to have preserved the enteric nervous system as an independent circuit.* It is only loosely connected to the central nervous system and can mostly function alone, without control by the brain.

Just like the brain in our head, the "brain in the belly" sends and receives impulses, records experiences and responds to emotions using the same neurotransmitters as the brain cells in our heads. The enteric nervous system is

---

* It is intriguing to note that as a human fetus develops, a clump of tissue called the "neural crest" forms early in the embryo. One section turns into the central nervous system while another piece migrates to become the enteric nervous system. According to Dr. Gershon, it is only later that the two systems are connected via the vagus nerve.

located in the sheaths of tissue lining the esophagus, stomach, small intestine and colon. Considered a single entity, it is a network of neurons, neurotransmitters and proteins that pass messages between neurons, support cells like those found in the brain and form a complex circuitry that enables it to act independently, learn and remember, producing "gut feelings."

Thus, you have the equivalent of a cat's brain in your belly. When everything is going its way, it purrs. But if it feels threatened it will go "psssst!" When the central nervous system encounters a threatening situation, it releases stress hormones that prepare the body to fight or flee. The enteric system contains many sensory nerves that are stimulated by this chemical surge – hence the experience we call "butterflies."

Recent studies also suggest that stress, especially early in life, can cause chronic gastrointestinal diseases. One doctor, in fact, reported that up to 70 percent of the patients he treats for chronic gastrointestinal disorders had experienced early childhood traumas such as loss of a parent, chronic illness, death of a significant other, etc.

It is interesting to note that traditional cultures on every continent have believed the belly to be a sacred "home of the soul." Japanese martial arts, Chinese healing arts, and the dances of Africa, India, Polynesia, Native America, the Middle East, and Old Europe all incorporate practices to energize the belly in order to awaken the "soul-power" within the body's center.

The abdominal center, which the Japanese call the *hara*, is considered in many martial arts and healing practices to be both a physical and energetic core. It is thought of as the locus of power and gravity, and it houses several bodily organs. The legs, extending from the *hara*, allow its connection with the earth, establishing rootedness as well as enabling mobility. Further, *hara* is understood as a life source and a type of "spiritual umbilicus." It is believed that its cultivation brings mastery, strength, wisdom and tranquility.

In the Japanese language, the word *hara* refers both to the belly and to the qualities of character that emerge as a person activates the "life force" concentrated in the belly.* A "person of *hara*" is one who lives with creativity, courage, confidence, purpose, integrity, and endurance. *Hara no aru hito* literally means an individual with "center" or one "with belly". Such a person is always balanced, tranquil, magnanimous and warm-hearted. Possessing calm, unprejudiced judgment, he or she knows what is important, accepts things as they are and maintains a balanced sense of proportion. The person is ready for whatever comes his or her way. When, through persistent discipline and practice, such a person reaches maturity, the person is said to be *hara no dekita hito*, a person who has "finished his or her belly."

In Chinese, the belly center is named the *tan tien*, a term which literally denotes a field to be cultivated for nourishment essential to the sustenance of life. The implication is that when a person activates his or her body's center with movement and breath, he or she engages the center of his or her being, soul-power and inner source.

Clearly, these linguistic expressions reflect the intuition and subjective experience that the "brain in the belly" is a key part of our somatic intelligence and a powerful resource. The following is a simple exercise and practice that you can use to cultivate access to your belly brain:

---

* Several Japanese phrases incorporate *hara* and indicate the belly's significance for living fully and well. "Belly art," for example, refers to any activity that a person accomplishes both perfectly and effortlessly. "A grand belly" refers to a person who is broad-minded, understanding, compassionate, and generous. "A clean belly" refers to a person who has a clear conscience. To "determine your belly" means to clearly define your intention. To "beat the belly drum" means to lead a contented life.

1. Sit comfortably in your "length" or your "vertical axis," with your spine erect yet relaxed, and your feet evenly placed on the ground. Place the palm of one of your hands on your belly, your thumb at belly button level and your fingers resting below. Place your other palm directly opposite on your lower back.

2. Relax and breathe deeply into your belly. Imagine a string running from the center of one palm to the center of the other. See it, feel it, describe it to yourself.

3. Find the string's midpoint. Focus your attention here for several breaths. Notice and feel whatever images and sensations are occurring at this point. Allow a felt sense of connection to your belly brain (belly center, *hara, tan tien*) to emerge. This should bring you a sense of centeredness, calm, relaxation and balance.

Finding your center in this way will be a key gateway and anchor to your somatic mind and the wisdom of the body.

Neurocardiology and the Brain in the Heart

In addition to the brain in the belly, there is also a growing body of research illustrating that your heart is not just a mechanical pump. The developing field of *neurocardiology* is demonstrating that the heart is, in fact, a highly complex, self-organized information processing center with its own functional "brain" that communicates with and influences the brain in our heads via the nervous system, hormonal system and other pathways. Through these pathways, the activity of our heart profoundly affects brain function and most of the body's major organs, greatly impacting our internal state and ultimately our quality of life.

Similar to the enteric nervous system, the heart's elaborate circuitry enables it to act independently of the brain in the skull – to learn, remember, and even feel and sense. The recent book *Basic and Clinical Neurocardiology*, edited by Dr. J. Andrew Armour and Dr. Jeffrey Ardell, provides a comprehensive overview of the function of the heart's intrinsic nervous system and the role of central and peripheral autonomic neurons in the regulation of cardiac function.

One of the early pioneers in neurocardiology, Dr. Armour has shown that the heart has a complex intrinsic nervous system that is sufficiently sophisticated to qualify as a "little brain" in its own right. The heart's nervous system contains around 40,000 neurons, called sensory neurites, which detect circulating hormones and neurochemicals and sense heart rate and pressure levels. Hormonal, chemical, rate and pressure information is translated into neurological impulses by the heart's nervous system and sent to the brain.

Thus, the heart has its own intrinsic nervous system that operates and processes information independently from the brain or central nervous system. This is what allows a heart transplant to work. Normally, the heart communicates with the brain via fibers running through the vagus nerve and the spinal column. In a heart transplant, these nerve connections do not become reestablished for an extended period of time, if at all. However, the transplanted heart is able to function in its new host through the capacity of its intact, intrinsic nervous system.

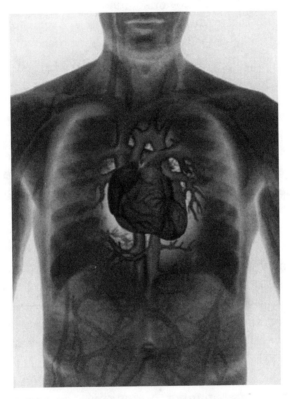

**The Heart Has Its Own Intrinsic Nervous System
That Functions Autonomously From the Brain**

In fact, the experiences of many heart transplant patients provide intriguing insights into the potential of the "heart brain" to store memories and influence behavior. Consider the example of a heart transplant patient related by Dr. Mario Alonso Puig, a specialist in General Surgery (and of the digestive apparatus) for more than twenty-five years, a Fellow in Surgery at Harvard University Medical School and a member of the American Association for the Advancement of Science. After the patient's recovery, he started exhibiting unusual behaviors. He began craving foods he had never liked before. He found himself obsessed with music that he had not previously enjoyed. He found himself attracted to places of which he had no conscious memory.

It was all a big mystery until the life patterns of the heart donor were investigated. The researchers discovered that the foods craved by the recipient had been the favorite foods of the donor, that the donor had been a musician who performed the music the recipient had become obsessed with, and that the places the recipient found himself going to were places where significant events had happened in the life of the donor. Due to strict confidentiality rules, neither the patient nor the doctors had previous access to information about the donor or his personal history. It seems that somehow the preferences had been transferred through the donor's heart.

This is only one of many examples. Claire Sylvia is another heart transplant patient who wrote a book about her experiences titled *A Change of Heart* (1997). According to her story, on May 29, 1988, she received the heart of a young man of age 18 who had been killed in a motorcycle accident. Soon after the operation, she noticed some distinct changes in her attitudes, habits, and tastes. She found herself acting more masculine, strutting down the street (which, being a dancer, was not her usual manner of walking). She began craving foods, such as green peppers and beer, which she had always disliked before. Sylvia even began having recurring dreams about a mystery man named "Tim L.", whom she had a feeling was her donor. As it turns out, he was. Upon meeting the "family of her heart," as she put it, Sylvia discovered that her donor's name was, in fact, Tim L., and that all the changes she had been experiencing in her attitudes, tastes, and habits closely mirrored those of her donor.

In his book *The Heart's Code* (1998), Dr. Paul Pearsal provides other remarkable examples based on 73 heart-transplant cases in which parts of the donors' personalities, memories and knowledge appear to have been transferred to the recipients.

In one instance, an 8-year-old girl received the heart of a 10-year-old girl who had been murdered. The recipient ended up at a psychiatrist's office, plagued by nightmares about her donor's murderer. She said she knew who the man was. After a few sessions, the psychiatrist decided to notify the police. Following the girl's instructions, the murderer was tracked down. The man was convicted on evidence stemming from clues provided first by her: the time, the weapon, the place, the clothes he wore, what his victim told him. Everything the girl said turned out to be true.

In another example, an 8-year-old Jewish boy who died in a car wreck had his heart transplanted in a 3-year-old Arab girl with a dangerous heart condition. As soon as the girl woke up from the anesthesia after surgery, she asked by name for a type of Jewish candy she could not have known existed.

These examples seem to confirm that the heart is much more complex and interesting than merely a muscle that pumps blood.

Similar to the belly, the heart has also been subjectively experienced as an important center of knowing and feeling throughout human history. Some of the earliest recorded civilizations, including the Greek, Mesopotamian and Babylonian, refer to the heart as harboring intelligence. The Greek philosopher Aristotle identified the heart as the most important organ of the body and the origin of the nerves. Noting that it was the first organ to form according to his observations of chick embryos, Aristotle believed it was the seat of intelligence, motion, and sensation—the center of vitality in the body.

HeartMath

Today, various groups, and most notably the Institute of HeartMath, in Boulder Creek, California, have been working on ways to tap into the intelligence of "the brain in the heart." Contending that "the heart is the most powerful generator of rhythmic information patterns in the human body," researchers at the HeartMath Institute claim that "as a critical nodal point in many of the body's interacting systems, the heart is uniquely positioned as a powerful entry point into the communication network that connects body, mind, emotions and spirit."

The essence of the HeartMath approach is that the heart communicates with the brain and the body in four major ways:

1. Neurologically through the transmission of nerve impulses via the vagus nerve and the spinal column.

2. Biophysically through the pulse. The heart sends energy in the form of a blood pressure wave, also known as blood pulse volume (BPV), which brings greater or lesser concentrations of blood supply to the cells of the body and brain. It has been shown that changes in the electrical activity of brain cells occur in relation to the changes in the blood pressure wave.

3. Biochemically through the release of neurotransmitters and hormones such as atrial peptide, a hormone that inhibits the release of other stress hormones.

4. Energetically through the electromagnetic fields generated by the heartbeat. The EKG used to measure heart rate, for instance, registers an electrical signal produced by the heart. This signal can be picked up anywhere on the body, and permeates the space around us. (We will be returning to this notion of energetic influence in more detail in the section on the field mind.)

The HeartMath research and methods focus mainly on the process of establishing a state of psychophysiological coherence. As they point out:

The latest research in neuroscience confirms that emotion and cognition can best be thought of as separate but interacting functions or systems, each with its unique intelligence. Our research is showing that the key to the successful integration of the mind and emotions lies in increasing the coherence (ordered, harmonious function) in both systems and bringing them into phase with one another.

Based on the assumption that greater coherence manifests as more ordered and efficient function in the nervous, cardiovascular, hormonal and immune systems, HeartMath methods promote a state they call *psychophysiological coherence*—a state involving a high degree of balance, harmony and synchronization within and between cognitive, emotional and physiological processes. Their research has shown that this state is associated with high performance, reduced stress, increased emotional stability and numerous health benefits.

HeartMath methods focus primarily on a distinct mode of cardiac function, termed the "internal coherence mode", which has been shown to accompany positive inner feeling states. Physiologically, internal coherence mode is registered in what is known as heart rate variability (HRV). Problematic and unproductive feeling states such as anger and frustration typically show a more random, jerky heart rate pattern, while sincere positive feeling states like appreciation can result in highly ordered and coherent HRV patterns, generally associated with enhanced cardiovascular function. The contrast is illustrated in the following diagram from the HeartMath website.

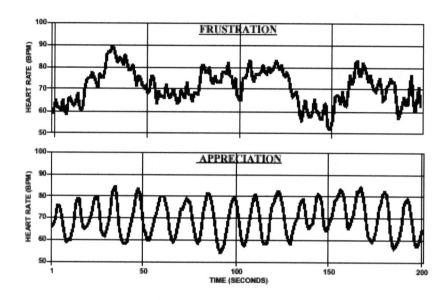

**Contrast of Incoherent and Coherent Heart Rhythms
Associated with Different Feeling States**

HeartMath has developed a number of simple tools whose purpose is to help people connect with and benefit from the intuitive intelligence of the heart brain in order to better make decisions, and to use the wisdom of the heart to manage the mind and emotions. An extensive exploration of these techniques, including supporting scientific data can be found in the book *The HeartMath Solution* (1999) by Doc Childre and Howard Martin. These tools have parallels to many fundamental NLP formats.

The most basic technique is called *Freeze Frame*. It is a one-minute procedure that can produce a significant shift in perception. It is especially useful in challenging or stressful situations. The following is simple summary of the steps:

1. Shift your attention out of your head, and focus on the area around your heart. Keep your attention there for at least ten seconds, continuing to breathe normally.

2. Recall a positive experience or feeling you have had in your life, and re-experience it as fully as possible. See it, hear it and especially tune into the felt sense in order to re-experience it fully.

3. Ask your heart brain: "What can I do in this situation to make it different?" or "What can I do to minimize stress?"

4. Listen to the response of your heart.

Even if you inwardly hear nothing, you will probably feel calmer and more relaxed. The answer may not come in words at all, but in the form of imagery or a felt sense. You may receive verification of something you already know, or you may experience a new perspective, seeing the situation in a more balanced way.

Cut-Thru is another HeartMath technique whose purpose is to help people better manage their emotions. The goal is to develop the ability to "cut through" complex, long-standing emotional responses, and dynamically transform and move through stuck states.

1. Be aware of how you feel about the issue or situation, focusing your attention on your heart.

2. Take an observer position to the situation. Act as though it were someone else's problem. Think of yourself in third person terms; i.e., "he" or "she" instead of "I" or "me." What kind of advice would you give yourself if you were a witness or coach to yourself?

3. Imagine bringing any distorted feelings or emotional energy that is out of balance into your heart. Let it soak there, as if you were soaking in a warm bath, so that it

relaxes, integrates and transforms. Practice letting the heart do the work for you.

The purpose of the Cut-Thru technique is to help people learn to accept, hold and transform difficult feelings rather than to repress them.

A third tool, *Heart Lock-In*, is about experiencing your heart at a deeper level in order to produce physical, mental and spiritual regeneration.

1. Move your attention from your mind into your heart and let it rest there.

2. Remember the feeling of love, connection or care you have for someone with whom those feelings come easily. Focus on a feeling of appreciation or gratitude for someone or something positive. Practice staying with that feeling for five to fifteen minutes.

3. Gently send that feeling of love or appreciation to yourself and others.

You can find out more about HeartMath research, methods and programs on their website: http://www.heartmath.org.

The Breath

Breathing is another key influence on the quality and effectiveness of both the cognitive and somatic minds. It is through the breath that we bring oxygen into the body, nervous system and brain. Mammals and other living organisms require oxygen to release energy in the form of the metabolism of energy-rich molecules such as glucose. Breath is also the mechanism through which we filter carbon dioxide and other gasses out of the body.

The *lungs* are the primary organs of respiration in humans. Our lungs add oxygen to the blood as it passes through them on its way back to the heart. When it reaches the heart, the blood is pumped to the brain and then throughout the remainder of the body. As blood passes through the brain and body, it deposits oxygen in the organs. The blood is almost depleted of oxygen and has a dull, dark color just before it reaches the lungs, where it is refreshed with oxygen and again looks bright red.

Lungs

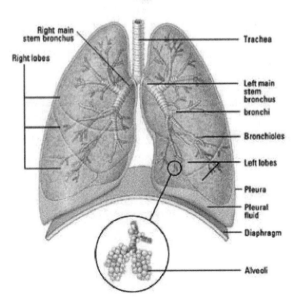

The organs used in the process of respiration include the mouth; the nose and nostrils; the pharynx; the larynx; the trachea; the bronchi and bronchioles; the diaphragm; the lungs; and the terminal branches of the respiratory tree, such as the capillaries and the alveoli—the tiny vessels through which the gas exchange with the blood takes place. Humans have two lungs, with the left being divided into two lobes and the right into three lobes. Together, the lungs contain approximately 1500 miles (2,400 km) of airways and 300 to 500 million alveoli. Furthermore, if all the capillaries that surround the alveoli were unwound and laid end to end, they would extend for about 620 miles. The lungs are thus very intricate and complex organs that connect us to our environment.

Breathing is essential for survival. We cannot live without breathing for more than a very short time before serious damage begins to occur. Typical resting adult respiratory rates are 10-20 breaths per minute with 1/3 of the breath time in inhalation. (The medical term for normal relaxed breathing is *eupnea*.)

Breathing is also essential for optimal performance, both mentally and physically. States of greater energy, exertion, focus, attention and awareness require higher levels of oxygen in the body, brain and nervous system, which means taking fuller and deeper breaths.

In what is referred to as *survival breathing* (the minimum level of breath required for survival) a person is essentially breathing just enough to make it to the next breath. Many of us breathe this way without being aware of doing so. To perform optimally and gain access to the full intelligence and wisdom of our somatic mind, we must breathe beyond survival breathing.

Breathing is one of the few basic bodily functions that, within limits, can be controlled both consciously and unconsciously. Intentional breathing is common in many forms of meditation, yoga and other awareness practices. In swimming, cardio fitness, speech or vocal training, one learns to discipline one's breathing, initially consciously but later subconsciously, for purposes beyond survival and "life support." In the practice of T'ai Chi Chuan, for example, aerobic training is combined with breathing to exercise the diaphragm muscles and to train effective posture, both of which improve the use of the body's energy.

Many ancient cultures have linked the breath to a "life force." The Hebrew Bible refers to God breathing the "breath of life" into clay to make Adam a living soul. It also refers to the breath as returning to God when a mortal dies. The words "spirit," "*qi*" (chi), and "psyche" are all terms related to the phenomenon of breath.

From the perspective of many of the world's great spiritual and philosophical traditions, our breath not only brings needed oxygen and other gasses to the physical body, but it can also bring, when we are conscious of it, other "energies" (i.e., prana, chi, and so on) needed to help nourish our "subtle bodies" or souls. In this view, breath is our most important connection with our environment, as we exchange breath with the universe. When we breathe out, we are giving our spirit through our breath to the world. When we breathe in, we are receiving spirit from the world through our breath.

Whatever we may believe about our soul and spirit, our breath and how we breathe are intimately connected with all aspects of our being.

It is no surprise, then, that many traditional approaches for increasing consciousness include practices that are based on breath awareness. The breath accompanies us from our first in-breath at birth to our last out-breath at the moment of our death. The breath is always happening in the present moment, and as such, is an excellent anchor for bringing our awareness into a present, ongoing connection to our somatic intelligence. By simply taking a few seconds to turn our attention to the sensation of the movement of the breath in the body, the sequential thought process of the mind that generally dominates our attention will loosen its grip, the body will relax to some degree, and we can then continue whatever we are doing with more presence and resources, more connected to ourselves and our somatic intelligence in the present.

One simple breathing practice you can undertake is to consciously follow your breathing in the many changing circumstances of your life. As you inhale, simply be aware that you are inhaling. As you exhale, simply be aware that you are exhaling. Try this exercise for 10 minutes or so at a time at least three times a day. It will help free you from your automatic thoughts and emotional reactions and thus enable you to live with more receptivity and clarity in the present moment. You may find this exercise especially useful at moments when you are anxious or angry.

To get a sense of this, take a moment right now to put your attention on your breathing. Feel the air coming in your nostrils and the expansion of your body on the in-breath. Feel the air pouring out through your nostrils or mouth and the corresponding release of muscular tension on the out-breath. Breathe at whatever rhythm happens naturally, and with gentle curiosity, feel the sensations breathing produces in your torso. Keep your attention on your breathing until you feel a change in your inner state. When you feel ready, turn your attention back to whatever you were doing (reading this page, for example), and allow a part of your awareness to remain present with your breathing. Notice also if there is any resistance (impatience, frustration, skepticism, "I'll do this later") to giving your attention for a few moments to your breath. Your cognitive mind may rebel against interrupting its activity, but you can reassure it that you will be right back.

Buddhist monk and spiritual teacher Thich Nhat Hanh suggests another simple breathing practice which extends this basic breathing exercise by adding some words to the in-breath and the out-breath:

> *"Breathing in* (breathe in), *I am calm."*
> *"Breathing out* (breathe out), *I smile."*

You can also add the phrases:

> (Breathe in) *"Dwelling in the present moment,"*
> (Breathe out) *"I know this is a wonderful moment."*

Another simple but powerful breathing practice is called 4 Square Breathing:

1. Breathe in for a count of 4
2. Hold for a count of 4
3. Breathe out for a count of 4
4. Hold for the a count of 4
5. Repeat

Notice the difference when you change the speed. Notice where your breath goes in the body, through the lungs, under the arms and into the back, etc. Follow your breath with your awareness.

Somato Respiratory Integration™

Somato Respiratory Integration™ (SRI) is a process developed by Donald Epstein, founder of Network Chiropractic or Network Spinal Analysis (NSA). Described in his book *The 12 Stages of Healing*, Somato Respiratory Integration™ exercises are designed to help the brain reconnect with the body and its somatic intelligence through the process of breath. According to Epstein, "These exercises reconnect breathing with awareness of the body and its natural rhythms. They help the individual experience his/her body more fully, instantly shift the individual's state of consciousness to one that supports trust for the body-mind and healing process, as well as promote increased peace and ease."

The following is an example of an exercise designed by Epstein known as *Stage One* of the SRI process (there are twelve stages in all).

1. Lie on your back or be seated. Touch your upper chest at the top of the sternum with both hands, palms facing your body, and breathe slowly and gently in through your nose and out through your mouth. Inhale just deeply enough to feel your breath meet the rhythm of your chest rising. Exhale just enough to feel the rhythm of your chest falling. Localize the area of motion and breath to just the zone under your hands. Do not allow other areas of the body to recruit motion. Repeat this process for a few breaths.

2. Now, do the same exercise with your hands placed at the bottom of your breastbone over your diaphragm and breathe the same way. Then place your hands on your abdomen (near your navel) and repeat. Remember to breathe gently just into the area where your hands are placed.

Notice in which areas this happens the most easily and brings a sense of peace and ease, and in which ones this seems more difficult to do or brings up any uncomfortable feelings.

3. Identify the area that feels most comfortable and at which you can focus the breath and movement with greatest ease. Place your hands there again, breathe gently and deeply and let the peace you experience there spread to any areas where you felt discomfort.

4. Once you have found the "connection" with the place of peace and ease and can focus the breath and motion into just that area, then alternate between touching and breathing into this area and the area of distress. When you hold the area of distress, you should attempt to get breath as close to that area of the body as possible and moan or make the sound of that area—the sound that area would want to make if it could speak.

5. After the sound is made in this area (no more than 30 seconds on this area of distress), place your hands back over the area of connection, ease and peace. Sigh or make a sound of peace, ease or relief at this area. Alternate between the area of connection or peace and distress for a few minutes (usually up to 10 minutes). Notice if there is more comfort or a sense of greater wellness, or if the sounds between both areas seem to merge.

More information can be found about SRI, Donald Epstein and Network Spinal Analysis at:
http://www.associationfornetworkcare.com.

The Spine

In human anatomy, the *spine* (backbone or vertebral column) is a column that houses and protects the spinal cord. It is made up of 7 cervical vertebrae, 12 thoracic vertebrae, 5 lumbar vertebrae, the sacrum and the coccyx (or tailbone). The ribs of the chest are connected to the thoracic spine.

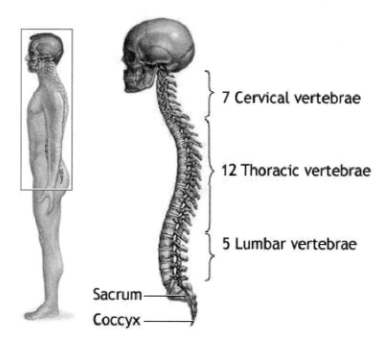

The Human Spine

The spinal cord is a bundle of nerve tissue and support cells about the width of a human finger that extends from the brain through the length of the vertebral column. These nerves are encased in the meninges sheath and surrounded by cerebral spinal fluid, which acts as a cushion to protect them from shock against the inside of the spinal column.

The spinal cord forks off in paired nerve branches at each level of the spine, except the top cervical vertebrae. These nerve branches leave the spine on both sides through spaces between each vertebra.

The *cervical nerves* connect to the shoulder, arm, neck and hands. These nerves also control the function of the throat, sinuses, nose, thyroid gland, lymph nodes and diaphragm.

The *thoracic nerves* run along the middle of the back, going to muscles, tissues and internal organs. These nerves affect the surface tissue of the elbows, hands, and fingers. They also affect the chest, abdomen, heart, lungs, liver, stomach, pancreas, spleen, adrenal glands, kidneys and the small intestine.

The *lumbar nerves* are responsible for coordinating the lower back muscles, thighs, legs, calves and feet. Nerves that exit from the lumbar nerves also control the large intestine, appendix, bladder, prostate gland and the male and female reproductive organs.

The *sacral nerves* are located in the sacrum and coccyx, more commonly known as the tailbone. Nerves exiting through these bones affect the buttocks, hips, thighs and legs. These nerves also affect the rectum and some pelvic tissues.

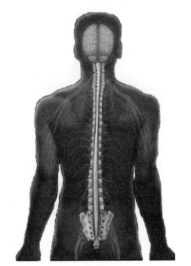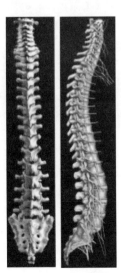

The Spinal Cord Branches from the Spine Between Each Vertebra

The spinal cord, then, is the main pathway for information connecting the brain, peripheral nervous system and the rest of the body. It functions primarily in the transmission of neural signals between the brain and the entire body but also contains neural circuits that can independently control numerous reflexes. Thus, the spinal cord has three major functions:

1. Transmit and distribute motor signals, which travel from the brain down the spinal cord.

2. Collect and relay sensory information, which travel from the peripheries of the body up the spinal cord to the brain.

3. Serve as a center for coordinating certain reflexes.

Like the belly and the heart, the spinal cord has some functions that are independent from the brain.

Nerve fibers going to every part of the body come through the spine. The position of the spine and the level of tension on the spinal cord can greatly affect the functioning of our body and nervous system. Damage to the nerves can cause pain, tingling, numbness or weakness in the area where the nerve travels. Damage to the spinal cord itself at any level can cause many symptoms, from paralysis to numbness to the disruption of proper functioning. Problems associated with the thoracic nerves, for example, include asthma, allergies, ulcers and kidney problems.

Body Posture

Anyone who has studied martial arts or yoga, or who has experience with different approaches to body work that focus on the structure and movement of the body (osteopathy, Alexander Technique, Feldenkrais, etc.) knows that our body posture and way of moving are a reflection of our inner life, and that, conversely, we can influence our internal states by practicing body awareness. Thus, another practice that can help us to learn to gain more access to our somatic intelligence is to develop awareness of our body posture. In any given moment, we can turn our attention to our physical body and become aware of our physical posture. This orients our attention to the present moment, and again slows down the sequential process of the thinking mind that tends to take us out of contact with the body. We can become aware of how we might be holding tension in the spine that is not useful and thus reduce excess energy expenditure in order to be more resourceful and energized in the present.

Without changing anything in your posture, become aware of how you are sitting (or standing) right now. Take the time to "visit" your body: shoulders, neck, face, spine, belly, chest, hips and any other part of your body that calls your attention. Sense where there may be excess tension (back of neck contracted), or a lack of vitality (chest sunk, shoulders rounded). Allow your body to gently adjust its posture. Use your breath to help your body do this. Use the out-breath to help release what is contracted or tense by gently "breathing out through those places." To tone those places where energy is lacking, allow the breath to fill them gently on the in-breath. Force nothing, but instead allow your body to find a more resourceful, balanced state as you give it your attention and "breathe with" it.

It can also be helpful to imagine your chest lifting and expanding. Move the center of your chest upward as you feel your heart area opening. At the same time, imagine your spine lengthening. As though there were a string attached to the center of the crown of your head, feel your head being gently, gently pulled upward. Think "head free," and feel the back of your neck lengthen, and your chin come slightly downwards and in. Feel the freedom in the occipital joint where the spinal column meets the skull. Imagine space between each vertebra all the way down your spine.

At the bottom of your spine, imagine that the sacrum and the coccyx ("tail bone") continue beyond the physical body and extend toward the floor, as though the spine lengthened into a "kangaroo tail" that goes all the way down to the ground. This may produce a sense of lengthening in your lower back and a general state of relaxation in the pelvic area. If it is useful, imagine that this "tail" continues to extend, like a root, deeper and deeper into the earth. Again, force nothing and continue to be aware of the sensations present in your body. When you are ready, give your attention back to whatever you were doing, keeping part of your awareness on the felt sense of your physical body.

Notice what changes are produced in your inner state by giving your attention to your spine and your body posture.

Network Spinal Analysis™ (NSA)

A good example of working with the spine as part of a larger somatic mind is *Network Spinal Analysis™*, developed by Dr. Donald Epstein whose process called Somato Respiratory Integration™ (SRI) is described in the section on the breath. Working initially within the traditional chiropractic paradigm, Epstein discovered to his surprise that a very gentle touch to the upper or lower spine could cause the entire spine to reconfigure itself. Deep respiration, along with wavelike undulations and dissipation of stored spinal tension were often associated with this gentle touch, and resulted in an overall enhancement of the patient's quality of life.

By using the spine as a key access point to a larger somatic intelligence, Epstein began to realize that in this non-linear approach to wellness, a small change in physiology, under the proper conditions, produced a disproportionate response in people's health and well-being. A strong force need not be applied to create a significant change in physiology. In fact, he discovered that applying a forceful touch could actually inhibit this process. He called this approach Network Spinal Analysis™ to distinguish it from more traditional chiropractic methods.

Working with the NSA approach, which assumes that body is not just a machine and the spinal cord a group of electrical cables connecting it to the brain, Epstein found that memories of childhood wounds, accidents, or other physical or psychological traumas are often stored as tension and energy patterns in the spine and other parts of the body. This energy, confined under tension, is somewhat like a powerful spring. Over time it manifests in physically tight muscles, joint fixations, resistance to full body motion, depression and shallow breathing. It also manifests as pain and disease.

The ability of our somatic mind to receive, circulate, and dissipate energy, coupled with our current and past conditioning, significantly affect our health and the way we interpret and respond to a given situation. Energy that is not free to circulate generates tension over time. When this energy is released (or converted from a confined state into a freer state), it becomes available for healing, creativity and other generative activities.

The severity of the symptoms, the duration of a condition, or the degree of pathology do not themselves determine the severity of the measures needed to be taken in order to heal. A small change, when perceived by the nervous system in the proper state, can release the stored energy and tension, allowing it to be utilized by the body for constructive purposes like healing and transformation.

As a personal example, author Robert Dilts injured his back in a water skiing accident at age 14. The resulting compressed vertebra and structural damage to the bone in the lower back created pain, weakness and postural problems for almost 30 years. After a few sessions with an NSA practitioner, Dr. John Amaral of Santa Cruz, the symptoms disappeared and were replaced by an increased sense of energy, vitality and stamina, which have remained for more than 12 years at the time of this writing.

Spinal adjustments, spinal entrainments, breathing practices and other exercises are some of the tools used by NSA practitioners.

More information on Network Spinal Analysis™ is available through the website:

http://www.associationfornetworkcare.com.

The Feet

Our feet are another part of our body that play a key role in accessing and optimizing the intelligence of our somatic mind. We often don't think about our feet as an important part of our nervous system, yet they have a significant effect on the way our body and mind function and interact with the world around us.

As mentioned earlier, in some traditions, the legs are considered to extend the *hara*, or belly brain, in connection with the earth, through the feet, establishing rootedness as well as enabling mobility. Physiologically, the sensory input of the foot has an important influence on balance and posture. When we are standing, our feet are our primary point of connection with the earth. Our posture is completely dependent on the way the bottoms of our feet contact the surface beneath us.

Similar to the palms of the hands, the soles of the feet are extremely sensitive to touch due to the high concentration of nerve endings necessary to make the constant subtle adjustments required to maintain our balance and posture. Increased awareness of the soles of the feet thus allows for greater stability, mobility and balance. Moshe Feldenkrais would sometimes spend as long as a half an hour to an hour with a person lying on their back as he gently touched the soles of their feet in order to help them improve their posture or to walk with improved balance and stability.

If necessary, the feet can do almost anything our hands can do. People who have lost their arms or hands (especially early in life) can frequently learn to do almost everything people do with their hands by using their feet, including eating, drinking, writing with a pen, typing at a computer, driving a car, etc. There are some fascinating and inspiring video examples that can be found on the Internet through Youtube. Search for Barbara Guerra (mother with no arms) and Jessica Parks.

Alternative approaches to health and healing, such as reflexology, maintain that different parts of the sole of the foot correspond to all the parts, glands and organs of the body. Reflexology, also called zone therapy, is based on the notion that all body parts are represented on the hands and feet and that pressing on specific areas on the hands or feet can have therapeutic effects in other parts of the body.

The individual's foot reflex areas reveal the individual's overall state of tension that has resulted from a lifetime of adaptation to stress. Stress cues in the feet are a roadmap to the reflexologist. Wherever stress cues are found on a foot, it is a sign that stress and its effects have begun to accumulate in the corresponding parts of the body.

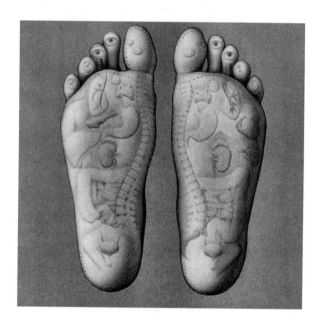

The Various Zones in the Sole of the Foot According to Reflexology

At another level, a large part of our nervous system is hard-wired to support survival through reflexes in various parts of the body. Our ability to move is a key part of our survival. It is a necessary part of both "flight" and "fight;" and we need our feet to move. If our feet become ungrounded, unbalanced or restricted for a long enough period of time, our survival may become at risk.

Most of the nerves in our bodies that are designed to detect how we're moving in space are located in the joints. After the skull and the hands, our feet are one of the most jointed parts of our body. If our joints become constrained or disturbed, those bones are prevented from doing what they were designed to do: to support us to move. This becomes interpreted as a threat signal by the rest of the somatic system.

Unbalanced or immobile joints signal to our body that there is a problem or threat. These subjective experiences relating to the feet are reflected in "organ language" such as: "I couldn't find my footing," "I need to learn to stand on my own two feet," "I got cold feet," etc.

For stability and balance (both physically and emotionally), our feet need to be firmly planted on the ground, which is not always as simple as it sounds. We often neglect our feet and don't treat them with much awareness. High heels, overly tight or worn down shoes, and shoes with inadequate arch support can all distort the foot's natural form and bring a great deal of tension and immobility to the foot. With this tightening of the tendons and muscles, the feet eventually become unbalanced and unstable.

Ungrounded and unsteady feet can lead to a misalignment of the entire body, creating tension throughout the somatic system. This tension can be the cause of leg pain, knee problems, hip issues, lower back pain, neck and shoulder discomfort and even headaches. It can also bring a sense of ungroundedness, unsteadiness and imbalance to your experience of your life and limit your access to the full potential of your somatic intelligence.

Gabrielle Roth, developer of the 5Rhythms®, places a tremendous emphasis on the feet. The fundamental principle of her transformational movement practice is to "follow your feet." Participants are encouraged to dance barefoot in order to free the feet, increase the sense of contact and rootedness with the earth and improve the capacity for mobility.

Foot Pad Release Practice

By spreading and massaging the muscles and tendons on the bottom of the feet, you can create a more stable and solid foundation on which to walk, thus avoiding eventual knee, hip and lower back problems.

Releasing the three foot pads (ball, side, and heel), allows your feet to once again come in full contact with the ground, restoring stability and balance throughout the body.

To rebalance and stabilize the foot pads, follow these three steps. Use firm pressure when applying these techniques.

1. *Ball Pad*: Place your fingers over the ball of the foot. Inhale. Exhale and drag your fingers up over the ball and through the toes while extending the foot. Repeat three times.

2. *Side Pad*: Place your fingers along the bottom surface, in the soft tissue or pink area of the foot. Inhale. Exhale and drag your fingers toward the outside of the foot while rotating the foot inward. Repeat three times.

3. *Heel Pad*: Place your fingers in the soft tissue area in front of the heel. Inhale. Exhale and drag your fingers over the heel surface while flexing the foot, with the toes pointing toward the sky. Repeat three times.

Once you have stabilized one foot, get up and walk around. You should feel a greater width and breadth of your foot pad as it strikes the ground, giving you a sense of greater balance, stability and connection with the earth. You should also notice a higher arch.

Then repeat the steps on the other foot pad.

The Cortical Homunculus – The Body In The Brain

So far we have been examining the various aspects of the nervous system within the body itself that make up our somatic intelligence—the brain(s) in the body. The so-called *homunculus* is a representation of how our brain perceives the body, which is another influence on our somatic awareness. The *cortical homunculus*, for example, depicts the relative number of cortical brain cells devoted to sensing or operating the various parts of the body, indicating the proportion of cells devoted to each body part. In other words, the cortical homunculus is a map of the relative amounts of the cortex associated with different body parts. It also reflects kinesthetic proprioception, the body as felt in motion.

Some parts of the body are linked to a greater number of sensory and motor cells in the cortex of the brain. These particular parts of the body are represented as being larger on the homunculus. A part of the body with fewer sensory and/or motor connections to the brain is represented to appear smaller. For example the thumb, which is used in thousands of complex activities, appears much larger than the thigh with its relatively simple movement.

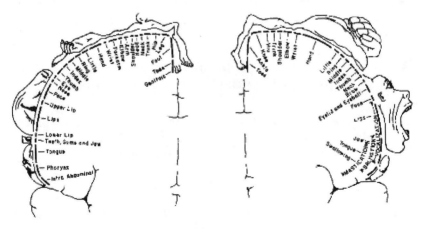

The Cortical Homunculus Shows the Relative Amount of Sensory and Motor Cells in the Brain Devoted to Various Parts of the Body

The cortical homunculus is the basis for our mental model of our body and physical self-image—i.e., the body within the brain. It reflects our cognitive, conscious awareness of our body, and the deletions, generalizations and distortions that accompany it.

If we translated that representation back into an actual body, the result would be a grotesquely disfigured human with disproportionately huge hands, lips, and face in comparison to the rest of the body.

The Human Body As It Would Be If It Looked the Way It Is Represented In the Cortical Homunculus

The cortical homunculus is a very deep example of the difference between "map" and "territory". We have both an actual arm and the brain's inner representation of that arm (the territory and map). They are not the same thing, and that difference is what makes it possible for people to experience "phantom limb" phenomena or to "negatively hallucinate" parts of their body and experience them as missing when they are still there.

Our brain's perception of our body is not our actual body nor is it the one that our somatic mind perceives. In addition to our actual belly and the brain's perception of the belly, there are also the enteric nervous system's perceptions of the belly. Clearly, what Gendlin referred to as the "felt sense" of our body includes more than the homunculus, integrating purely somatic as well as cortical perception.

The somatic mind and the cognitive mind naturally give priority to different parts and aspects of our body and physiology. The cortex is heavily devoted to processing information coming in from our teleceptors—the senses oriented toward the outside world. Our somatic nervous system manages our inner world.

The cortex was the last part of the human brain to evolve. Its structures and purposes are thus more recent than the parts of our nervous system with more ancient roots (such as the enteric system, neuro-cardio system, spinal cord, "reptilian brain," etc.). Our cortex, which is unique to humans, developed to help us manage social, cultural and environmental interactions. This is why the homunculus puts so much emphasis on our hands, lips, tongues, etc. These are the parts of our bodies used for communication and the manipulation of our external world. The cortical homunculus is a more socially, culturally and environmentally oriented representation of ourselves.

There is also evidence that the cortical homunculus is shaped by our life experiences. It has been shown that the cortical homunculus develops over time and differs from one person to the next. The representation in the homunculus of the hand in the brain of an infant, for example, is different from the representation of the hand in the brain of a concert pianist. We could also predict that in the case of the people mentioned earlier who had lost their hands and arms and learned to eat, write and drive using their feet, a much larger portion of their motor homunculus would probably be devoted to their feet than in the case of a person who still has and uses both of his or her arms and hands.

An important implication of this is that, within limits, our degree of awareness and use of a particular part of our body can alter its representation within the neural homunculus. The types of practices provided in this book, then, could alter the neurolinguistic structure of our brain (and perhaps other parts of our nervous system). This can help us to have a more balanced and integrated felt sense of our bodies and ourselves.

Exploring Your Subjective Homunculus

Our cortical homunculus is mirrored in our *subjective homunculus*—our personal perception of our own body. If you bring your attention to your own introspective sense of your body, you will no doubt notice that some parts of your body spontaneously stand out in your awareness more than others. Exploring your subjectively perceived homunculus involves noticing which parts of your body are more or less in your conscious awareness at a particular point in time. This can give you a lot of feedback about your relationship with different parts of your body and the type of activity going on in your somatic mind.

If you pause and put your attention on your body right now, which parts of your body (e.g., spine, hands, eyes, belly, pelvis, etc.) most easily come to your attention? Remember that the homunculus is not a register of emotional responses, but rather relates to physical sensations and movement.

Some parts of your body may not be in your awareness at all. Are there any parts of your body (soles of the feet, ear lobes, elbows, lungs, left big toe, etc.) that have been absent from your awareness at this time?

It can be both insightful and useful to assess your subjective homunculus when you are in different internal states or functioning at different levels of performance. As an example, try out the following exercise:

1. Recall an experience in which you found yourself in an unresourceful state (stuck, confused, anxious, etc.) or at a poor level of performance.

2. Relive the experience as fully as possible. As you do, become aware of which parts of your body are most in the foreground. Which ones do you feel most intensely? Which ones do you feel in the most detail? Are there any distortions? Which parts are in the background? Do some body parts seem to run together or seem indistinguishable from each other at a feeling level? Which are you not aware of at all?

3. Clear your mind and release that state from your body.

4. Identify an experience in which you were in a resourceful state (confident, relaxed, creative, centered, etc.) or at high level of performance.

5. Put yourself into that experience as fully as possible. Again, be aware of which parts of your body are most in the foreground. Which ones do you feel most intensely or in the most detail? Which parts are in the background? Which are you not aware of at all?

6. Clear your mind and reflect upon any differences that make a difference. Orient yourself to the present moment where you can consider both experiences and identify the differences in your perception of your body between the resourceful and non-resourceful states or the low and high instances of performance.

People often have very interesting insights when doing this type of exploration. It is fascinating to realize that our perceived body image can sometimes vary quite dramatically. People who have substance addictions, for example, will usually have highly distorted perceptions of their body and anatomy when they are craving the substance. Such body distortions indicate that one does not have access to the full range and power of his or her somatic intelligence and resources. These distortions act to prevent us from gaining full somatic connection, creating a type of downward spiral or vicious cycle that bring about a collapse into the problem state.

It is interesting to explore such problem states and reduce the deletions, distortions and generalizations present in the subjective homunculus. Following are two possible explorations:

1. Put yourself back into the unresourceful experience or instance of low performance that you explored above, but keep a more balanced overall body awareness. What is different in your subjective perception of the state or the situation?

2. If a particular body part feels especially distorted or absent, practice bringing an even focus of attention to that part. Then maintain that same level of awareness as you shift in and out of that experience.

Another very interesting example of the impact of body awareness is the following version of the Foreground-Background technique.

Steps of the Somatic Foreground-Background Process

1. Identify an automatic limiting response that occurs in a well-defined context and is testable *(e.g., anxiety related to making an oral presentation)*.

2. Associate into a specific example of the limiting response enough that you experience its effects on your physiology.

    a. Introspectively attend to your body image (subjective homunculus) within that experience. Identify what is in the *"foreground"* of your awareness—i.e., which parts and sensations in your body seem MOST amplified at the time the limiting response is happening *(e.g., awareness of pounding heart rate and tense jaw)*.

    b. Identify what is in the *"background"* or neutral with respect to the state—notice which parts of your body you are not aware of during the experience and that seem to have no involvement in it *(e.g., soles of feet, earlobe, left elbow)*.

2. Identify a resourceful *counter example* experience—that is, a time when you could or should have had the limiting response but did not. If there is no counter example, then identify an experience that is as close to the limiting one as possible in all respects but where there is no limiting response. Associate into this experience *(e.g., telling a joke or story to a group of new acquaintances)*.

    a. Again become aware of which parts of your body you are MOST aware of *(foreground)* *(e.g., a sense of energy in the spine and calmness in the belly)*.

    b. Also identify what is in the *background*, neutral or absent from your subjective body awareness *(e.g., knee cap, soles of feet and earlobe)*.

3. Reflecting on both examples, find some parts of the body that are in the background of, or absent from, *both* the problematic *and* resourceful experiences (*e.g., little toe and left elbow*).

4. Return to the resourceful experience and really get a full felt sense of it. Expand your body awareness while in that state to produce a more balanced sense of your whole body, especially including the parts of the body that you discovered in the previous step (*e.g., little toe and left elbow*).

5. Now go back to the limiting experience. Access it fully, but this time focus your attention on the parts of the body that had previously been in the background of both states (*e.g., little toe and left elbow*). You should notice an immediate and automatic dissipating of the problem response and a shift of your state toward a more positive and resourceful experience.

More information and a more comprehensive version of the Foreground-Background Process are available in the *Encyclopedia of Systemic NLP* (2000).

Biofeedback

What is known as *biofeedback* is another resource for developing a deeper connection with somatic awareness and somatic intelligence. "Biofeedback" involves providing a person with feedback (either auditorily or visually) about a particular biological or bodily response in order to help create a greater link between cognitive and somatic processes. These processes are generally those occurring in the involuntary, or "autonomic," nervous system, such as heart rate, vascular responses (often indirectly measured as skin temperature), brain waves, and the activity of the pores and sweat glands (measured by the electrical responses of the skin).

The autonomic nervous system has two basic branches, the sympathetic and parasympathetic systems. The *sympathetic* branch is the part of the nervous system that moderates our fight/flight reactions and other survival strategies. It is essentially excitatory in its function. When the sympathetic system becomes active, it speeds up the heartbeat, increases the rate of breath, stimulates adrenaline flow, constricts blood flow to the periphery of the body, opens the pores which causes an increase in perspiration, etc., essentially readying the body for action. These reactions accompany both the stimulation of excitement and the stress of survival strategies.

The parasympathetic nervous system tends to calm and relax the body and is responsible for regenerative functions. When the parasympathetic system is activated, the heartbeat slows, breathing becomes slower and deeper, the micro muscles around the blood vessels and capillaries relax, increasing blood flow to the hands, feet and peripheries of the body, perspiration decreases, etc. This makes it possible for the body to relax, reenergize and rebuild resources.

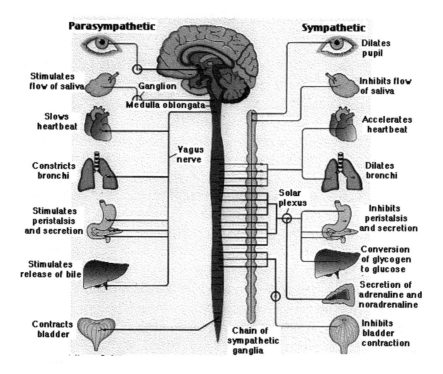

Parasympathetic

Sympathetic

Stimulates
flow of saliva

Ganglion

Dilates
pupil

Medulla oblongata

Inhibits flow
of saliva

Slows
heartbeat

Accelerates
heartbeat

Vagus
nerve

Constricts
bronchi

Dilates
bronchi

Stimulates
peristalsis
and secretion

Solar
plexus

Inhibits
peristalsis
and secretion

Stimulates
release of bile

Conversion
of glycogen
to glucose

Secretion of
adrenaline and
noradrenaline

Contracts
bladder

Chain of
sympathetic
ganglia

Inhibits
bladder
contraction

The Autonomic Nervous System is Divided Into Two Branches: the Sympathetic and Parasympathetic Systems

Biofeedback provides a very powerful means for people to recognize and explore the relationship between cognitive mind and these vital body functions (between the central nervous system and the autonomic nervous system). By measuring "autonomic" functions and "feeding back" the result to the individual through a tone or graph, the individual is able to recognize in what ways he or she is able to harmonize with and influence that aspect of physiology.

As a result of extensive research in the area of biofeedback, the "autonomic" system—which was previously thought to be completely "self-regulating"—was found to be surprisingly responsive to the influence of the central nervous system.

The use of biofeedback has demonstrated that potentially dramatic gains can be achieved by teaching psychosomatic techniques to patients with medical problems. Biofeedback has been used to positively influence a number of biological responses that cause health problems, such as headaches, chronically taut muscles from accidents or sports injuries, asthma, high blood pressure, and heart arrhythmia. It is often used instead of, or as a complement to, drugs in pain treatment.

Biofeedback has been particularly effective in helping people to reduce the impact of stress and to achieve more optimum states of physical and mental functioning. This is because such feedback brings greater awareness of our internal state and increases our ability to intentionally influence it in a positive way.

As was pointed out earlier, when a person experiences stress or excitement, there is an activation of the sympathetic nervous system. This increases breathing rate, sweat gland activity (and consequently skin conductance) and heart rate. The variability of the heartbeat also becomes uneven and sporadic. Relaxation, calm and stillness, however, result from the activation of the parasympathetic system, which reduces and deepens breathing, decreases sweat gland activity and skin conductance, and produces a slower, smoother and more rhythmic heartbeat pattern.

By helping us to better recognize and calibrate our inner state, and learn (both consciously and intuitively) what types of thoughts and actions trigger and influence that state, biofeedback refines our ability to choose and direct the quality of our internal state, similar to the way we learn to ride a bicycle.

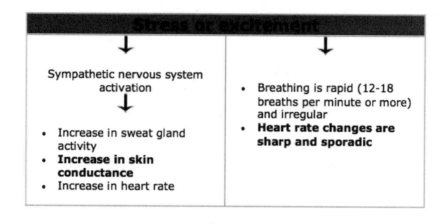

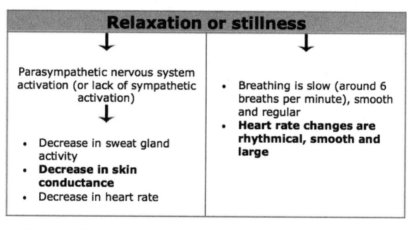

**Common Somatic Responses Associated with States of
Stress or Excitement and Relaxation or Stillness**

Biofeedback training methods are relatively simple, although they require the appropriate instrumentation. Initially, the learner must choose the appropriate type of feedback that is most relevant to his or her goals. For example, learning to relax certain muscles may be somewhat useful in many stress related disorders, but may not be the most effective treatment for other physical issues. An anxious patient with tachycardia (rapid heartbeat) may benefit much more by learning to slow his or her heart rate and bring it into psychophysical coherence rather then by learning to relax muscles.

After the desired mode of feedback has been selected, the learner is connected to the appropriate sensor. Information about the particular autonomic nervous system function being measured is then fed into a computer or some other type of display, and the response is presented back to the learner. The learner's conscious awareness of the feedback is registered in his or her central nervous system, which, in turn, influences the autonomic nervous system. This influence is usually intuitive and outside of the awareness of the learner.

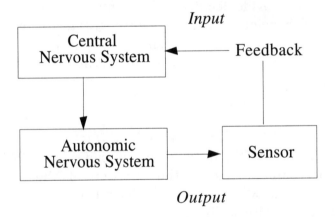

Input

Central Nervous System ← Feedback

Autonomic Nervous System → Sensor

Output

Process of Traditional Biofeedback

A learner may be given either "binary" or "analog" feedback. "Binary" or "digital" feedback involves setting a certain target or threshold value for the autonomic reaction. Whenever the learner's physical response reaches that target or crosses the threshold, a light or tone indicates that the learner is succeeding. This is the primary mode of training for producing an EEG "alpha" state. Feedback is provided whenever the learner is producing brain waves in the range of "alpha" (8-12 Hz).

"Analog" feedback involves supplying the learner with an ongoing representation of a particular autonomic function, such as heart rate, temperature, or skin resistance. In this way, the learner develops the ability to calibrate and control a particular autonomic process, and establishes his or her own internal feedback mechanism.

Regardless of the particular mode of feedback given, the learner is eventually able to develop a sense of deep connection with fundamental somatic functions without needing an external device.

Many techniques of NLP actually employ the principles of biofeedback in which the guide or facilitator functions as the "sensor" to provide feedback to clients or learners about aspects of their internal states. Other NLP techniques (such as calibration and internal inventory) help people to develop their own personal feedback mechanisms and skills.

NeuroLink and MindDrive

In the early 1980s, co-author Robert Dilts began to apply NLP principles to the development of biofeedback tools and methods, culminating in the creation of the patented NeuroLink and MindDrive technology. Dilts sought to provide learners with a different logical level of feedback. He believed that people would learn to connect with and influence autonomic functions more quickly and effectively if they were given feedback about the degree of change they were able to effect, rather than the specific state of that function. As an example, in addition to being shown a reading of his or her heart rate, the learner would also be given feedback about the rate and degree of *change* in heart rate he or she was able to produce.

This approach has proven effective in accelerating a person's ability to feel a sense of conscious alignment and influence with respect to a particular autonomic function and thus strengthen his or her mind-body connection. It was also found that this approach could be used to assist people in controlling certain devices, such as a video game or robot, through their autonomic nervous system. This has led to applications allowing people with central nervous system damage (such as multiple sclerosis, cerebral palsy, spinal injury, etc.) to be able to play computer games and communicate more effectively. It also led to the development of consumer oriented "thought controlled" video games. Thus, not only does such an approach extend the therapeutic value of biofeedback, it is able to expand people's capabilities to develop and use their nervous systems and somatic intelligence.

SomaticVision

The latest embodiment of this approach is the *SomaticVision* mind/body integration tools developed by Ryan DeLuz in collaboration with Robert Dilts. SomaticVision software operates on the Wild Divine "LightStone" hardware, which senses heart rate and skin conductance (GSR) and transmits it to a laptop computer.

**SomaticVision Products Allow People to Practice
Biofeedback on Their Laptop Computers**

SomaticVision software tools collect this somatic data and represent it in the form of dynamic computer graphics, 3D games, graphs, and music. The tools help people to deepen and fine-tune their conscious connection with the body. This, in turn, makes it possible to more intentionally:

- Increase relaxation

- Restore balance and vitality

- Improve physical & mental well-being

Some of the SomaticVision tools include:

Particle Editor, which provides continuous feedback in the form of unique moving particle displays that respond to somatic changes in your body. Shifting your state instantly alters the activity on the screen allowing you to become aware of how specific sensations, feelings and thoughts produce particular graphical changes.

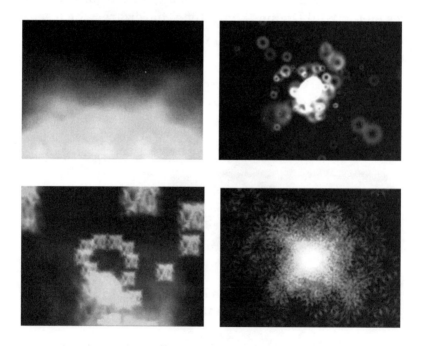

**Images from SomaticVision Particle Editor
Biofeedback Program**

Inner Tube and *Dual Drive* are real time 3D games that use heart rate and skin conductance to operate a space ship or an off road vehicle. The speed of the vehicle changes with your inner state of relaxation or excitement. The more you relax, the faster you go. It is a very entertaining way to learn how to manage your inner state.

A Screenshot from the SomaticVision 3D Game *Dual Drive*

NLPace is a coaching tool (for either self-coaching or coaching another person) to help people become aware of, understand and record subtle changes in their mental, emotional and physical state. By using this tool you can observe and verify somatic changes as a result of a session as well as get constant feedback during a process:

1) During a session you can watch changes in heart rate and skin conductance as signs of mental or emotional changes of state.

2) You can verify at the end of a session that the session was effective, by testing the somatic response to an event that was previously difficult or troubling. For instance, if you have public speaking anxiety, you can imagine speaking in public and notice your somatic response.

3) By choosing to record a session, you can analyze the changes that occurred during the session. This can be done in addition to, or instead of, watching the changes during the session.

4) Recording also allows you to keep track of change over many sessions.

While working with the NLPace coaching tool, it can be useful to experiment with relaxation techniques, either while watching the measurement feedback directly, or by looking at the feedback afterwards, using the graphs. It may be helpful to close your eyes (or look away from the feedback) when applying any of the following techniques. Although it is important to learn how the relaxation technique impacts you, it can also be distracting if you are constantly evaluating the changes instead of fully focusing on the experience inside.

The following relaxation exercise was designed to be explored using feedback from the SomaticVision software. However, it can be just as valuable if you use your own introspective awareness to observe your level of calm and relaxation.

1) Let go of disturbing mental thoughts about work, yourself, relationship, etc.

2) Gently allow yourself to breathe with relaxed, slow, steady breaths (without straining, try counting to five or six on your in-breath, and then to five or six again on your out-breath).

3) Think of someone you love or something that is very enjoyable. You may wish to close your eyes for a moment and revel in that feeling. Notice if that creates any change, but do not attempt to create a change. Just cultivate the positive feelings, memories, and warmth associated with that person, place, animal, etc.

4) Focus on progressively relaxing all the muscles in your body. Especially release your face, neck, shoulders and even your tongue.

5) Imagine a relaxing warmth flowing through your arms, legs, hands, feet, back, belly, face, neck and head.

6) Imagine a very positive situation or being in a relaxing environment. Experience the situation or environment as vividly as possible.

7) Notice the physical sensations in your body. Notice the feeling of your feet on the floor. Notice the feeling of your heart beating. Feel each heart beat in your chest or fingertips.

8) Allow yourself to experience positive feelings such as love, joy, deep peace, etc.

Much of our ability to perform effectively and maintain healthy lives is a result of what is called *adaptive control*. For instance, we must keep our stress level within a certain "tolerance band" or suffer the consequences. In order for an athlete to perform effectively, he or she needs to maintain the state of his or her heart rate, blood pressure, temperature, etc., within a certain tolerance band. The timing or distance the athlete is able to achieve with respect to the activity he or she is performing is a function of how well he or she has been able to stay within the range defined by the tolerance band. Biofeedback and tools like SomaticVision help us to greatly increase our capacity for adaptive control, which makes it easier to manage things like stress and fatigue (such as jet lag) with more resilience and resourcefulness.

For more information about SomaticVision products, you can go to the website at: http://www.somaticvision.com.

Somatic Syntax

There is an old proverb from Papua New Guinea that states, *"Knowledge is only a rumor until it is in the muscle."* This saying defines one of the basic premises of *Somatic Syntax*. In 1993, authors Judith DeLozier and Robert Dilts originated the principles and practice of Somatic Syntax as a way to further deepen and utilize the connection between the somatic and cognitive minds. As we saw at the beginning of this chapter, the term "somatic" comes from the Greek word *soma,* which means "body." *Syntax* is a Greek word meaning, "to put in order" or "arrange."

Somatic Syntax has to do with "body language". It is about the way in which we organize our physiology in order to process and express our experience and the meaning we attribute to it. Similar to the rest of NLP, somatic syntax focuses more on the form, deeper organization and patterns of relationship in our body language than it does on its content. Somatic Syntax is less concerned with which parts of the body are involved in these processes as it is with their deeper structure. Rather than focus on physical details, Somatic Syntax emphasizes the overall pattern and organization of movement and the formation of cognitive-somatic (i.e., "mind-body") expressions. Take, for example, a fundamental deep structure like "opening". We can "open our eyes". We can "open our heart", "open our arms", "open our mouth", etc.

One of the primary objectives of Somatic Syntax is to mobilize and utilize the "wisdom of the body." As author Morris Berman points out in his book *Coming to Our Senses*:

> *Western academic understanding, including philosophy and anthropology as well as history, tacitly assumes that the body had nothing to tell us, has no knowledge or 'information'; that for all practical purpose, it isn't even there. And yet the life of the body is our real life, the only life we have.*

A fundamental principle of Somatic Syntax is that there is information and wisdom in the body and knowledge in "the muscle." It is a way to access and take advantage of the full capacity of "the brain in our body."

NLP has long acknowledged the influence of our physiology on our thinking processes. Micro behavioral "accessing cues," such as NLP's celebrated eye movement patterns, are considered to be both reflections of specific mental processes and triggers for internal activity relating to the sensory representational systems. Through such physical cues we can detect as well as promote certain aspects of our cognitive strategies. This is one of the foundations of the "programming" aspect of "Neuro-Linguistic Programming."

These specific types of cues, however, are not the only kind of mind-body link. Disciplines like the Feldenkrais and Alexander methods, yoga, aikido, t'ai chi, dance and transformational movement practices such as Gabrielle Roth's 5Rhythms®, explore a variety of other interactions between movement and mental processes. These disciplines emphasize the systemic nature of our bodies, and focus more on the pattern and quality of movement than on the specific parts of the body involved. Until the development of Somatic Syntax, NLP had not applied methods that take full advantage of the role "whole body" movement plays in human thought and programming.

Darwin's Thinking Path

A fascinating article in **Natural History** magazine from 1996 provides a simple but powerful example of the relationship between our somatic mind and our cognitive functioning. The article is essentially a reflection on the country estate of Charles Darwin (1809 - 1882), the English biologist and naturalist whose theory of evolution via the mechanism of natural selection revolutionized our understanding of natural history and shifted our perception of human origins.

Darwin acquired Downe House a few years after his return from his historic voyage aboard HMS *Beagle*. Darwin spent some 20 years after returning from his travels on the HMS Beagle working out his theories and their relationship to the evidence he had gathered and the observations he had made. It was at Downe House that he wrote his classic works *Origin of Species* and *Descent of Man*.

In describing the estate, the author of the article notes:

> *Soon after settling at Downe, Darwin constructed a sand-covered path, known as the sand walk, that still winds through the shady woods and then returns toward the house along a sunny, hedge-lined field. He strolled it daily, referring to it as "my thinking path." Often he would stack a few stones at the path's entrance, and knock one away with his walking stick on completing each circuit. He could anticipate a "three-flint problem," just as Sherlock Holmes had "three-pipe problems," and then head home when all the stones were gone.*

Reading this description, it is easy to imagine Darwin, deep in thought, strolling along his sand walk and contemplating some key aspect of his theory of evolution and natural selection. The fact that Darwin called the sand walk his "thinking path" indicates that he considered his walks along this path to have some significant connection with his thinking process. An intriguing question from the NLP perspective would be: "What, specifically, *is* the link between "thinking" and walking along such a path?"

Movement and Mind

As we mentioned earlier, the traditional NLP approach to interpreting and utilizing the relationship between thought and behavior has been to relate specific categories of body movements (such as eye movements, breathing patterns, facial expressions, gestures, etc.) to specific mental events - i.e., "eye movement up and to the left accompanies visual memory," "stroking the chin indicates internal dialogue," "lower, deeper breathing increases access to feelings." NLP *accessing cues* usually focus on very subtle behaviors and address the more transient microstructure of our thinking process

On the other hand, repetitive physical movements and activities involving major muscle groups (such as walking, swimming, biking, playing tennis, etc.), influence our overall state of mind, and thus provide a more general context for our thinking processes.

As the allusion to Sherlock Holmes' pipe in the quotation about Darwin's Thinking Path indicates, the notion that some form of repetitive activity facilitates deep contemplation is a familiar one. In addition to his pipe, the fictional Holmes is also reported to have played a violin when needing to work out some particularly challenging aspect of a case.

Similar patterns may be found in many famous non-fictional thinkers as well. Similar to Holmes, Albert Einstein played the violin during times of productive thinking, claiming that it was in some ways an extension of his thinking and that it helped him to solve particularly tricky problems. Einstein also loved to sail regularly, reportedly hastily scribbling away in his notebook whenever the wind died down. Leonardo da Vinci played the lyre.[*] Wolfgang Amadeus Mozart claimed that many of his best musical ideas came while he was walking or riding in a carriage. Similar to Darwin, other famous thinkers, such as Emmanuel Kant, walked as part of their daily regimen.

We authors have our physical practices that support us to creatively meet and process tricky problems and challenging situations. Deborah, for example, regularly dances the 5Rhythms®. Robert runs every morning. His running paths

---

[*] In fact, it was for his prowess as a musician rather than a painter that Leonardo was first brought to Milan by the powerful Duke Lodovico Sforza.

have been the birthplace and nursery of many seminars, software programs, books and articles.

We have noticed that the different qualities of movement associated with various activities seem to bring out particular qualities of mind. Different "whole body" physical patterns seem to help access and integrate different qualities of mental processing. That is, certain types of activity seem more conducive to addressing certain types of outcomes and issues.[*]

During Robert's extensive study of effective leadership, he interviewed the founder of a large Scandinavian shipping company. Even as an older person, this man claimed that he used different physical activities to help him solve various problems. For certain issues, he would have to go out and play golf to get into the frame of mind required to deal with the issues. For other problems, he would go out and ride his bicycle in order to think about it effectively. He was so specific about which type of physiology to use that he would say, "You can't golf on that problem. That's the kind of problem you have to ride your bicycle on."

It seems natural to conclude that patterns of physical activity stimulate and organize patterns of neurological activity, not just in the brain but also throughout the whole body and the various somatic functions we have been exploring in this chapter. Riding a bicycle is an example of one way to activate and maintain a particular internal state.

There are some who might even go so far as to contend that mind *is* movement, and that wisdom and intelligence come from the quality of that movement.

---

[*] You can try this as an experiment for yourself. Choose three different physical activities that are rhythmic and to some degree cyclic or repetitive. They may be sports or some other type of activity. Think of a particular problem you are trying to solve and begin to engage in one of the physical activities. When you have completed that activity, check on your perception of the problem you have chosen. Repeat this same process with the other two activities. Notice what types of insights emerge from the practice of each physical activity.

Transformational Grammar

A key inspiration for the development of Somatic Syntax comes from Noam Chomsky's theories of *transformational grammar* (1956, 1966) which are the foundations for the NLP Meta Model language patterns. According to Chomsky, sensory and emotional experiences (*deep structures)* may be expressed through a variety of linguistic descriptions (*surface structures*). In other words, we can use quite different sentences and types of linguistic modalities (literal description, poetry, song, etc.) to express the same feelings and ideas. This is known as a *generative grammar*.

Another characteristic of generative grammar is that a relatively small number of words may be recombined in different ways to form a practically infinite number of expressions. For example, all of the ideas expressed by the human race so far (from Jesus to Shakespeare to Hitler to Mother Teresa to Madonna and so on, including the ones in this book) can be expressed in the English language through a working vocabulary of around 30,000 words.

The same words can take on different meanings and implications based on their order and relationship to one another. We can rearrange the words "The man saw the cat chase the rat," to create different meanings: "The man saw the rat chase the cat," "The cat saw the man chase the rat," "The rat saw the man chase the cat," "The cat saw the rat chase the man," and so on. If we leave out or repeat certain words, we can begin to create even more expressions: "The man saw the rat," or "The man saw the man chase the rat," etc. The point is that many different things can be expressed with the same small number of words rearranged in different orders.

Central to the theory of transformational grammar is the notion that deeper structures reach a particular surface expression after a series of transformations. These transformations act as a sort of filter on the experiential deep structures they are attempting to manifest. According to Grinder and Bandler (1975), the movement from deep structure to surface structure necessarily involves the *deletion, generalization* and *distortion* of some aspects of the original deep structure. When we say, "The cat chased the rat," for example, we have left out how fast, how far, in which physical setting, the size and color of the animals, etc.

Bandler and Grinder discovered that they could use the principles of transformational grammar to create a model of the intuitions that effective therapists use when listening to clients and asking questions. Books such as *The Structure of Magic* and *Patterns of the Hypnotic Techniques of Milton H. Erickson, M.D.,* describe the therapeutic processes used by these individuals explicitly in terms of transformational grammar. They found that effective therapists had important intuitions about which of these deletions, distortions and generalizations were problematic, and about how to use language to enrich their clients' internal maps of the world.

Bandler and Grinder formulated the Meta Model as a description of the intuitions of the therapists they studied. The function of the Meta Model is to identify problematic generalizations, deletions or distortions through the analysis of the *syntax* or form of the surface structure and provide a system of questions so that a more enriched representation of the deep structure may be attained. The Meta Model applies the notion that verbal expressions that may be "well-formed" in casual conversation are not necessarily "well-formed" in therapy. Therapists (and other professional communicators) must specify or recover certain information related to a client's deep structure in order to successfully facilitate the person to change in an effective and ecological way.

NLP has gone on to widen the use of the notions of "deep structure" and "surface structure" to include more than linguistic processes and representations. NLP considers deep structure to be composed of fundamental sensory and emotional experiences—or "primary experience," derived from

sensory input coming from the world around us. NLP techniques work with the whole range of "neuro-linguistic" filters
that perform the "transformations" operating on our primary
experience to give it meaning and expression. In this way,
Somatic Syntax applies the principles of verbal language to
body language.

Consider the following example of the relationship between deep structure and surface structures. Most of us
learned to write using our right or left hand. Yet, once our
hand has learned this skill, it can be immediately transferred to other parts of the body. For instance, we can easily
write our name in sand with our left big toe or make letters
by holding a pencil in our mouth, even though the physical
structures of these parts of our bodies are completely different. The deep structure related to the form of the letters is
not tied to any particular part of the body. It can be
generalized to many surface structures.

Deep Structure

Resource

Physical and Verbal Expressions
Movements   Words
Surface Structures

Somatic Syntax essentially uses the movement of the body as
a way to strengthen, integrate and expand the expression of
deep level resources. By exploring the physical form and organization of the movements associated with a particular state, we
can learn to better express or manifest that state in more
situations, thus increasing our flexibility. In this way, Somatic
Syntax helps to deepen our understanding and ability to utilize
knowledge by bringing it more "into the muscle."

At another level, because physical movement taps into more structures within our nervous system beyond the brain, exploring Somatic Syntax can bring us closer to certain experiential deep structures. Thus, another application of Somatic Syntax is to help recover and express parts of deeper structures that may be deleted or distorted by verbal or other forms of expression. In the words of the famous dancer Isadora Duncan, "If I could say it, I wouldn't have to dance it."

The Body as a Representational System

The perspective of earlier generations of NLP has been that all our information about the world around us is relayed by the senses to the brain, where it is centrally represented and processed. One of the tenets of Somatic Syntax is that the body itself is a "representational system." Rather than considering the body as simply some kind of mechanical shell for inputting and outputting signals to and from the brain, Somatic Syntax views the body as a means for representing and processing information within the "belly brain," "heart brain" and other nervous system structures within the body.

According to Somatic Syntax, we can use our bodies to make a model of the world just as we do with our other representational systems. We can represent key relationships in the world around us and in our personal history through the relationship between parts of our body. For example, our perception of the relationship between our mother and father could be represented by the relationship between our left and right hands, or between our chest and our belly.

In addition to being able to input, process and output information, all representational systems have the capability to represent information in at least two ways: *literally* and *figuratively*. That is, each of our sensory systems can form maps that have either a direct correspondence or a more metaphorical connection to the phenomenon we are representing. For example, we can visualize the white cells of our bodies as we have seen them under the microscope, or as looking like octopi or video game characters. Similarly we can speak of our brains literally as "a network of neurons," or figuratively as being "like a computer." Likewise, we can experience a particular emotional symptom as a certain set of kinesthetic body sensations or as a "knot" in the stomach.

As a representational system, our bodies have a similar double capacity. We can express movements that are the literal response to a particular situation, or create expressions that are more metaphorical, as through dance and mime. A state of anxiety, for instance, may be literally represented by reproducing the physical effects which accompany a feeling of anxiety (such as tensing up the muscles in one's face and shoulders), or figuratively represented by placing one's arms over one's head and eyes, as if hiding from something dangerous.

As is the case with our other representational modalities, metaphorical representations are often more meaningful and impactful than literal ones because they carry multiple levels of information. According to anthropologist Gregory Bateson, the mode of representation characterized by Somatic Syntax is the primary way in which most animals communicate. An adult male wolf, for example, may treat another adult male wolf with the same behavior used by a mother wolf toward her cub, as a sign of rapprochement or dominance.

Applying Somatic Syntax

Somatic Syntax is the active study of how movement may be used to help bring knowledge *into* the muscle, and to help draw out knowledge *from* the muscle. It is a means to access the "wisdom of the body." According to Somatic Syntax, repetitive structures of movement can form the framework surrounding a particular thinking process, and thus influence its conclusions. As Moshe Feldenkrais pointed out (in *Body and Mature Behavior*, 1949):

> *A recurrent emotional state always appears together with the attitude of the body and the vegetative state with which it was conditioned earlier. Therefore, when an individual emotional complex has been resolved, a specifically individual body habit is resolved simultaneously.*

The most fundamental tool we have for conducting our lives and building our futures is our own body and nervous system. Certainly the manifestation of our thoughts and dreams must eventually come through our body or physiology in some way. Our mental activity becomes manifested into the world through our words, voice tone, facial expression, body posture, the movement of our hands, etc. And the way in which we use these fundamental instruments of life is greatly influenced by the types of physical practices and disciplines we adopt.

A healthy and creative mental and physical life is often accompanied by some kind of movement as was previously illustrated by Darwin's thinking path. Or the example of Mozart who wrote that his musical ideas flowed "best and most abundantly" during times of movement, such as "traveling in a carriage, or walking after a good meal."

Somatic Syntax Exercises

The following exercises were developed by authors Robert Dilts and Judith DeLozier as ways of exploring and applying Somatic Syntax to develop one's own resources more fully, model the resourceful states of others, communicate more effectively and transform problematic responses and "stuck states".

Exercise 1: Getting a Resource "In the Muscle"

This exercise helps to identify particular patterns of movement associated with a resourceful internal state, in particular those that operate to enhance or diminish that state.

1. Identify a resource state (creative, confident, centered, etc.) that you would like to have more of in your life.

2. Fully experience the resource and identify any spontaneous physical expressions associated with the resource state (i.e., body posture, breathing pattern, movements, gestures, etc.).

3. Explore the organization (deep structure) of the physical expressions by changing the "syntax" (or form) of various aspects of these expressions (i.e., quality, speed, parts of the body involved, sequence, direction, etc.).

4. Notice which of these changes:

   a. Intensify/make more of the state.

   b. Dampen/make less of the state.

   c. Change the state to a different state.

Exercise 2: Generalizing the Resourceful Pattern

This exercise helps to increase access to a particular internal state by incorporating key patterns of movements associated with that state into other actions and activities.

Choose three common actions or "macro" behaviors (e.g., walking, carrying something, sitting, writing). For each action:

1. Start making your best version of the physical expressions associated with the resource state you have been exploring in the previous exercise.

2. Begin the action (walking, sitting, etc.) and adapt the physical expression of the resource (breath, posture, gestures, movements, etc.) to blend with and fit that activity in the way that is most natural and preserves the full experience of the resource.

Exercise 3: Applying the Resourceful Pattern

In this exercise, you take the pattern associated with the resource you have been exploring in the first two exercises into situations in which it would be (or would have been) useful.

1. Identify a specific context or situation in which you would like to have more access to the resource you have been exploring in the previous exercises.

2. Internally project yourself into that situation, imagining that you are actually there. Notice the body posture, breathing pattern and movements that spontaneously emerge as you put yourself into the situation. Physically express the posture, breath, movement, etc.

3. Begin to blend the physical expression of the resource that you have been exploring with the pattern of movement spontaneously associated with that situation. Notice what begins to shift in your posture, breath and quality of movement.

4. Adapt the physical expression of the resource so that it integrates and "fits" into the situation most appropriately and elegantly.

5. Notice how bringing the resource movement pattern into the situation transforms or enriches your experience of that situation.

Exercise 4: Modeling Resources with Somatic Syntax

In this exercise, you explore how to use Somatic Syntax to model resourceful states from other people.

1. Identify a resource state (confident, playful, open, etc.) that you would like to access more fully.

2. Find a person (a role model) who is able to easily express that resource state.

3. Ask the person to put him/herself into the resourceful state and observe the spontaneous behaviors (posture, gestures, breathing pattern, etc.) that accompany the state.

4. Imitate the resource movement of the role model (i.e., from your own perspective or 1st position, reproduce the other person's pattern of movement as accurately as possible).

5. Now, put yourself "into the shoes" of the role model (take 2nd position) and repeat the movement (i.e., act as if you are the other person doing the pattern of movement).

6. Reflect on the resource movement from an observer perspective (3rd position). What do you learn about yourself, the role model and the resource?

7. Return to your own perspective (1st position), taking with you some aspect of the other person's resource (deep structure and/or surface structure) that is both appropriate and enriching to you. Express it as a movement. You do not have to take the whole pattern, nor do you have to do it exactly as the role model did it. Adapt the pattern to fit yourself.

Exercise 5: Widening Your Scope of Self-Expression— Somatic Syntax of Self

Sometimes, when we begin to explore or enrich our inner resources through the outer expression of Somatic Syntax, it can initially feel insincere or like "acting." This exercise can help to expand our scope of expression by helping to link behavioral expressions to your sense of "self."

1. Identify a resource that you have explored in yourself or modeled from another person that you would like to express more fully in yourself.

2. Put yourself into an inner state in which you feel centered, aligned and fully "yourself."

3. Begin to recall and enact the physical pattern of expression and quality of movement associated with the resource state you would like to experience and express more fully. Explore the organization and syntax (deep structure) of this movement or quality of movement by changing different aspects of it (i.e., speed, parts of the body involved, direction, etc.).

3. Notice which of these changes:

    a. Intensify the state or make you feel more like "you."

    b. Dampen the state or make you feel less like "you."

    c. Shift you into a state or experience that you can't label (as indicated by the "?" in the diagram below).

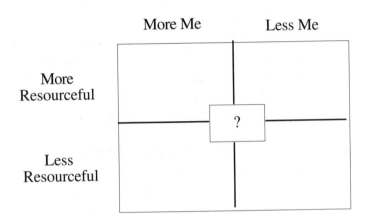

4. If a particular movement dampens your state, changes it to a different state or diminishes your sense of self, explore what other physical changes you would have to make in other parts of your body in order to reaccess and maintain the original resource state and sense of self. For example, if some gesture with your hands or arms seems "fake" or "insincere," what could you adjust in your posture or your breath or elsewhere that would make the same gesture feel more authentic and "like you.")

Exercise 6: Transforming Stuck States Through Somatic Syntax

There is an old story about two actors about to go on stage. One is an older and seasoned performer. The other is younger and inexperienced. The younger one approaches the older actor saying, "Gosh, I am so nervous. I feel like I have a ton of 'butterflies' in my stomach. After all of your years of performing, do you still get 'butterflies' in your stomach?" Smiling knowingly, the older actor replies, "Oh yes, I still get butterflies every time I am about to begin a performance. I don't think that will ever change. When I was younger, they bothered me so much I used to try to kill them. I learned over time that it was much better to teach them how to fly in formation.

In the previous exercise, you may have discovered certain patterns of movement that, while they feel like they are authentically you, make you feel unresourceful, stuck or anxious. This exercise is a way to help to transform stuck or unresourceful internal states into a more resourceful expression (i.e., to teach the "butterflies in your stomach" how to fly in formation).

1. Identify a situation in which you experience resistance, interference or a "stuck" state with respect to being yourself in an aligned and resourceful way.

2. Using memory and/or imagination, put yourself fully into the experience of the stuck or unresourceful inner state. Become aware of and physically express the somatic patterns associated with the movement your body made going from your normal or neutral state into the stuck state—i.e., bent body posture, constriction of breath, tension in shoulders, arms or hands, finger pointing, etc.

3. Physically step away from the problem situation, but maintain the physiology associated with the stuck or unresourceful state. Center yourself internally and explore the syntax and organization (deep structure) of the movement by repeating it several times very slowly and with heightened awareness. As you do, consider the positive intention of the movement. What is it trying to do or accomplish for you?

4. Keeping the positive intention of this movement in mind, explore ways in which you could complete this movement in such a way that it brings you back to a more centered and resourceful state. Make the smallest changes in physical expression that you can at any point in time. Avoid making large movements or big changes in posture, breathing, etc. The more the movement and change are subtle, the better.

5. Practice beginning with the physical expression of the stuck state and then slowly and subtly completing it in a way that brings you back to a more centered and resourceful state several times, until you feel the new pattern is "in the muscle."

6. When you feel ready, put yourself back into the situation in which you had previously experienced the stuck state. Let your body and "somatic mind" react intuitively. You should feel a natural and spontaneous shift in your response.

Using Somatic Syntax to Enhance Non-Verbal Communication

Body language and Somatic Syntax are a powerful way to add impact and richness to our verbal communication. The following exercises can enhance your ability to communicate with greater vividness and influence.

1. Identify an idea, principle or message that is important for you to be able to communicate clearly and effectively to others. Create a simple and clear verbal expression of the message; e.g., "Knowledge is only a rumor until it is in the muscle." Or "It is important to connect the wisdom of the body to our cognitive understanding."

2. For each key part of your message, identify a gesture or physical expression that can accompany the words. Imagine you were a mime or a person speaking sign language. How could you say the same thing with your body that you saying are with your words?

3. Speak your verbal message while simultaneously making your non-verbal gestures and expressions.

   E.g., "Knowledge (point finger to the head) is only a rumor (wave hands above head) until it is in the muscle (place both hands on the body and take a deep breath)."

   E.g., "It is important (hold both hands out in front of the chest facing one another and breathe deeply) to connect (clasp hands together) the wisdom of the body (place one hand on the belly and the other hand on the heart while taking a full breath) to our cognitive understanding (place both hands on sides of the head)."

Exploring Somatic Metaphors to Enhance Non-Verbal Communication

1. Identify an idea or subject that is important for you to be able to communicate clearly and effectively to others.

2. Identify a simple physically based metaphor that helps to illustrate that idea or subject; e.g., building, fishing, cooking, fencing, etc.

3. Verbally express or describe the subject or idea while simultaneously acting out the metaphor with your body. Do not mention or incorporate the metaphor in your verbal presentation or description.

"Somatic Fractal" Format

A fractal is a complex geometric pattern that can be subdivided into parts, each of which is (at least approximately) a smaller copy of the whole. Fractals are generally "self-similar" (the bits look like the whole) and independent of scale (they look similar, no matter how close you zoom in). Benoit Mandelbrot, the discoverer of the Mandelbrot set, coined the term "fractal" in 1975 from the Latin fractus meaning "to break." Because fractals are generally made of irregular curves or shapes repeated at every scale they are difficult to represent with classical geometry, and have developed into their own branch of mathematics.

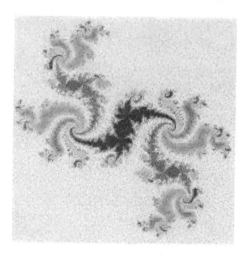

**The Fractal Dragon
(Benoit B. Mandelbrot/IBM)**

Many mathematical structures are fractals; e.g. the Sierpinski triangle, Koch snowflake, Peano curve, Mandelbrot set and Lorenz attractor. Fractals also describe many real-world objects that do not have simple geometric shapes, such as clouds, mountains, turbulence, and coastlines. Fractal type equations are also used as the generative engines behind many "artificial life" simulations.

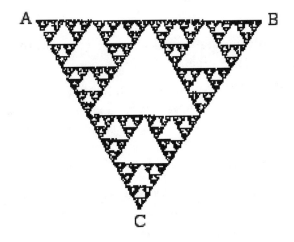

The Sierpinski Triangle

From an NLP perspective, fractals are a good example of how a simple process at the level of deep structure can generate a complex pattern at the level of surface structure. Many behaviors could be considered to be types of "neurolinguistic" fractals. Dance, for instance is a type of somatic fractal. Many forms of music are a type of auditory fractal (consider Ravel's Bolero, or Pachelbel's Canon in D, for example).

The following exercise combines Somatic Syntax with the principles of the fractal to create and enhance personal resource states.

Creating a Somatic Fractal for a Resource State

1. Identify and associate into a resourceful state (e.g., creativity, confidence, focus, etc.)

2. As you fully "relive" what it is like to be in this state, notice a physical pattern or quality of movement that accompanies the resource state. What sensations are there? Where are they in your body? What are the patterns and qualities of the movement of the sensations in the body?

3. Mindfully make a few subtle variations in this movement, and notice the impact they have on your experience of the resourceful feeling. This will help you get a sense of its deeper structure.

4. Transfer the pattern and quality of movement to some other part of your body. For example, if the movement naturally involved your arms, transfer it to your shoulders. Make any adaptations you need to until it seems natural, and you can feel the sense of the resourceful state as a result of making the movement with this other part of your body.

5. Transfer the resourceful movement to as many parts of your body as you can (i.e., face, feet, eyes, breathing, hips, etc.). In this way, your whole body should be alive with the resource.

Dancing S.C.O.R.E. Format

While many aspects of these particular exercises are unique to Somatic Syntax, the principles and use of Somatic Syntax can be adapted to fit with many other NLP techniques and models. Somatic Syntax is a powerful way to supplement and augment practically any change process.

The Dancing S.C.O.R.E. format is a simple but powerful example of the application of Somatic Syntax. It was developed by author Judith DeLozier in 1993 as a means of using physical movement and spatial sorting to maximize intuition and the "wisdom of the body" in problem solving. The Dancing S.C.O.R.E. format incorporates the principles of Somatic Syntax with the NLP S.C.O.R.E. Model in order to promote effective mind-body relationship, access and mobilize deep resources, and create a self-organizing pathway towards a particular desired state.

As we described in the previous chapter, the letters "S.C.O.R.E." stand for: Symptoms, Causes, Outcomes, Resources and Effects. These elements represent the minimum amount of information that needs to be addressed in any process of change.

1. *Symptoms* are typically the most noticeable and conscious aspects of a present problem or problem state.

2. *Causes* are the underlying elements responsible for creating and maintaining the symptoms. They are usually less obvious than the symptoms they produce.

3. *Outcomes* are the particular state or behaviors that will take the place of the symptoms.

4. *Resources* are the underlying elements (skills, tools, beliefs, etc.) responsible for removing the causes of the symptoms and for reaching and maintaining the desired outcomes.

5. *Effects* are the longer-term results of achieving a particular outcome.

a. Positive effects are often the reason or motivation for establishing a particular outcome to begin with.

b. Negative effects can create resistance or ecological problems.

The Dancing S.C.O.R.E. involves placing each of the S.C.O.R.E. elements into a sequence or "time line," such that the cause of the symptom is the first step in the sequence, at a location representing the past. The symptom can be placed in a location representing the present or ongoing time frame. The desired outcome would be positioned slightly beyond the present to a location representing the time frame in the future, in which the outcome is to be achieved. And the effect would be placed somewhere just beyond the outcome.

One advantage of using physical locations is that they help to more easily and clearly sort out the different parts of the S.C.O.R.E. and keep them separate. It also makes it possible to tangibly and experientially explore the physiological patterns (such as posture, breathing, movement, etc.) associated with each element.

According to Webster's Dictionary, dance is "a series of rhythmic movements which have as their aim the creation of a visual design by a series of poses and tracing of patterns through space and time." Dance often starts as simple emotional expression, but then develops into a design—a planned organization of patterns of movement incorporating space, sequence and rhythm. When a particular physical pattern of expression has its own set of steps, gestures, and dynamics—it becomes a specific dance.

The Dancing S.C.O.R.E. brings the powerful resources of the somatic mind and the wisdom of the body into the process of problem solving.

Steps of the Dancing S.C.O.R.E. Format

1. Think of a problem state or challenging issue that you want to work with.

2. Lay out four locations in a sequence representing the cause, symptom, outcome and desired effect related to the problem or challenge, as in the sequence shown below:

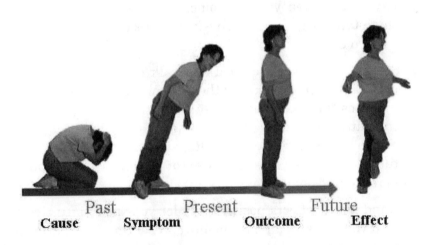

Physical Layout of the Starting Positions for the Dancing S.C.O.R.E.

3. Physically associate into the experience of the physical symptom. Use your body as a "representational system." Create a pattern of movement that represents and expresses that symptom. Also, allow the internal state you feel in that location to expand and become more fully expressed through the pattern of movement.

4. Take a step backwards into the cause space. Allow the feeling and movement associated with the symptom to intuitively guide you to the cause of that symptom. Fully express the experience of the cause in movement. (Notice

how this pattern of movement is related to the symptom
movement.)

5. Shift your state and completely leave the problem experience, physically stepping to the side. Move into the
outcome location and create a full associated experience of
your desired state. Fully represent and express this state
through the movement of your body.

6. Step forward into the effects space and feel the results of
having achieved your outcome. Spend special time with
this state to get a full physical representation of these
desired effects.

7. Starting in the cause location, walk slowly through the
entire sequence, repeating the movements associated with
each position. Go very slowly between the symptom and
the outcome locations to notice how your body intuitively
connects these two spaces. Repeat this process several
times until there is a sense of a single, continuous
movement from cause to effect (the dance).

8. Stand in the effects position and let your body intuitively
lead you to a special movement representing the appropriate resource to add to the "dance" sequence.

9. Starting in the cause location, incorporate the resource
movement into the other movement associated with that
location. Walk through the other locations, adding the
resource movement to the other movements until you
have reached the effect space.

10. Repeat the movement through cause, symptom, outcome
and effect until you have transformed it into a kind of
"dance."

Gabrielle Roth's 5Rhythms®

One of the purest expressions of Somatic Syntax is rhythm. With respect to the body, *rhythm* can be defined as "a regular, repeated pattern of movement." In NLP, we view these repeating patterns of movement as somatic deep structures that can mobilize and integrate various qualities of knowing and processing within our somatic minds. Different rhythms can function as somatic "accessing cues" and "meta programs" that organize fundamental patterns of relationships.

Similar to the way that the various types of brainwaves in our cerebral cortex (i.e., alpha, beta, delta, theta, etc.) bring about different states of consciousness in our cognitive minds, rhythms in the body bring out different states of awareness and functioning in our somatic minds.

Gabrielle Roth's 5Rhythms® are a good example of the transformational capacity of rhythm and somatic syntax. The 5Rhythms® are the result of Gabrielle Roth's many years of observation of how energy moves in people and in life. As she points out in *Sweat Your Prayers* (1997), "Energy moves in waves. Waves move in patterns. Patterns move in rhythms. A human being is all of those: energy, waves, patterns and rhythms."

She identifies five rhythms—flowing, staccato, chaos, lyrical and stillness—that form a type of "meta model" for change and transformation. These 5Rhythms® are expressions of "archetypal" patterns of energy that organically emerge in a particular sequence that forms a type of larger pattern or *wave*.

The 5Rhythms® are both a set of maps and a movement practice. As a somatic experience, the body moves through the five rhythms of the wave, beginning in the rhythm of *flowing*. This starts by being rooted in the feet, feeling their connection with the ground and inviting them to begin to move through space. The body follows the feet and begins to move in continuous easy movement. Nothing is forced. The movement is grounded, connected and circular. Roth says flowing is the rhythm of the feminine, of the physical body and the earth. If we lose connection with the ground or with our center while flowing, we experience its shadow. We become stuck in inertia, move mindlessly and automatically, or begin to "blow with the wind."

Gabrielle Roth's 5Rhythms® Follow the Form of a Wave

Flowing is the rhythm where we practice connection and receptivity, breathing in and "being with" our experience in movement. As we connect to our bodies and ourselves and receive our own flow, we gain energy, just like a wave beginning to form.

As our energy increases through the grounded and fluid rhythm of flowing, the second rhythm *staccato* emerges naturally. In staccato, the rhythm of the masculine and of the heart, the wave continues to build and we feel the strength that comes from being deeply connected to ourselves and to our environment. Out of the continuous movement of the rhythm of flowing, the body gives distinct shape to the expression of our energy in staccato. It is the yang to the yin of flowing, the out-breath that follows the in-breath. The centered form of staccato includes focus, concentration, commitment and setting clear boundaries. The uncentered or shadow form can become rigidity, aggression and violence.

As the feet, the body and the heart join the beat in the rhythm of staccato, our level of energy continues to build and reaches a point where it becomes difficult to contain. The structure of staccato dissolves into the third rhythm of chaos, similar to the way a wave churns as it reaches its peak.

In the rhythm of *chaos* we surrender, letting go of the neck and head as fixed structures dissolve from our bodies and our minds. With the foundation of the feet firmly rooted in flowing and the courage and commitment ignited in staccato, we arrive in chaos with a safe container in which to let go. Chaos allows us to experience the deep letting go of old patterns. When their stuck energy is released, we experience renewal, a feeling of being refreshed by freely flowing water. The uncentered, shadow side of chaos is confusion, disorder, feeling overwhelmed and out of control. But the positive function of chaos is to allow us to release ourselves into the freedom of our unique expression in the rhythm of lyrical.

Lyrical is the rhythm of spontaneous creativity, the expression of whatever is true, unique and alive in the moment. It is both deeply connected and profoundly free. It is often light and playful like the foam and spray of a wave after it crests, but it can take on the form of anything we are experiencing after moving through the first three rhythms. After grounding in flowing, engaging in staccato and letting go in chaos, lyrical allows us to experience being original, unpredictable, and exquisitely alive. Like the air, in lyrical we are attached to no form in particular, thus able to embody whatever form is appropriate to the moment. However, if we are not grounded in the body and connected deeply to our self, it is possible to land in the shadow side of lyrical, which would be superficiality, shallowness or escape.

The lightness and freedom of lyrical expands into the rhythm of *stillness*, just as a wave does when it reaches the shore. Rather than the absence of energy, stillness is the full presence of energy in a form that allows us to connect both to ourselves and beyond ourselves. Gabrielle Roth says stillness is the rhythm through which we open ourselves into the field. The shadow side of stillness — which can emerge when we are not grounded in our feet and body, present and connected with our own source of energy — is lethargy, dissociation, and becoming disembodied and lost in the field. Centered stillness is a form of disappearing while being simultaneously fully present—you are the stillpoint of the moving center, connected with the greater field surrounding you.

While practicing the 5Rhythms®, dancers are invited to develop their awareness of the space around them and to learn to move attention into different parts of the body. They are reminded to continually "move into the empty spaces." They are invited to explore different ways of moving through space, of moving body parts, thus progressively expanding their repertory of ways of moving.

There was an interesting study done some time ago regarding human movement. Researchers observed infants, older children and adults for an hour, recording the number of unique (discreet and non-repeating) movements they made in that period. They discovered that, in the space of an hour, infants made somewhere around 1,000 unique movements. In older children, however, by the time they were around 10 years old, the number of unique movements had dropped to around 300. In adults of age 30, the number of unique movements they made in an hour was down to about 100.

Of course, one implication of this study may be that as we age, we use our bodies more elegantly and purposefully, better conserving and directing our energy. Another implication, however, is that we begin to become more unconsciously limited and restrained in our repertory of physical expression.

As Gabrielle Roth teaches, what we do on the dance floor while practicing the rhythms is a mirror for what we do elsewhere in our lives. Moving through the rhythms teaches us about our relationship to the different principles contained in each rhythm. Moving with awareness through the structure of the wave allows us to bring movement to unconscious patterns and to develop new patterns that progressively bring more freedom, flexibility and choice. Movement works like running water, bringing space, renewal and new information to our existing somatic patterns.

Gabrielle asks: "Do you have the discipline necessary to be a free spirit?" As a movement practice, the 5Rhythms® teach us how following process contained in a clear structure can bring new awareness, insights, transformation and more choice. A somatic practice like the 5Rhythms® helps us to regain our flexibility of expression and gain access to all dimensions of ourselves.

In Gabrielle's words:

In flowing you discover yourself. In staccato you define yourself. Chaos helps you dissolve yourself, so you don't end up fixed and rigid in the self you've discovered and defined. Lyrical inspires you to devote yourself to digging deep into the unique expression of your energy. And stillness allows you to disappear into the big energy that holds us all so you can start the whole process over again.

Each of these rhythms can have many forms of expression, dance and "somatic syntax" being the most obvious. They also, however, have corresponding visual and auditory expressions (as in art and music). They are apparent at the process level of various techniques.

In NLP, the Swish Pattern is clearly an application of a staccato rhythm in order to produce a clear demarcation in behavior. The Dancing S.C.O.R.E. is more like a wave that starts in staccato (each part is first experienced separately and discretely) then adds flow (all of the elements are linked together into a unified sequence of movements) and then lyrical (resourceful/transformational energies are brought in through the sequence of movements).

Riding the Wave of Change

1. Create a location that represents your current state. Put yourself into your present experience of that problem or situation. See what you see, hear what you hear and feel what you feel regarding that situation. Allow your body to create a somatic expression—a gesture and/or repetitive movement—of how you experience your present state.

2. Move forward several steps into a location the represents your desired state. Put yourself into your experience of how it would be. See what you see, hear what you hear and feel what you feel regarding that experience. Again, allow your body to create a somatic expression—a gesture and/or repetitive movement—of how you experience your desired state.

3. In between the locations for your present and desired states, make a space into which you can bring each of the five rhythms: flowing, staccato, chaos, lyrical and stillness.

4. Go through the following process, accessing each of the five rhythms:

   a. Go to the location of your present state and make the gesture and/or movement associated with that experience. Step forward and bring that movement into the rhythm of *flowing*. Let your body follow your feet and begin to move in continuous easy movement that is grounded, connected and circular. Practice connection and receptivity, breathing in and "being with" the present state experience in movement. End by flowing into the somatic expression associated with your desired state.

b. Return to the location of your present state and again make the gesture and/or movement associated with that experience. Step forward and bring that movement into the rhythm of *staccato*. Ground in your feet and let them find a repetitive beat, marking it out with strength in your steps, feeling deeply connected to yourself and to your environment. Sense your heartbeat and as you breathe out, make strong, clear and distinct movements and gestures with your body. Practice bringing focus, concentration, commitment and clarity into the present state experience. End by moving strongly and confidently into the somatic expression associated with your desired state.

c. Start again the location of your present state, making the gesture and/or movement associated with that experience. Step forward and bring that movement into the rhythm of *chaos*. Keeping a firm rooting in your feet, alternate your steps from side to side. Let go of your neck and head and let your body move as if it were made of jiggling rubber. Allow yourself to release any tension or rigidity and bring flexibility into old patterns. Free up any stuck energy associated with the present state experience. Finish by bringing the looseness and release of chaos into the somatic expression associated with your desired state.

d. Beginning in the location of your present state and the somatic expression associated with that experience, step forward and bring that expression into the light and free rhythm of *lyrical*. Let yourself explore spontaneous creativity and express whatever is true, unique and alive for you in the moment. Allow yourself to be original, unpredictable, and fully alive. Play with whatever physical and energetic forms seem appropriate to bring lightness to the present state experience. Ride that sense of freedom into the somatic expression associated with your desired state.

e. Once more, go back to the location of your present state and the somatic expression associated with that experience. Step forward and bring that expression into the final rhythm of *stillness*. As you make the movements and gestures associated with the present state, move slowly and mindfully, breathing deeply, pausing from time to time. Feel the full presence of energy in a form that allows you to connect both to yourself and beyond yourself to a larger field. Experience yourself as the stillpoint of a moving center, connected with the space surrounding you. Let yourself smoothly arrive at the somatic expression associated with your desired stat

5. Reflect on what you have learned from each rhythm.

The 5Rhythms® and the Dancing S.C.O.R.E.

You can combine Riding the Wave of Change with the Dancing S.C.O.R.E. Begin by laying out spaces for the Symptom, Cause, Outcome and Effect and explore the spontaneous somatic expressions associated with each location. Then, one by one, bring in each of the five rhythms as a resource for the situation that you have mapped out.

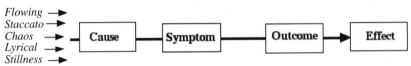

As with Riding the Wave of Change, repeat the movement from Cause to Symptom to Outcome to Effect bringing each of the five rhythms into the gestures and movements associated with each location. Each journey through the phases of the S.C.O.R.E. should bring new awareness and help add to the momentum to move in the direction of the Outcome and Effect.

Start with flowing. Root in your feet and begin moving fluidly and continuously. Integrate this quality of movement with the somatic expression associated with the Cause location. Notice what types of shifts and "differences that make a difference" this rhythm brings to your experience of the Cause. Then move to the Symptom location, continuing to bring the quality of flowing to whatever somatic expression is connected with your experience of the Symptom. Again notice the impact this has on your experience of the Symptom. Continue moving through the locations for the Outcome and Effect, bringing the quality of flowing to the somatic expressions associated with those locations.

Follow Your Feet!

Like all true works of genius, the 5Rhythms® are universal and can seem deceptively simple. As with any discipline— such as learning NLP—to become skillful in guiding others through the map and into the territory requires many, many hours of dedicated practice and training. While the 5Rhythms® are based on a series of maps, the learning happens first and primarily in the body. The intelligence of the somatic mind will nurture the cognitive mind, but this is a learning process that begins in (and never leaves) the feet, rather than trying to go from the head down.

We encourage you to experience this process "in the muscle" by dancing it yourself. Gabrielle Roth and her group The Mirrors have created CD's for dancing the Rhythms. The music itself will guide you through the 5Rhythms®.

Bones: Tracks 2 - 6
Initiation: Tracks 1 - 5
Trance: Tracks 4 - 8
Tribe: Tracks 1 - 5
Jhoom: Tracks 1 - 5
Endless Wave, vols. 1, 2 (Gabrielle's voice guides you through a wave)

In many parts of the world, you can find workshops and courses led by teachers who have gone through extensive training with Gabrielle. She has also written three inspiring and practical books, *Maps to Ecstasy*, *Sweat Your Prayers* and *Connections* that will deepen your relationship with your practice. Consult her website www.gabrielleroth.com for information about classes, teachers, music and books. You can also check www.movingcenter.com for more classes and workshops.

As you explore Gabrielle's 5Rhythms® remember to breathe, stay grounded and follow your feet!

Chapter 3

The Field Mind

Overview of Chapter 3

- **Field, Spirit and Purpose**
  - **Studying the Subjective Experience of Field and Spirit**
- **Neurophysiological Mechanisms of the Field Mind**
  - **Mirror Neurons**
  - **The Human Energy Field**
- **Exploring the Field Mind**
  - **Feeling Your Field**
  - **Connecting Through Your Center**
  - **Energetic Mirroring**
  - **Generating a "Second Skin"**
- **Creating a Generative Field**
  - **Evolving a Shared Resource (A "We-Source")**
- **Generative Collaboration**
  - **Creating a Generative "Container"**

Overview of Chapter 3 (continued)

- **Enriching the Group Field**
- **"Intervision"**
- **Accessing the "Larger Mind"**
  - **Active Dreaming**
    - Active Dreaming Exercise
  - **Seeing the "Field"**

The Field Mind

The emphasis on the notion of *field* or *field mind* is one of the defining characteristics of Third Generation NLP. A "field," in the Third Generation NLP view, is essentially a type of space or energy produced by relationships and interactions within a system of individuals. Central to this view of field is the idea that relationship itself is a "third entity" generated between those involved, similar to the way that hydrogen and oxygen can combine to produce the third entity of water. The relationship becomes a container that holds, processes and evolves the thoughts, emotions and experiences of those involved.

In physics, a field is defined as "a region of space characterized by a physical property, such as gravitational or electromagnetic force or fluid pressure, having a determinable value at every point in the region." A field, in physics, relates to the movement of energy through a widely dispersed area of space.

**In Physics, a Field Is Represented as "Lines of Force"
Extending Out into Space**

An electromagnetic field is typically represented in terms of "lines of force" that extend out infinitely in every direction and which produce an influence on objects in the "field" created by those lines of force. It is the gathering of these lines of force that determines the density and intensity, and thus the influence, of the field.

This stands in contrast to the notion of a "particle," which is an object that exists only in a very limited and defined region of space. A field is less tangible than a particle, and is more about movement and relationships than "things" themselves. A field is both generated by relationships between objects and exerts an influence on the behavior or actions of objects. A gravitational field, for instance, is a function of a fundamental attraction between all objects in space. The pull of gravity does not exist without the presence of the objects being drawn toward one another. The gravitational field generated between two objects (say, two planets) will also affect the behavior of other objects (a spaceship, for example) that enter the range of influence of that field.

The idea of a physical field has important implications (both direct and metaphorical) for psychology, management, therapy and NLP. Hypnotherapist and early NLP explorer Stephen Gilligan (1997) talks about a felt "relational field" that exists between human beings, which he considers a fundamental and necessary aspect of change and healing. German family therapist Bert Hellinger (1996) bases his work on the notion of a "family field" that extends into the entire history of a family system and includes the influence of members that are no longer living.

The sense of being a part of a larger system or field is a common subjective experience of almost every human being. We often speak of the feeling of "team spirit," for instance, which is a sense of being part of a group that includes us but is bigger than ourselves. This experience of belonging to a larger collective is expressed in NLP through the notion of *Fourth Perceptual Position*, or "We" position (Dilts & DeLozier,

1998). First, Second and Third Perceptual Positions (self, other and observer) relate to the significant points of view with respect to a system of human interaction, which define the "space" of the interaction. A type of relational "field" is created by the patterns of relationship and interaction that occur in that space. Fourth Position simultaneously includes and transcends the other three positions. The qualities of this "field" are often shaped by and reflected in the physical positioning or "psychogeography" between the individuals involved in the interaction.

Subjective experiences such as that of "team spirit," then, emerge from a felt sense of the "relational field" arising from the interactions between our own nervous systems and those of other people, which form a type of larger collective nervous system. This collective nervous system produces results that are sometimes referred to as a "group mind" or a "collective intelligence." This group *mind* can have characteristics and qualities of intelligence that are quite different from the individual minds of the members of the group, similar to the way that water has quite different properties than the hydrogen and oxygen atoms from which the water is formed.

According to the French psychologist Gustave Le Bon (1895):

> *The most striking peculiarity presented by a psychological group is the following. Whoever be the individuals that compose it, however like or unlike be their mode of life, their occupations, their character, or their intelligence, the fact that they have been transformed into a group puts them in possession of a sort of collective mind which makes them feel, think, and act in a manner quite different from that in which each individual of them would feel, think, and act were he in a state of isolation. There are certain ideas and feelings which do not come into being, or do not transform themselves into acts except in the case of individuals forming a group.*

Le Bon goes on to add:

> *The psychological group is a provisional being formed of heterogeneous elements, which for a moment are combined, exactly as the cells which constitute a living body form by their reunion a new being which displays characteristics very different from those possessed by each of the cells singly.*

These phenomena are an expression of what writer, philosopher and transpersonal theoretician Ken Wilber calls a *holarchy*. Holarchies are arrangements of related *holons* (a concept central to the writings of Arthur Koestler and the works of Gregory Bateson). The notion of the holon is that every entity and concept shares a dual nature: as *a whole unto itself, and as a part of some other whole.* For example, a cell in an organism is a whole and at the same time a part of another whole, the organism. Another example is that a letter is a self-existing entity and simultaneously an integral part of a word, which then is part of a sentence, which is part of a paragraph, which is part of a page, and so on.

Everything from quarks to matter to energy to ideas can be looked at in this way. Each entity *includes and transcends* the holons from which it is made. In this manner, collective fields can also be created by other creatures and beings, and even by our environment.

According to Gregory Bateson, when some holarchies reach the appropriate level of interconnection and integration, they display key qualities of "mind." He claimed that systems with the appropriate amount of complexity, flexibility and feedback can show "self-organizing" characteristics. Such systems often appear to have "a mind of their own":

> *[A]ny ongoing ensemble of events and objects which has the appropriate complexity of causal circuits and the appropriate energy relations will surely*

show mental characteristics. It will compare . . . it will "process information" and will inevitably be self-corrective either toward homeostatic optima or toward the maximization of certain variables.

With enough interconnection and feedback, a system is able to reach a higher level of integration and show characteristics of self-organization. The so-called *Gaia hypothesis*, proposed by NASA researcher James Lovelock (1979), is a good example of this. Lovelock used the term "Gaia" (in honor of the Greek primordial goddess of the Earth) to describe "a complex entity involving the Earth's biosphere, atmosphere, oceans, and soil; the totality constituting a feedback or cybernetic system which seeks an optimal physical and chemical environment for life on this planet."

Lovelock suggested that life on Earth provides a cybernetic, homeostatic feedback system that operates to maintain stable surface temperature, atmosphere composition and ocean salinity. The global surface temperature of the Earth, for example, has remained constant, despite an increase in the energy provided by the Sun of 25% to 30% since life began on the planet. The atmospheric composition of the Earth (79% nitrogen, 20.7% oxygen and 0.03% carbon dioxide) also remains constant, even though it should be unstable. Ocean salinity has been constant at about 3.4% for a very long time. Salinity stability is important as most cells require a constant salinity and do not generally tolerate values above 5%.

Lovelock proposed that these facts are evidence that the planetary ecosystem of the Earth's biomass regulates variables such as these to make conditions on the planet more inhabitable.

Physicist Peter Russell applied and extended this principle in his concept of *The Global Brain* (1983, 1995). Russell perceives the process of evolution as the progressive collecting together of units (holons) into larger systems—from elementary particles to atoms, to molecules, to cells, to tissues, and so forth, up to self-conscious organisms. Each leap to a larger unit establishes a new self-organizing pattern.

According to Russell, the increasing population density of the planet and the accelerating developments in communications technology have produced a situation in which human beings have the potential to reach a higher level of integration and act as a type of nervous system or "brain" to the rest of the planet.* (People are like neurons, and cell phones, television, radios, the Internet, etc. are like the synaptic connections between them.)

Russell's view of the "global brain" is echoed in Gregory Bateson's assertion that:

> *The individual mind is immanent but not only in the body. It is immanent in pathways and messages outside the body; and there is a larger Mind of which the individual mind is only a sub-system. This larger Mind is comparable to God and is perhaps what people mean by "God," but it is still immanent in the total interconnected social system and planetary ecology.*

One implication of Bateson's statement is the possibility that we can tap into networks of intelligence greater than our individual minds. This is a notion that has certainly been reflected throughout human history in the subjective experience of shamans, healers, parapsychologists, mediums, artists, people of traditional cultures, and some of the world's most creative geniuses.

---

* Russell postulates that the human race is poised to achieve a whole new level of "consciousness" and self-organization – perhaps comparable to the shift between the Neanderthal and the Cro-Magnon. While considering Russell's hypothesis, keep in mind that the threshold required for a new level of integration does not have to be large. The DNA of humans and chimpanzees, for instance, is 98% the same.

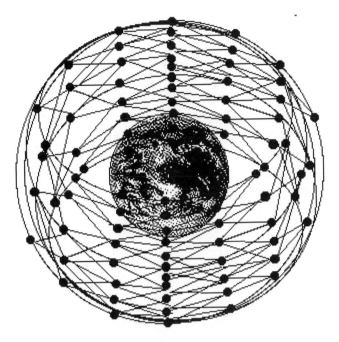

Gregory Bateson Postulated that Our Individual Minds Were Part of a "Larger Mind" Emerging from the "Total Interconnected Social System and Planetary Ecology"

In his work on *Strategies of Genius,* for instance, author Robert Dilts points out that almost every well-known creative genius in history, from Leonardo da Vinci to Einstein to Mozart to Michael Jackson, maintains, in some way or another, that his or her most creative works and ideas come "through" and not "from" him or her as an individual. Of his musical ideas, for example, Mozart wrote, "Whence and how they come, I know not; nor can I force them." He did, however, mention that these ideas came most easily when he was in certain types of internal states, in which the creative process unfolded "in a pleasing lively dream."

In his notebooks, Leonardo da Vinci described how he would stare at "walls spotted with various stains or with a mixture of different kinds of stones" in order to "stimulate and arouse" his mind "to various inventions." Leonardo claimed he was able to see in the walls "various different landscapes adorned with mountains, rivers, rocks, trees, plains, wide valleys, and various groups of hills" as well as "figures in quick movement, and strange expressions of faces, and outlandish costumes, and an infinite number of things."

Similarly, Albert Einstein claimed his ideas and theories arose spontaneously from certain types of "thought experiments" and "did not grow out of any manipulations of axioms" or rational, cognitive forms of thought.

These descriptions imply methods of connecting to creative intelligence beyond the confines of the individual cognitive mind. Besides the notion of "God" mentioned by Bateson, the "larger Mind" to which Bateson refers is perhaps what is meant by "intuition," the "creative unconscious" in the works of Milton H. Erickson, or the "collective unconscious" in Carl Jung's writings.

Freud had assumed the unconscious to be something personal, contained within an individual. Jung, on the other hand, saw the personal unconscious mind as sitting atop a much deeper universal layer of consciousness, the *collective* unconscious – the inherited part of the human psyche not developed from personal experience.

According to Jung, the collective unconscious is expressed through *archetypes*, universal thought-forms or mental images that influence an individual's feelings and actions. Noting that the experience of archetypes often does not conform to local tradition or cultural rules, Jung suggested that they were innate projections. In Jung's view, a newborn baby was not a blank slate but came hardwired, ready to perceive certain archetypal patterns and symbols. The reason children fantasize so much, Jung believed, was because they have not experienced enough of reality to cancel out their mind's connection to archetypal knowledge and imagery.

Archetypes have been expressed throughout history in various forms of myths, fairy tales, sacred texts, art, literature and even advertising. They show up at a personal level in dreams and visions. Plato described them in philosophical terms as "elemental forms" of thought and experience.

Another phenomenon of what Bateson called the "larger Mind" is what Rupert Sheldrake termed *morphic fields*. Sheldrake proposed the idea of morphic fields to explain phenomena which involve action at a distance, from the development of embryos to healing through prayer and the "the hundredth monkey" phenomenon*—i.e., situations in which change in a part of a population stimulates change in another member of the population, or the group as a whole, without any direct physical contact.

Essential to Sheldrake's model is the process of *morphic resonance*. This is a feedback mechanism between the field and the corresponding elements (i.e., holons) from which it emerges. The greater the degree of similarity between the individual elements or holons, the greater the resonance, making the existence, strength or persistence of that particu-

---

* The hundredth monkey phenomenon refers to a sudden, spontaneous and mysterious leap of consciousness achieved in dispersed populations of individuals when a "critical mass" point is reached through enough of the individuals in the population sharing a particular behavior or idea. The idea of the hundredth monkey phenomenon comes from Dr. Lyall Watson in his book *Lifetide* (1979) in which he wrote about several studies done in the 1960's by Japanese primatologists observing populations of macaque moneys who inhabited islands off the coast of Japan.

According to Watson, one monkey taught another to wash sweet potatoes. The second monkey in turn taught another who taught another and another until soon all the monkeys on the island were washing potatoes where no monkey had ever washed potatoes before. When the "hundredth" monkey learned to wash potatoes, suddenly, spontaneously and mysteriously monkeys on other islands, with no physical contact with the potato-washing group, started washing potatoes.

While the scientific accuracy of the studies has since been disputed, there are many other examples of phenomena that appear to be a result of this type of morphic effect; such as the simultaneous formulation of certain ideas and theories by people on different parts of the planet (e.g., the discovery of calculus by Newton and Leibniz).

lar form of thought or behavior contained in the larger field more likely.

Consider, for example, the phenomenon of the US soldiers who so brutally tortured prisoners at the Abu Ghraib prison (including physical, psychological and sexual abuse, rape, sodomy, and murder of prisoners) during the early phases of the US occupation of Iraq in 2003 - 2004. At the trials of these soldiers, defense attorneys brought out witness after witness who testified that their particular clients had no history of violent and sadistic behavior and were essentially normal, average people. How is it possible then, that a normal person could become an "inhuman monster," with seemingly no human empathy or compassion? One explanation would be a type of morphic field proposed by Sheldrake, in which violence engenders and perpetuates violence through morphic resonance between the US soldiers, compelling them to act in opposition to their own individual nature and personality.

Sheldrake proposes that the process of morphic resonance leads to stable morphic fields, which are significantly easier to *tune into*. He suggests, for instance, that this is the means by which simpler organic forms synergetically self-organize into more complex ones, and that this model allows a different explanation for the process of evolution itself, as an addition to Darwin's evolutionary processes of selection and variation.

It is very important to remember, however, that, as Bateson points out, "The mental characteristics are inherent or immanent in the ensemble as a whole." When we separate ourselves or become disconnected from the larger system, we lose access to the intelligence that it holds.

Another way of understanding what happened at the Abu Ghraib prison, for example, is that the soldiers became trapped within a disturbed, disconnected and unintegrated field permeating their environment, thus losing connection with themselves.

This need for connection with ourselves and the larger fields around us is why it is so critical to develop neurolinguistic tools that help us to connect or reconnect to ourselves and the larger Mind to which Bateson referred. Tools and processes that open us and connect us to various levels of field and field mind include the development of special or altered states, meditation, trance, psychogenic drugs and other substances; prayer, singing, dreams, poetry, dance, movement, somatic syntax, yoga; even making love.

Michael Dilts, for instance, has been exploring the connection between NLP and Shamanism to create Shamanic coaching processes (http://www.shamancia.com/). Using drumming as a means to create a connection between the human nervous system and field intelligence, Michael helps people to access archetypal wisdom in order to find deep level resources and solutions.

Field, Spirit and Purpose

The notions of field and field mind are clearly connected to what has been known throughout human history as "spiritual" experience. The term *spiritual* is used in Third Generation NLP to refer to the subjective experience of being part of a "larger system"; one that reaches beyond ourselves as individuals to our family, community and global systems. This level of experience is considered one of the six fundamental levels of learning and change in Robert Dilts' NeuroLogical Levels model. "Spiritual" level experience relates to what could be called *the larger "S" self*—a sense of being that goes beyond our own image of ourselves, our values, beliefs, thoughts, actions or sensations. It relates to our connection with *who else* and *what else* are in the larger system surrounding us. Change at this level of experience typically comes in the form of an "awakening" to this greater context that gives our lives meaning and purpose.

Depending on the individual or culture, the subjective experience of the spiritual may be represented in terms of a personal "God," a whole realm of gods and spirits, a diffuse energy connecting everything in the universe, a vast impersonal order, or as an initiating power, coming to human life and touching it from beyond itself.

Spiritual experiences are at the root of religion but are not themselves inherently "religious." Religions typically stem from the attempt to form a community around shared spiritual experiences and beliefs. Religion involves the institutionalization of specific beliefs, values and ethical codes that are an attempt to socially reflect or represent something derived from the personal experience of "Spirit."

Because we cannot perceive intricate, complex and invisible relationships that make up a field directly, our subjective representations of them are often symbolic and non-literal. The revelations that typify spiritual or religious experience are often characterized by sensory distortions or unusual combinations of sensory qualities (or submodalities). For example, as a visual image gets farther away, it typically appears smaller, dimmer and less clear. Religious "visions," however, are often characterized by distant images that are large, bright, and clear. Similarly, when a sound or a voice is far away, it becomes quieter and less distinct. "God's" voice, however, is usually represented as distant but loud and clear. As another example, most people who are aware of "inner" voices, talk to themselves, and are thus used to hearing their own distinctive tonal qualities associated with that voice. It is unusual to hear someone else's voice in the location of one's own "inner dialog," as people do when they hear guiding "inner voices."

Another characteristic of spiritual or religious experiences is that they often include "synesthesias," or overlaps between sensory experiences. That is, people not only see something, but hear and feel it at the same time (as a musician might "see" and "feel" music).

The common thread that unites all spiritual level experiences, however, is that they have to do with our sense of being part of something, on a very deep level, that is beyond ourselves. It is the awareness of what Gregory Bateson called *the pattern which connects* all things together into a larger whole. We, as individuals, are a subsystem of this larger system. Our experience of this level is related to our sense of purpose and mission in life. It comes from asking the questions, "For whom and for what do I devote my energy and actions?"

Spiritual pursuits, in the form of accomplishing one's "vision" and "mission," are the motivation behind some of the greatest human achievements. Of his work in the area of physics, for example, Albert Einstein claimed:

> *I want to know how God created this world. I am not interested in this or that phenomenon, in the spectrum of this or that element; I want to know his thoughts; the rest are details.*

From the perspective of Third Generation NLP, the notion of the *spiritual* may be likened to what Einstein was referring to as "God's thoughts." Many of the world's most important leaders and geniuses acknowledge the significance of some type of spiritual guidance in their lives and work.

Studying the Subjective Experience of Field and Spirit

Clearly, the subjective experience of the *Field* and *Spirit* is one of the most intense and profound available to human beings. As NLP is by definition *the study of the structure of subjective experience*, the exploration of the structure of the subjective experience of field, the larger Mind and of spirituality is of great relevance to NLP. Field and spiritual level experiences and the processes that influence them, however, are a relatively new area of study in NLP. Many developments in this area were pioneered by author Robert Dilts and NLP trainer Robert McDonald in their work *Tools of the Spirit* (1997). Similarly, the overall purpose of many *NLP New Coding* distinctions (Grinder and DeLozier, 1987) was to shift the focus of attention in NLP from specific elements in an interaction to the larger relational field of interaction between elements.

One does not have to look very far to establish that the perception of various types of fields is a common subjective experience. The three main types of fields that people experience are:

1) A personal field or "life force" associated with our physical body and being;

2) An interpersonal field between oneself and others or between individuals within a group;

3) A progressively larger field or mind, of which we and others are parts as a subsystem of a greater whole with an intelligence beyond our individual minds.

In this chapter we will be examining some of the "neurolinguistic" mechanisms of field and the field mind and exploring processes and procedures through which we can access the greater intelligence of the field to help us heal, create, think outside of the box, make wiser decisions and better manage our lives.

Neurophysiological Mechanisms of the Field Mind

Mirror Neurons

One of the neurological bases for the Third Generation NLP notion of field is what is known as *mirror neurons*. Mirror neurons were discovered in the early 1990's at the University of Parma in Italy. A neuroscientist named Giacomo Rizzolatti and his graduate students were recording electrical activity from neurons in the brain of a macaque monkey. The tips of very thin electrodes were placed within individual neurons in the monkey's premotor cortex, which is known to be involved in the coordination of movements.

As expected, the researchers observed that when the monkey moved its arm to grab an object, certain neurons in the premotor cortex fired, creating a specific crackling sound in their equipment.

One day, when the research team was breaking for lunch, they forgot to turn off their equipment. Being Italian, one of Rizzolatti's graduate students decided to have some gelato for dessert and brought the ice cream cone with him back into the lab. As he licked the ice cream, he suddenly heard the distinctive crackling sound of the monkey's neurons firing, as if the monkey was moving its own arm. When he looked at the monkey, it was motionless, but watching him intently.

To the student's surprise, each time he licked the cone, neurons in the part of the brain the monkey used to coordinate motor activity fired, despite the fact that the monkey was sitting still and only observing the action of the student.

The same group of researchers had earlier noticed a similarly strange phenomenon with peanuts. The same brain cells fired when the monkey watched humans or other monkeys bring peanuts to their mouths as when the monkey itself brought a peanut to its mouth. Later, the scientists found cells that fired when the monkey broke open a peanut or heard someone break a peanut. The same thing happened with bananas, raisins and all kinds of other objects.

They called these brain cells "mirror neurons" because they "mirrored" actions that the monkeys observed in others.

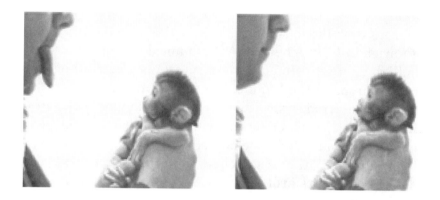

A Baby Macaque Monkey "Mirroring" a Human Sticking Out His Tongue

Subsequent experiments have confirmed the existence of mirror neurons in humans. These experiments further revealed that, in addition to mirroring physical actions, the cells reflected sensations and emotions. Humans, it turns out, have mirror neurons that are more sensitive, flexible and more highly evolved than any of those found in monkeys. This fact, according to scientists, reflects the evolution of humans' sophisticated social abilities.

The human brain has multiple mirror neuron systems that specialize in carrying out and understanding not just the actions of others but their intentions, the social meaning of their behavior and their emotions.

"We are exquisitely social creatures," Dr. Rizzolatti points out. "Our survival depends on understanding the actions, intentions and emotions of others. Mirror neurons allow us to grasp the minds of others not through conceptual reasoning but through direct simulation. By feeling, not by thinking."

Mirror neurons are clearly the foundation of empathy, compassion and what is known in NLP as *second position* – our ability to put ourselves into perspective of another individual and get a sense for how they are feeling, thinking and experiencing a particular situation or interaction. They are also clearly a key element in explaining how people, and in particular children, are able to learn vicariously by simply observing someone else perform an action.

Mirror neurons, however, can also potentially account for some of our experience of what we have referred to as *fourth position* in NLP - our experience of being part of a collective. Through mirror neurons we literally share the experiences of others with whom we are interacting. This is reflected in our use of the word "we" to describe the experience of being part of a group that includes but transcends ourselves.

Mirror neurons are also one of the physiological mechanisms at the basis of the phenomena of introjection and imprinting. Both are processes by which we internalize the behaviors and feelings of significant others.

Through mirror neurons, the behaviors, responses and emotions of others enter our nervous system without the filters of conscious decision or choice. They clearly make up part of the way that we take on the actions and energy of other people (and beings) in our surrounding environment.

The Human Energy Field

Another mechanism contributing to what we have been calling the "field mind" is the *human energy field*. It has long been known that the activities of cells and tissues in the human body generate electrical fields that can be detected on the skin surface. These electrical signals include: brainwaves (EEG—electroencephalogram), skin conductivity (GSR—galvanic skin response), micro muscle activity (EMG—electromyogram) and heartbeat (ECG—electrocardiogram). Such measures are at the foundation of biofeedback and polygraph (lie detection) technologies.

The electrical currents associated with these signals, however, also generate a corresponding magnetic field in the surrounding space. In fact, it has been discovered that all tissues and organs produce specific magnetic pulsations, which have come to be known as *biomagnetic fields*.

Instruments such as the SQUID magnetometer, for instance, are able to detect the biomagnetic field projected from the human heart and measure magnetic fields around the head produced by brain activities. In some areas of medicine, traditional electrical recordings, such as the electrocardiogram and electroencephalogram, are now being complemented by biomagnetic recordings, called *magnetocardiograms* and *magnetoencephalograms*. In fact, mapping the magnetic fields in the space around the body can provide a more accurate indication of physiology and pathology than traditional electrical measurements.

Such biomagnetic fields not only reflect the activity of the body's cells and organs but can also influence their functioning. Studies have shown, for instance, that neurons change their firing properties under the influence of magnetic fields.

In one exploration of the influence of the human energy field, researchers at the *HeartMath Institute* in California conducted studies concerned with energetic communication by the heart, which they refer to as *cardioelectromagnetic communication.* These studies (McCraty, Atkinson and Tiller, 1999) explore the possibility that the electromagnetic field generated by the heart may transmit information that can be received by others.

According to the HeartMath researchers, the heart is the most powerful generator of electromagnetic energy in the human body, producing the largest rhythmic electromagnetic field of any of the body's organs. The heart's electrical field is about 60 times greater in amplitude than the electrical activity generated by the brain. This field, measured in the form of an electrocardiogram, can be detected anywhere on the surface of the body. Furthermore, the magnetic field produced by the heart is more than 5,000 times greater in strength than the field generated by the brain. This field not only envelops every cell of the body but also extends out in all directions into the space around us. The cardiac field can be measured several feet away from the body.

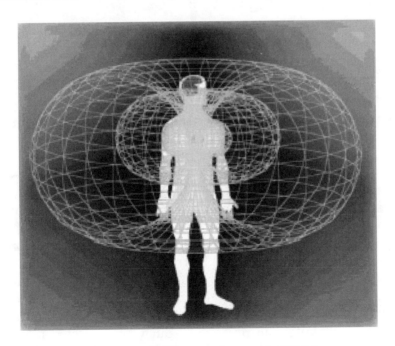

The Heart's Electromagnetic Field

HeartMath's research indicates that the electromagnetic signals generated by the heart have the capacity to affect others around us. Their data shows that in subjects separated by several feet, synchronization can occur between the alpha waves in one person's EEG and the other's ECG signal. In other words, when two people are at a conversational distance, the electromagnetic signal generated by one person's heart can influence the other person's brain rhythms.

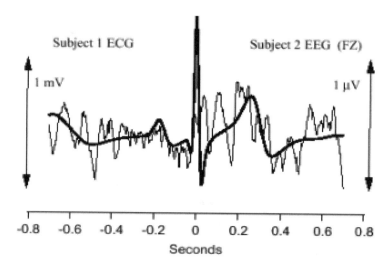

HeartMath Graph Showing the Heartbeat (ECG) of One Person Superimposed on the Brainwaves (EEG) of Another

HeartMath's findings also indicate that as individuals stabilize and align functions in their own inner psychophysiological state (referred to as physiological "coherence") these individuals become more sensitive to the subtle electromagnetic signals communicated by those around them.

These results suggest that cardioelectromagnetic communication may be a source of information exchange between people, and that this exchange is influenced by our emotional states and internal processes. Such phenomena may be expressions of what Rupert Sheldrake termed "morphic resonance."

Other studies have shown that pathology alters the body's biomagnetic fields. Some researchers have suggested that diseases can be detected in the energy field of the body before physical symptoms appear, and postulate that some diseases may be prevented by altering the energy field.

Such studies reveal the physiological underpinnings of subtle, ongoing energetic forms of communication between people through mechanisms such as biomagnetic fields. Similar to the synapses that connect nerve cells in the body and brain, biomagnetic fields may function as energetic synapses that connect us with each other and with other organisms in a larger virtual nervous system.

The combination of the activity of mirror neurons with the phenomena of human energy fields provides a rich basis for understanding more about how we can access and utilize the resources of the field mind. In the next section, we will be exploring exercises and techniques through which you can deepen your connection to personal and interpersonal fields, and ultimately to the extended fields of what Bateson called the "larger Mind."

Exploring The Field Mind

As you read over and try out the following formats, remember that what we are exploring is not necessarily about objective reality. The purpose is rather to enrich your subjective experience and personal map of the world. Whether what you experience is verifiable in "objective reality" is less important than the quality of resourcefulness it brings you. The ultimate measure of all NLP processes is whether or not they are useful to you in some way.

There are many belief systems relating to the phenomena of field, field mind and "spiritual" level processes. These belief systems are not necessary for the direct subjective experience of these phenomena and often will even distort or contaminate our experience. When we get caught up in beliefs and stories about our experience, and we are not somatically centered, connected and grounded in our bodies, we can become lost in field phenomena or experience its problematic or "shadow" sides.

According to Third Generation NLP, the body and somatic intelligence are the gateway to field awareness and the field mind. It is through the body that we know the field most directly. The conscious cognitive mind primarily operates through the linear logic of conscious purpose. Key to Third Generation NLP is the ability to center in the somatic core (coming home to the body) and then open to the field. This makes it possible to include, yet transcend (i.e., get outside of the box of), the cognitive structures of the ego.

Thus, the first step of these processes generally involves some type of centering and connecting with the somatic mind, incorporating elements from the previous chapter.

Feeling Your "Field"

The purpose of this first exercise is to help you become more aware of your own personal energy field and how, through it, you can connect to the bigger field around you (the "larger Mind") in order to access and strengthen fundamental resources.

1. Center yourself somatically and become fully present in your body. Rub your hands together in order to make them warm and sensitive.

2. Hold the palms of your hands facing one another so that they are almost touching. Bring presence and awareness into your hands and let them become so sensitive that you can feel the energy of your body between the palms of your hands. You may experience it as a type of warmth, tingling or subtle pressure.

3. Move your hands a little further apart until they are about 3 or 4 inches (8-10 centimeters) away from one another. Keeping your awareness in your hands, begin to sense the field of energy between them at this distance. Are the qualities any different from when your hands were almost touching? Keep in mind that reducing your cognitive thinking processes, especially your inner dialog, will help you to be more tuned into the subtle dynamics of your body's field. Moving your hands very slightly toward and away from each other can also help you to get a better sense of this field.

4. Continue to move your hands a little further apart until they are about 10 inches (25 centimeters) away from one another. Keeping your awareness in your hands, sense the field of energy between them at this distance. Notice the qualities of this field. How do they compare to those of the previous two distances?

5. Keep moving your hands apart until your arms are almost fully extended. Staying centered in your body and maintaining your sense of presence and awareness in your hands, feel the field of energy between your hands as the distance increases. Continue to notice the qualities of the field between your hands as well as if and how they change as you move your hands farther apart.

6. Keeping your arms extended, allow your hands and arms to move into a position as if you were about to embrace someone. Notice if you can feel a sense of embracing the field of energy emanating from your body. Also become aware of any energetic sensations on the backs of your hands and arms (on the outside of your embrace).

7. Open your arms fully and allow the palms of your hands to face outward from your body. Notice how far you can feel a sense of your field extending into the space around you.

8. Set an intent to bring some resource (such as serenity, inner peace or wisdom) from your sense of connection to the larger field around you and move your arms and hands back to the extended embrace position. Become aware of an increased sense of fullness or richness in your field.

9. Slowly bring your hands towards your body, continuing to feel an increasing sense of fullness and richness in the field between your hands and your body.

10. End by placing your hands on top of one another and putting them on the part of your body that feels most appropriate to receive the resource that you have brought through your connection between your personal energy field and the larger field around you.

When you have finished, reflect upon how easy this type of experience was for you. How natural was it for you to be subjectively aware of these field phenomena?

Did you experience any interferences? Sometimes you will encounter limiting beliefs or critical internal thoughts. It can be useful to be aware of them so that you can be sure you have a choice about them.

Like every other skill, your facility with this basic capacity to become aware of your own field and connect it with a larger field will increase with practice. If you found this process useful or feel that it may be useful to you at some time, we encourage you to repeat it at regular intervals, like a type of meditation. As Aristotle pointed out, "We are what we repeatedly do. Excellence then is not an act, but a habit."

Connecting Through Your Center

The purpose of the next format is to explore how you can connect your personal field with that of another person in order to create and experience an "interpersonal" field that includes and integrates both of your individual fields, similar to the way that hydrogen atoms and oxygen atoms combine to make the third entity of water.

Key to this process is your ability to first be grounded and connected to yourself. Transformational teacher Richard Moss points out that *the distance between ourselves and others is the same as the distance between ourselves and ourselves.* The implication of this is that our relationships to others and to the world around us is a mirror for our relationship with ourselves. Thus, our relationship to ourselves forms the ground from which emerges our relationships to others and to the external world.

According to Moss, when two people are each connected to themselves and present with each other, the natural feelings that emerge are compassion, empathy, genuine interest in each other, spontaneity, authenticity and joy. These feelings are the foundation for all effective personal and professional relationships.

1. Stand facing your partner. Close your eyes and allow your attention to go inside your body to a felt sense of your "center." Connect fully with the feeling of your center, bringing a sense of awareness and presence into your body.

2. When you feel centered and present within yourself, put your hands on top of one another and place them on your body where you most feel the sense of your physical and personal center.

3. Staying in contact with the felt sense of your center, open your eyes and look into your partner's eyes. When you are sure you can do this and maintain the felt sense of connection with your own inner center, "anchor" it by lifting your right hand from your body and extending it toward your partner. Take each other's right hand as if you were gently shaking hands. Feel the sense of connection with your partner through your right hand.

4. Gently release your partner's hand and bring your attention back into yourself, placing both hands over your center and allowing your eyes to close again.

5. Feel a sense of awareness and presence in your body, but this time become aware of your center as a "center point" of the field or space of your body.

6. When you can do this, begin to move your hands slowly and gently away from your body. Feel the field or energy of your presence and awareness expand into the space around your body indicated by the distance between your hands and your body. Again, be aware of your center as the center point of this space or field.

7. Keep slowly moving your hands farther and farther away from your body, maintaining the sense of your center as the center point of a field or space that extends from your body to the distance that your hands have moved.

8. Keep widening the sense of your field or space until your arms and hands are fully extended out from the sides of your body in a gesture of opening to the world. Feel your center as the center point of this vast space or field.

9. Once again open your eyes and look into the eyes of your partner, maintaining the feeling of the center point within yourself. Bring your left hands toward one another and take each other's hand as if you were gently shaking hands. Feel the sense of connection with your partner through your left hand. Notice any differences between this sense of connection and the one you felt when you took each other's right hand.

10. Release each other's hands, return to the open gesture. Then let your arms relax and come down by your sides.

11. Shift your state by moving around a little; i.e., turning around and shaking your arms and legs.

12. Face your partner again. Look into each other's eyes and take a breath together at the same time, then reach out with both hands. Take your partner's right hand with your right hand and your partner's left hand with your left hand, as if you were shaking right and left hands simultaneously. Notice the presence of both ways of experiencing your center at the same time.

13. Feel the rich sense of connection with your partner that this produces. What feelings naturally emerge from this connection? What are the qualities of the "third entity" that your connection produces? Silently send a blessing or gift to your partner through this connection. Then gently release your partner's hands and give each other a hug.

When you have finished, again reflect upon how easy or challenging this type of experience was for you. Were you able to sense the "third entity" or field produced by your connection?

Were there any interferences such as fear, vulnerability or uncomfortable self-consciousness? If so, were there limiting beliefs or critical internal thoughts associated with these interferences about which you can have more choices?

If you found this level of connection useful or fascinating, there are ways in which you can create it without having to formally go through all of the steps. Often, simply coming present in your own body, centering yourself and holding the intention to connect with another person will produce the subjective experience of this type of interpersonal field.

Energetic Mirroring

According to Rupert Sheldrake's notion of *morphic resonance*, the greater the degree of similarity between individuals (or holons), the greater the level of resonance. This, in turn, enriches the quality of the morphic field between them.

A key purpose of this exercise is to help you develop a high quality of morphic resonance between yourself and another person through "energetic mirroring," by matching the quality and level of intensity of each other's personal field. This increases the degree of resonance produced by the interpersonal field between you.

1. Center yourself and become fully present in your body. Rub your hands together in order to make them warm and sensitive.

2. Stand facing your partner and lift both of your hands so that the palms of your hands are facing the palms of your partner's hands, almost touching them. Put your awareness into your hands and become very aware of the energy field between your hands and your partner's hands. Feel a sense of connection to your partner through this field.

3. Together with your partner, begin to move your hands farther apart, until they are about 4 inches (8-10 centimeters) from each other. Keeping your awareness in your hands, increase your sensitivity to your partner until you can feel the field of energy between your hands and those of your partner. Moving your hands very slightly toward and away from each other can help you to get a better sense of this field. Notice the qualities of this field. How is it similar to, and different from, what you experienced at the previous distance? Maintain your feeling of connection with your partner through this field.

4. Step slowly back from your partner until your hands are about 10 inches (25 centimeters) away from one another. Keeping your awareness in your hands, sense the field of energy between your hands and your partner's hands and your connection at this distance. Notice the qualities of your mutual field at this distance. How does it compare with the other two?

5. Continue to step back slowly from your partner keeping your hands facing one another, feeling the field between you and your sense of connection through that field. Move only as far away from one another as you can and still feel your connection through the field that you sense between you with your hands.

6. Begin to slowly move back toward one another, feeling the field between your hands and your partner's hands, until your hands once again are almost touching. Then allow your hands to gently make physical contact.

7. Push on each other's hands, putting pressure on one another's hands until you are moving each other's hands slightly back and forth.

8. Adjust the pressure you are putting on each other's hands until you are mirroring back exactly the same amount of pressure that you feel coming from your partner's hands.

Both your and your partner's hands should become perfectly still. Tune into this sense of matched pressure and
energy between each other's hands and feel the increased
sense of connection that comes with it.

9. Together with your partner, move your hands slightly
apart until they are once again almost touching and you
can feel the life force field between your hands. Stand
with your hands facing your partner's hands until you can
feel that you are both mirroring back the same amount of
energy as you feel coming from the hands of your partner.
Again, notice the increased sense of connection to one
another that comes with it.

10. Repeat steps 3-5 of the exercise adding the process of
mirroring back each other's energy through the field
between your hands at each successive distance.

11. Once again, move slowly back toward one another,
mirroring back the energy you feel in the field between
you and your partner's hands, until your hands once
again are almost touching. Then allow your hands to
gently make physical contact and stand mirroring back
the physical pressure you feel from one another. Feel the
strength of the connection between you and your partner.

12. When you are ready, you can release your connection with
your partner's hands and give each other a hug.

Reflect again upon how easy or challenging you found the
exercise to be. Such exercises and experiences can frequently
produce a sense of vulnerability as we more intimately open
ourselves to the energy of another person. It can be especially
challenging if their energy is overly intense, unintegrated or
disturbed. When someone uses an expression like: "If looks
could kill," or "That person is throwing daggers through their
eyes," these are descriptions of energetic "attacks." A major
challenge in opening to the field mind is how to receive these
"attacks" skillfully and work with them positively.

It is important to have a sense of security and trust in order to open to the field of another person. This is why one of the most important resources we can learn in order to safely develop our experience of the Field Mind is to create what our colleague Stephen Gilligan (2009) calls a "second skin."

Generating a "Second Skin"

A *second skin* is a type of energetic insulation that protects us from potential disturbances coming from the various fields around us without disconnecting us from the important knowledge and information contained in those fields.

The metaphor of a "skin" here is crucial. Unlike a barrier or "armor," skin is both *receptive and selective*. It allows you to be visible without being exposed, and to be present without being overly vulnerable or fragile. Accomplishing this requires a balanced energy field that is neither too soft nor too hard. The phenomenon of a "second skin" allows you to open safely and confidently into the world, without either dominating others with your own energy or being pushed around because your energy is too weak.

Skin is a type of membrane that has pores that filter the flow of energy, material and information that pass between what is outside of the membrane and what is held within it. What Gilligan calls the second skin determines, on the one hand, how much of our own energy is contained on the inside and how much is released into the world. On the other hand, it connects us to the outside world through touch, but also regulates the impact of outer energies and influences by filtering what aspects of them are allowed to enter.

The following format can help you to subjectively create healthy and resilient energetic "skin" that can be a resource for you in your interactions with others.

1. Identify a relationship context in which you become overwhelmed, lost or assaulted by a disturbed or "shadow" field; i.e., a situation in which you feel caught in or in the spell of some type of negative energy or vibration (e.g., fearfulness, aggression, sadness, depression, fatigue, etc.). This does not have to be connected with any specific behavioral content or expression. It may be a sense that you pick up in that context.

2. Select a location in front of you, step into it and put yourself into that situation, imagining that you are there now, seeing what you see, hearing what you hear and feeling what you feel. Take an internal inventory of what it is like subjectively. How do you experience the impact of this negative energy? How do you feel? What happens to your thoughts?

3. Step out and away from the situation and shake off the state. Center and ground yourself, becoming fully present in your body. Rub your hands together in order to make them warm and sensitive.

4. Hold the palms of your hands facing one another so that they are almost touching. Bring presence and awareness into your hands and let them become so sensitive that you can feel the life force energy of your body between the palms of your hands. Imagine that your grounded center is an energy generator. Imagine the energy from your center moving out your arms and through your hands. Feel the presence of this energy in the space between your hands.

5. Move your hands a little further apart until they are about 3 or 4 inches (8-10 centimeters) away from one another. Keeping your awareness in your hands, continue to sense the field of energy between them at this distance. Moving your hands very slightly toward and away from each other can help you to get a better sense of this field.

Note: Stay present and in your body. If your mind begins to wander or leave the present you will not be able to feel the field.

6. Continuing to feel the presence of the field generated from your center, slowly allow your hands and arms to move into a position as if you were about to embrace someone. Notice if you can feel a sense of embracing the field of energy emanating from your center and your body. Also become aware of any energetic sensations on the backs of your hands and arms (on the outside of your embrace).

7. Holding the sense of this field in your hands and arms, begin sculpting and creating a "second skin" around that yourself. The metaphor of skin is important here. It is neither armor nor a force field. Skin allows you to be both connected and selective at the same time. The skin of your body both protects your delicate internal organs and also connects you in an intimate way with your environment. This energetic skin will do the same thing with the field. Take extra time to make sure this second skin is in place at the places over your body where you have felt most vulnerable (heart, stomach, throat, etc.). When you feel the presence of your second skin clearly in place, take a few steps to practice moving with your second skin accompanying you as you move.

Note: If it helps, you can add other representational systems as well; i.e., visualizing the skin as an energy field or a certain color of light.

8. Feeling strongly the presence of your second skin, now step into the location where you explored the disturbing situation. Feel the sense of both safety/selectivity and connection with the environment around you. As you re-experience the problem context and situation notice how it is different for you.

9. Future pace by imagining the next time you will be in that situation, being inside of your second skin.

If you are guiding someone else through this process, center yourself and generate a field with your hands as you are guiding your partner. As you are explaining and demonstrating what to do, you can reinforce your partner's second skin by mirroring it back through sculpting it with your hands.

If you do this, however, it is important that, as a coach, you do not try to put any of your own qualities or energy into your partner's "second skin." Your role is simply to acknowledge and sponsor the presence of the second skin in your partner by mirroring through the sculpting movements of your own hands where you observed him or her place his or her own second skin.

Creating a Generative Field

When we are grounded in ourselves and connected appropriately with others, interpersonal fields can be an extremely powerful source of resources for us. Through our interactions with others, we discover and strengthen archetypal knowledge and energy, creating what we call a "generative field."

A generative field is one that is able to bring out or release something new, remarkable or unprecedented within the individuals involved in creating that field or within the interaction between them. As Le Bon pointed out, "there are certain ideas and feelings which do not come into being, or do not transform themselves into acts" except through people's participation in groups. In other words, we have resources and potential capabilities and behaviors that can only be discovered and developed through our relationships and interactions with others.

This is similar to the dynamic of DNA that makes up the physical structure of our bodies. Genes are activated (i.e., "turned on" or "turned off") by their interactions with other molecules around them. Our genes represent our potential, which may or may not become expressed. The fact that we have a genetic predisposition to something does not necessarily mean that it will in fact manifest, or manifest properly. This is determined by its interaction with its local environment.

Consider, for example, the capacity for verbal language in humans. Language ability is believed to be innate. That is, language will emerge naturally and spontaneously from human interactions with one another. All human populations on the planet possess some form of verbal language. The release and development of such innate (archetypal) capacities, however, appear to require interaction between people in order to become expressed. Language will apparently develop spontaneously whenever there are two or more people living together. It will not, however, emerge in humans who are isolated from other humans.

In perhaps the earliest psychology experiment ever done, Greek historian Herodotus recounts how the Egyptian pharaoh Psammetichus I (Psamtik) sought to discover the origin of language by giving two newborn babies to a shepherd. The shepherd was instructed to feed and care for them, but was ordered not to speak to the children as they grew up. The idea was to see if the children would develop language on their own and, if so, to determine what language it would be. The hypothesis was that their first words would be uttered in the root language of all people.

Apparently, the children did begin to spontaneously speak on their own. When one of the children cried *"becos"* with outstretched arms, the shepherd supposedly concluded that the word was Phrygian because that was the sound of the Phrygian word for "bread." [As a result, they concluded that the Phrygians were an older people than the Egyptians, and that Phrygian was the original language of men.]

The natural development of language, such as in the two Egyptian infants, however does not occur in reported incidents of isolated or so-called "feral children" raised by wolves or other animals. In fact, feral children typically have trouble learning to walk upright and display a complete lack of interest in the human activity around them. They often seem mentally impaired and have almost insurmountable trouble learning a human language if they are discovered after a certain age.

As an interesting demonstration of mirror neurons, feral children tend to take on characteristics of the animals that raised them. In a recent incidence (December 2007), a child was discovered in central Russia who had been living with a pack of wolves. The boy reportedly expressed typical wolf-like behavior and reactions, and was unable to speak any human language.*

---

* From this perspective, it is interesting to reflect on the fact that it has been noted that the word "becos," supposedly uttered by the Egyptian child in the account of Herodotus is a sound quite similar to the bleating of sheep.

The conclusion of these observations seems to be that relationship and interaction with other humans are required in order to create the necessary degree of "morphic resonance" (perhaps through mirror neurons) needed to activate even basic human capacities such as walking upright and using verbal language. In other words, we might say that it is not so much that language is innate within individuals as it is innate in the field between individuals.

In his book *Outliers* (2008), Malcolm Gladwell points out that the accomplishments and performance of remarkable and successful individuals are shaped by their environment and social context as much as they are by their internal make-up. Gladwell asserts that success requires more than individual intelligence, ambition, hustle and hard work, concluding that "what we do as a community, as a society, for each other, matters as much as what we do for ourselves."

As an illustration, if Albert Einstein had been isolated as a child or raised by wolves, he would clearly not have developed and expressed his unique genius. As Einstein himself claimed:

> *The individual, if left alone from birth, would remain primitive and beast-like in his thoughts and feelings to a degree that we can hardly conceive. The individual is what he is and has the significance that he has not so much in virtue of his individuality, but rather as a member of a great human society, which directs his material and spiritual existence from the cradle to the grave.*
>
> *A man's value to the community depends primarily on how far his feelings, thoughts, and actions are directed towards promoting the good of his fellows. We call him good or bad according to how he stands in this matter. It looks at first sight as if our estimate of a man depended entirely on his social qualities.*

And yet such an attitude would be wrong. It is clear that all the valuable things, material, spiritual and moral, which we receive from society can be traced back through countless generations to certain creative individuals. The use of fire, the cultivation of edible plants, the steam engine -- each was discovered by one man.

Only the individual can think, and thereby create new values for society -- nay, even set up new moral standards to which the life of the community conforms. Without creative, independently thinking and judging personalities the upward development of society is as unthinkable as the development of the individual personality without the nourishing soil of the community.

Thus, we grow and evolve ourselves through our interactions with others. As a coaching client once said to one of the authors, "I like who I am when I am around you." We have certainly all experienced how being around certain people can bring out energies and qualities in ourselves that would not be there were we on our own. Falling in love is a classic example of this.

There is a very instructive and inspiring music video segment that we often like to show in our workshops and seminars that illustrates the phenomenon of generative field quite beautifully. The video is an excerpt from the recording of a concert put on by the New Age musician Yanni at the Acropolis. The segment is of a brief improvisational performance by two violinists — an African American woman with a background in jazz and a man of Middle Eastern descent who has been classically trained. As the two musicians take turns playing during their improvisational duet, it is obvious that there is a positive and creative rapport between them which shows up in the somatic enthusiasm and playfulness that they demonstrate as they both play and listen to one another. As they continue to perform, they begin to incorporate musical ideas and melodies that they have just heard from each other and take those ideas in new and creative directions.

The end result is an inspired performance in which each musician has clearly given the best of him or herself and elevated each other, playing things that would never have entered into either one of their minds had they played by themselves. It is also clear that the result was not simply a consequence of their obvious high level of skill with their instruments. It is a function of the somatic energy within their bodies and the generative field formed between them.

Evolving a Shared Resource (A "We-Source")

Author and humanist Morris Berman states, "*The energy of the universe originates in the body, and is generated as a field between bodies.*" The purpose of this next exercise is to explore how we can release, harness and creatively utilize our energy through what we have termed a "generative field."

Similar to the example of the two musicians cited earlier, the process involves interacting with a partner to draw out and enrich resourceful states and creative expressions from one another. Instead of the language of music, however, you will be working with somatic syntax, the language of the body.

The steps are as follows:

1. With a partner, enter a centered and resourceful state of harmony, balance and generativity. Feel the positive energy of this state in your body. Expand your awareness to include your partner and sense the qualities of the field or "third entity" between you.

2. Notice what resourceful feeling or inner state seems to emerge naturally through your connection with your partner. Both partners (A and B) allow a physical movement to emerge that expresses your current felt sense of your own resource state.

3. Person A demonstrates his or her movement to Person B. Person B observes, allowing his or her "mirror neurons" to take in A's somatic expression and the accompanying energy.

B then shows his or her movement to Person A. Person A observes, allowing his or her "mirror neurons" to take in B's somatic expression and the accompanying energy.

4. Keeping his or her attention on the field he or she is creating and holding with Person B, Person A mirrors some part of Person B's resource movement and allows it to spontaneously inspire a new movement that adds to or extends B's somatic syntax.

5. Keeping his or her attention on the generative field he or she is creating and holding with Person A, Person B mirrors some part of Person A's new movement and allows it to spontaneously inspire a new movement that further adds to or extends it.

6. Person A, in turn, mirrors some part of Person B's new movement and allows it to spontaneously inspire another new movement that adds to or extends it.

7. After repeating this process several times, Persons A and B then begin to move at the same time, feeling the energy or "field" that connects them and finding the movement that expresses the unique character of the generative field between them.

8. [Optional] If the exercise is being done with a group of people, each pair can find another pair and repeat this same process; this time using the movement they created together as a couple in step 7. Then repeat it again in foursomes, etc., until you have found a common movement for the whole group.

Hopefully this exercise will give you a clear experience of the generative capacity of interpersonal fields. When we do it in our seminars and workshops the feeling of energy and connection among participants invariably increases dramatically.

Generative Collaboration

The phenomenon of a generative field can easily be extended to a group or team to create a state of creative performance that we call "generative collaboration." Working together with others in groups and teams is an increasingly common and important part of modern business and contemporary life. High performing groups and teams demonstrate the characteristic of *collective intelligence*. The fruit of effective teaming and collective intelligence is what is known as *generative collaboration*. This relates to the ability of people in a team, group or organization to think and act in an aligned and coordinated fashion to create a whole that is truly greater than the sum of its parts.

Collaboration literally means to "work together." There are many ways in which people work together and collaborate. Some are more effective than others. In fact, group performance could be categorized into three types:

1. In an *under performing* group or team, the performance or output of the group as a whole is actually *less* than it would be if the individuals were working separately.

2. In an *average* group or team, the performance or output of the group as a whole is about *the same* as it would be if the individuals were working independently.

3. In a *high performing* group or team, the performance or output of the group as a whole is much *greater* than it would be if the individuals were working by themselves. This is a result of *generative* collaboration.

We can say that an under performing group or team is essentially lacking the capacity to collaborate effectively. Not only are the individuals failing to work together, their interactions are actually impeding their ability to accomplish even their individual tasks effectively (a type of "degenerative collaboration" or "negative sum" interaction).

An average group can be said to have reached a basic level of collaboration. *Basic collaboration* involves a group of individuals working together to reach a specific objective. Basic collaboration requires that people have a certain degree of rapport with one another, communicate effectively and each performs the task required of them in coordination with other partners or group members. The goal of basic collaboration is for people to perform according to what is expected of them in order to produce a result equaling the sum of the individual contributions. Basic collaboration requires that group members are able to support each other as guides, coaches and, at times, teachers.

Generative collaboration involves people working together to create or generate something new, surprising and beyond the capacities of any of the group members individually. Through generative collaboration, individuals are able to utilize their abilities to the fullest and discover and apply resources that they did not yet realize that they had. They draw new ideas and resources out of each other. Thus, the performance or output of the group as a whole is much *greater* than it would be if the individuals were working by themselves.

Consider the following example involving a large, well-known multinational telecommunications company. The company was struggling to stay competitive and knew it needed to develop a product for a very important area of its market. The situation was so critical that the company assembled a team of 1000 people to develop the new product. It turned out, to their surprise and embarrassment, however, that one of their competitors was able to create a better product in a shorter time that cost much less—completely outperforming them in the marketplace—and they did it with a team of just 20 people!

Of course, the burning question for the large telecommunications company was, How is it possible that 20 people can so completely outperform 1000?!" The difference that made the difference is what we are referring to as the capacity for "generative collaboration." In reflecting upon how the team of 1000 people had worked together, it became obvious that they operated in "silos," largely isolated from one another. The team members simply worked to carry out the task they had been assigned by the project leader who viewed people as essentially parts of a machine or computer software program.

The group of 20 people, on the other hand, were in constant communication and interaction, challenging, stimulating and supporting each other to be and give the best of themselves and think "outside of the box." Generative collaboration is a function of people stimulating and supporting one another to move forward in new ways and create something unprecedented. It requires that the group members share abilities such as vision, multiple perspectives and the capacity to create a strong relational field based on trust and mutual respect. This involves the ability of group members to support each other as mentors, sponsors and "awakeners."

As we have pointed out, generative collaboration of this type results in the development of a group mind or collective intelligence in which the knowledge and know-how of individuals combine to produce a larger collective intelligence and creativity that is impossible without the presence of the other partners or group members. This process is similar, as we have said, to what happens when two hydrogen atoms combine with an oxygen atom to create the third and new entity of water.

Yet, in order to create water, oxygen must remain fully oxygen and hydrogen must remain hydrogen. In the words of the philosopher Ken Wilber, the new relationship expressed by the creation of water "includes and transcends" the individual entities which make it up, producing something which contains both, but is at the same time completely new.

An important principle at work here is that individuality and people's personal interest and passion are necessary for generative collaboration. It has been said that "there is no 'I' in team," and perhaps this is true of basic collaboration, but not of generative collaboration (there is literally an "i" in both the words "generative" and "collaboration"). To produce generative collaboration, people must be firmly rooted in themselves, somatically centered in their unique energy and personal resources, and personally passionate about seeing their visions become realities. When people "sacrifice their own interests for the good of the team," the team itself loses the full passion, creativity and energy of its members.

As an illustration, in basic collaboration, a group of six or seven people would get together, arrive at a consensus regarding a particular project and work together to achieve that project; thus producing one project as a result of the sum of their interaction. Applying the principles of generative collaboration, the group of six or seven would produce at least six or seven projects, plus several possible synergies between some of those projects.

As American founding father Thomas Jefferson said, "If two people get together and exchange a dollar, they both walk away with one dollar. But if two people get together and exchange an idea, they both walk away with at least two ideas." In fact, they probably walk away with even more, resulting from the combinations and synergies between the ideas they have shared. Generative collaboration is a good example of this type of economics of ideas.

A good metaphor for understanding the dynamic of generative collaboration is the interplay of bubbles. In this analogy, a bubble would represent a particular vision or idea. In basic collaboration, all of the partners or team members work together to create one bubble. Generative collaboration would involve each of the group members creating his or her own bubble and then noticing how that bubble joined together with the bubbles formed by the other group members.

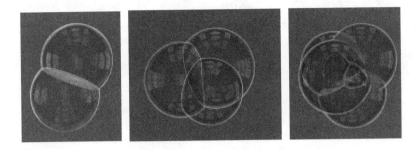

**Similar to Bubbles Joining Together to Make a Larger
Whole, Generative Collaboration Involves the Integration
of Complementary Visions and Ideas**

Many successful developments and accomplishments in
our modern world have not been the result of the vision of a
single person, but are rather the consequence of combining
multiple visions and ideas.

The creation of the Internet is a good example. The seeds
of the Internet began in 1969 as the Arpanet, a U.S. Depart-
ment of Defense research project to develop a network
architecture for military use, as well as a way to get the most
economical use out of scarce large-computer resources. Universities, research labs and defense contractors soon discovered the Internet's potential as a medium of communication
between "humans" and linked up in steadily increasing
numbers. In the 1980s and the early 1990s, more and more
pieces of the original government network were sold to major
telecommunications companies until the Internet backbone
had become completely commercialized. In 1994, mainstream
computer users discovered the Internet, attracted by the
hypertext and multimedia features of the World Wide Web.
Today, the globally-extended Internet has become the key
unifying communications technology for people across the
planet.

However, as one of the original developers of the Arpanet pointed out, "Nobody back then had the vision of *The Internet.* What has developed today was not envisioned by anyone at that time."

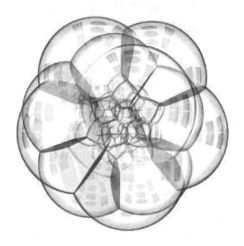

The Result of Generative Collaboration Is a Unique Collective Vision

Entrepreneur Don Pickens echoes this perspective when he claims, "Visionary leadership is not just having a vision; it is weaving that vision with other visions."

Creating a Generative "Container"

The following exercises explore how to create the conditions for generative collaboration. In doing so, it is important to distinguish between the *container* (the relationship or field between the members of the group or team) and the *content* (the visions, ideas or issues to be addressed by the group or team).

Essential to generative collaboration is the creation of a relational "container" built on trust, mutual respect and the recognition of each group member's unique resources and contributions. This is known as "sponsorship" in Third Generation NLP.

Transformational teacher Richard Moss claims that "the greatest gift we can give to ourselves or another person is the quality of our attention." *Sponsorship* involves seeing, sensing and affirming positive qualities and potential in others. One way to encourage mutual sponsorship among a group of people is to have them practice looking for and acknowledging what they perceive and appreciate about their fellow group members.

The following process, initially developed by NLP trainer Robert McDonald, encourages people to sponsor one another by having them focus on what they perceive and authentically like about one another.

Group members take turns being Person A, the person to be focused on by the rest of the group. It is important that each person volunteers only when they feel ready to be the focus.

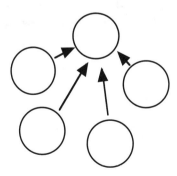

Each Group Member Volunteers to Be the Focus of the Group

Starting at Person A's left and going clockwise around the group, each member of the group is to comment on one thing that he or she <u>sees</u> (or observes) and likes about Person A, and something he or she <u>senses</u> and likes about person A. "Seeing" is based on our literal sensory-based observations of another person's behavior. "Sensing" is a somatic, intuitive impression about the deeper essence of the other person.

Each group member is to use the following format:

"I see_____. And I like it."

"I sense that you _____. And I like it."

Repeat this process until everyone in the group has the opportunity to be Person A and receive these comments from all of the other group members.

It is important to keep in mind that to be observed so intimately by others can create a feeling of vulnerability in many people. Thus, it is important to be sure that group members are centered in themselves with a healthy "second skin" as they begin this process.

When done properly, this practice can create a rapid and deep experience of trust and connection between group members, even if they have not had a great degree of previous familiarity with one another.

Enriching the Group Field

A key principle of generative collaboration is that the more each person is able to bring his or her own special energy and resources to the group, the more the group will benefit. Likewise, the more of that resource the group can bring out of the person, the more both the person and the group will benefit.

The following exercise is designed to help establish and support the positive feedback loop between the individual and the group as a whole.

As an individual:

1. Identify a state of resourcefulness that you would like to bring to the group as your contribution, and have the group bring out of you even more.

2. Put yourself fully into that state. Feel the energy of that state and let it become a physical expression in the form of a movement (somatic syntax). Also identify the word or label that you would use to characterize the state. The name may be literal (i.e., "confidence," "humor," "wisdom," "generosity," etc.) or it may be symbolic or metaphoric (i.e., "starlight," "deep roots," "radiant blue energy," etc.).

As a group:

3. One at a time, each member of the group expresses and demonstrates the state and energy he or she would like to bring to the group field. As he or she does so, the individual will make the invitation, "See my (resource state/energy)."

4. The rest of the group is to carefully observe the person who is making the invitation, then go to "second position" by taking on the somatic syntax of the individual. When group members have a sense of the individual's special

state and energy, they are to return to their own first position perspective and say, "I see your (resource state/ energy)."

5. The individual then says, "See me."

6. Each group member is to sense the deeper presence of that individual (his or her "superposition") and say, "I see you."

7. Repeat the process until each group member has made both of the invitations, ("See my (resource state/energy)", and "See me"), and has been acknowledged by the rest of the group.

8. After each group member has demonstrated and been sponsored with respect to his or her resource, all the group members begin making their unique resource movements at the same time. Then all the group members together begin to incrementally change and blend their individual movements into a single "group resource" movement. This will create a type of shared "fourth position."

Once the "container" of the group field has been established and enriched, it is possible to begin to tap the "collective intelligence" of the group members. One powerful method of doing this is through a process we call "intervision."

"Intervision"

The richness of a generative field comes from the fact that people have different maps of the world, different backgrounds, different resources and different perspectives. When these differences are brought together in a way where they complement one another, they form the basis for effective generative collaboration. The process of *intervision* is a way to promote synergies and constructive overlaps between the diverse visions, ideas and perspectives of people forming a group.

In "supervision" there is an implied hierarchical relationship between people; the supervisor provides the "right map" to the other person. In "inter-vision" it is assumed that people are peers and that there is no single correct map. There is also an important implication in the term "vision." One of the goals of the intervision process is to apply visual and symbolic thinking strategies in a group context.

A key benefit of intervision has to do with the influence of our way of representing and conceptualizing our ideas and visions. The way that somebody else represents a particular individual's vision or idea can automatically help to enrich the other group members' perception of it. For this reason, the intervision process is best done in a group of at least four people in order to get a wide enough range of diversity.

Another important aspect of intervision is for each group member to be inspired by the visions and ideas of the others. In terms of the relationship of the group members, the goal of the intervision process is for each person to share his or her vision with the others taking on the attitude, "This my future, can you contribute?" And asking, "What is your vision so I can contribute?"

In a typical intervision format, each member of the group takes turns presenting his or her vision, idea or situation to the other group members in as brief and concise a form as possible. As the other group members listen, they are to let the words and ideas of the presenter touch and inspire them.

When the presenter has finished, the other group members draw a symbolic or metaphoric picture of their understanding of what they have received and understood, and what has been inspired in them. It can be any kind of a diagram or a sketch. For example, somebody might draw a tree or landscape; another person may just draw a group of symbols like rectangles, circles and stars and connect them with lines and arrows. What is certain is that the other members will not represent the explorer's description in the same way. Everyone will have a different map of the territory.

When drawing, each person makes his or her own representational map individually without looking at the other drawings. Each group member, including the presenter, is to draw his or her own individual picture of what the presenter's vision, idea or situation has inspired in him or her.

Group members are then to consider what resources they can freely offer to the presenter. A "resource" in this case would be something that the group member can contribute to help the presenter to better manifest his or her vision or idea. Resources, for example, could be a book, article, website, contact information for a person or organization that could be helpful, etc. A resource could also be in the form of a suggestion, advice or guidance drawn from your own experience.

It is important the resource be something that the group member can offer to the presenter without asking for anything in return.

Once group members have completed their pictures and thought of the resources they can offer, each person explains what he or she has drawn and makes his or her contribution using the following format:

1. "This is my picture of your idea or vision . . ." (Briefly explain the drawing as is necessary.)

2. "What your vision inspires in me is . . ." (Share any feelings, ideas, new perspectives, etc., the presenter's words or ideas have triggered in you.)

3. "A resource I can freely offer that can help you to implement your idea or vision is . . ."

At the end, the presenter is to give feedback to the group in terms of how his or her own map of the vision or idea has been enriched.

If there is time, the group can also explore creating a drawing or picture that represents overlaps or common areas of their visions.

Accessing the "Larger Mind"

As we have stated earlier, generative fields can extend beyond interpersonal interactions. They can also arise out of our interaction with what Bateson called the "larger Mind" held within our natural environment, planetary ecology and collective unconscious. The following exercises provide procedures designed to help tap into the intelligence of the larger fields around us.

Active Dreaming

"Active dreaming" is a way to practice gathering information from the field through a state of "not knowing." Active dreaming is a process inspired by certain Native American groups. It involves setting an intention to be achieved during either sleep or daydreams. The intention may be to get an answer, solve a problem, make a decision, get more information, understand something better, etc. Intentions are typically stated in more general terms than a specific goal or outcome. For example, a person might say, "My intention is to dream about something that I can safely and ecologically let go of." The intention serves as a filter or guide that directs unconscious processes.

Answers may be either literal or symbolic. One person might awaken the following morning, and realize, "It is time for me to let go of the anger that I have been holding onto about a relationship that ended five years ago." Another person may go for a walk, and find herself fantasizing about leaves falling from a tree. The person may have no conscious understanding of what the leaves symbolize, but feel lighter and more at ease.

One way to explore the symbols is to take "second position" with them — imagining being the leaves or the tree, for instance. Returning to one's own perspective or an observer position, one can then explore the relationship between the symbols and one's original intention.

Active Dreaming Exercise

To explore active dreaming, try the following exercise:

1. Center yourself in your body and open your awareness to the larger field around you (see the exercises on *Feeling Your Field* and *Connecting From Your Center*). Place an "intention" in the back of your mind; for example, a decision you are making, a problem you are solving, something you want to be more creative about, an issue about which you want more information, etc.

2. Create a state of "not knowing" or "up-time" by:

   a. Shifting to peripheral (as opposed to foveal, or a more focused) vision.

   b. Focusing your hearing on external sounds (turning off any internal dialog).

   c. Entering a relaxed physiology (no excess emotional or physical tension).

3. Commit to this state for a ten-minute walk. While walking, notice what appears to "jump out at you," or where your attention is pulled; i.e., a tree, grass, the wind, the sound of a bird, etc.

4. As these phenomena present themselves (there may be more than one), take second position with each symbol or object. What are the characteristics of that object or symbol? What would be your attributes if you were a tree, for example? Time would probably change, the speed with which objects or people move would be different, you would be stationary on the bottom with movement on the top, etc.

5. Take all of the knowledge and characteristics that you have discovered by taking second position with the objects or symbols and create a third position or meta position with respect to your original intention. Explore what new news, data, or understandings you have gained with respect to your original intention.

Seeing the "Field"

Albert Einstein claimed, "Our thinking creates problems that
the same type of thinking will not solve." Most of our formal
education focuses on steps and methods oriented toward
applying the functions of our conscious cognitive mind. Many
of our most important life challenges and decisions, however,
are not resolvable through the rational and linear logic of our
conscious cognitive minds. This frequently leads us to a state
of "impasse" in which we have reached "our wits' end."

An *impasse* is defined by Webster's Dictionary as "a deadlock
or a situation in which no progress is possible." The following
exercise helps you to connect with the intelligence of the field
mind to move through areas where you have reached an
"impasse" in your life, career or personal relationships.

Accessing the field mind allows us to get outside of the box of
our own cognitive limitations. The world's most well-known
creative geniuses and greatest thinkers all acknowledge the
importance of methods and practices that connect them with a
level of intelligence that includes but transcends the limits of
their own ego and rational intellect.

Seeing the field involves focusing on the deeper structure of a
situation as opposed to the particular content or conditions
through which it is being expressed. As we pointed out earlier,
field dynamics are too complex and subtle for us to perceive
them literally. Because we cannot directly perceive the intricate
and invisible relationships that make up a field, our subjective
representations of them are generally symbolic and non-literal.

1. Identify an experience where you have reached an impasse
   and select a physical location to be associated with it.
   Associate into that experience as fully as possible and
   step into the physical location you have chosen.

2. Step away from the physical location to an observer
   position. Center yourself and open to the field. With your
   eyes closed, imagine you are looking through your center

at the field or energy dynamics influencing the system. Allow a symbolic image to emerge.

3. Reflect upon your desired state and select a different physical location with which to associate it. Staying centered, step into that location and get a feeling for the desired state. Pay attention to the field or energy dynamics of this state. Allow a symbolic image to emerge.

4. Step back into an observer position. Center yourself and open to the larger field that includes and transcends both the symbols of the impasse situation and desired state. With your eyes closed, imagine you are looking through your center. Set the intention to discover what resource would allow the impasse situation to transform into the desired state. Do not think logically or rationally about the situation. Allow a symbolic image to spontaneously emerge. As you hold this image in your awareness, bring it into your body as a felt sense of the resource so that it becomes somatically expressed as a movement or gesture.

5. Taking the symbolic image and somatic expression that emerged in the previous step, put yourself back into the impasse location and experience how it spontaneously transforms as you bring the resource from the larger field fully into this location.

6. Then, move to the desired state, taking the symbolic image and somatic expression of the resource with you. Notice what strengthens, deepens or enriches as you bring the resource from the larger field fully into this location.

7. Finally, stand in a location halfway between the impasse and the desired state, bringing the symbolic image and somatic expression of the resource. Again, notice what strengthens, enriches or transforms as you bring the resource from the larger field fully into this location.

Out beyond all ideas of right doing and wrong doing there is a field. I'll meet you there.

When the soul lies down in that grass, the world is too full to talk about.

Ideas, language and even the phrase "each other" doesn't make any sense.

   —Rumi

Chapter 4

Applying Next Generation NLP

Overview of Chapter 4

- **Applying Next Generation NLP**
  - Fitness for the Future
  - Survival Strategies
  - Promoting Generative Change
- **The Adaptive Cycle**
- **Choice**
- **Awareness: The Basis for Choice**
  - Unconscious Programming and Thought Viruses
- **Coaching with Third Generation NLP**
  - Large "C" and Small "c" Coaching
- **Coaching and the "Inner Game"**
  - The Example of the "Miracle On The Hudson"
  - The Importance of Practice

Overview of Chapter 4 (continued)

- **Practicing Being in the Zone: COACHing Versus CRASHing**
  - Finding Your Zone
  - Learning From Apple Juice
  - The Power of Presence
- **Creating a COACHing Container™**
- **Moving From CRASH to COACH**
- **Bringing Archetypal Energies into the COACHing Container™**
  - Exploring the Influence of Archetypal Energies
- **Holding Difficult Feelings**
- **Belief Barriers and Belief Bridges**
- **Working With Archetypes of Transition**

Applying Next Generation NLP

The applications of Third Generation NLP combine and utilize all three of our minds: *cognitive, somatic* and *field*. When we integrate these three sources of intelligence, we have a greater ability to accomplish many different types of activities and endeavors (results) with greater ease and elegance. At the same time, we are also often able to address more profound and complex issues and achieve outcomes that are not possible to reach through any one of the intelligences alone. Thus, Third Generation NLP processes have the characteristic of being both simple and also deeply transformational.

The practices and techniques of Third Generation NLP are founded upon the understanding that *at our core we are inherently generative*, that *the seed of a solution is held within any problem*, and that *we can learn how to create the space for solutions to unfold in an organic way by holding the source of a problem within a larger field of resources*.

From the perspective of Third Generation NLP, times of crisis, growth and transformation in our lives are usually accompanied by the need for evolution and "awakening." These are products of *generative change*. To "generate" means to *create something new*. Thus, generative processes are those that promote expansion and growth.

Truly creating something new involves shifts in "deep structure" as well as "surface structure." *Deep structures—* such as the laws of physics, the DNA of living creatures, the machine code or operating systems of computers, the core values and mission of an organization, etc.—are fundamental forms that become expressed through a variety of concrete surface structures. Biologically, for example, the evolutionary change of a species occurs as it interacts with and adapts to changes in its environment. When these adaptations and changes alter the deep structure (DNA) of the species, this results in new developments and expressions in the form of the species; i.e., metamorphosis. The purpose of these generative changes is to help the species become more fit for the future.

Fitness for the Future

A core criterion for both the survival and success of any system is its *fitness for the future*—that is, the degree to which the system is able to adapt to change and move effectively toward a sustainable and healthy future state. Fitness for the future involves the abilities of an individual, group or organization to perceive weak signals and adjust behavior in order to deal with constraints, successfully avoid or address dangers, and take advantage of opportunities that arise, in many cases unexpectedly or spontaneously—as Arthur C. Clarke so eloquently pointed out, "The Future just isn't what it used to be."

There is an old proverb that "an ounce of prevention is worth a pound of cure." When resources are developed and in place ahead of time, a person, group or organization is able to rise to the challenge instead of scrambling to deal with unnecessary problems. Fitness for the future involves being prepared for the challenges and opportunities of the future that we have not yet even imagined or anticipated.

The capacity for generative change is thus a key aspect of our fitness for the future. While generative processes may be used to address specific problems or reach specific outcomes in the present, they do not need to be applied or developed in relation to a particular current problem or objective. Generative processes are based on the presupposition that the resources needed to produce solutions already exist in some form within the field of any system. Those resources may be mobilized through strategies and tools that help to unveil, release and strengthen latent capabilities. In this sense, "generative" processes are about making more from what already exists.

Generative techniques for change help support people to solve problems and achieve goals in a more systemic and organic way. When new resources are discovered, released and developed, problems that are ready to be solved by those resources naturally emerge and resolve without effort.

Generative change, then, is essentially about the discovery, creation, enrichment, strengthening and elaboration of resources. It is about finding the "deep structure" of a resource and facilitating the expression of that resource into many other contexts where it has yet to be applied. Generative change involves identifying dormant resources and activating them, making them more available and "holographic." It focuses on developing higher-level processes that can function in an evolutionary way towards new possibilities.

Survival Strategies

The opposite of evolution and generative change is regression into survival strategies. As their name implies, survival strategies are activated by a perceived threat to our physical or psychological survival. They are a part of our deepest programming that we share with all other animals. All creatures must develop some form of survival strategies.

The primary survival strategies are *fight* (attack), *flight* (escape), *freeze* (paralysis) or *surrender* (submit). Survival strategies are deep and often unconscious internal patterns that are usually established at a very early age. They form a part of our core programming and function as a type of fundamental meta program which shapes our approach to life and relationships.

These fundamental strategies can take many forms in our daily life, such as rebelling, withdrawing or acquiescing, feeling the need to shrink, trying to become small and invisible, going blank, dissociating from feelings, becoming passive, seducing others, believing in the necessity to hold one's ground at all costs, etc. "Survival" in many cases, extends beyond physical survival to include the preservation or protection of our sense of identity and personal integrity, key beliefs and values, significant roles and relationships to which we have devoted ourselves, and so on.

As with all behaviors, it is most effective to have a range of possibilities with respect to our survival strategies and apply them flexibly according to the context. The challenge with most survival strategies is that they are driven by fear which, when excessive, can cause us to become disconnected, shut down and contracted. This leads us to act inappropriately, and frequently produces a paradoxical result in which we actually exacerbate the situation and end up putting ourselves even more at risk in some way.

Most survival strategies are designed to preserve what exists and avoid taking risks. Thus, they are not generative; i.e., they do not promote transformation, growth or change. When a survival strategy is applied excessively due to fear, it begins to limit us and hold us in a state of inertia. There is a significant difference between surviving and thriving.

Survival strategies naturally emerge when we are facing change or unknown territory, especially if there is a possibility of the breakdown or loss of the current structure. In this way, survival strategies can be either a complement or an interference to evolution and generative change. Growth and evolution clearly involve surviving (i.e., continuing to exist), but without becoming lost in the survival strategy, which will hold us back. This is only possible when there is an expansion of consciousness and awareness. Thus, it is important to periodically review, enrich and update our survival strategies, expanding our options to include new possibilities.

Acknowledging, addressing and updating survival strategies is a key skill of generative change. Because they are so deep and vital to our existence, changing survival strategies is not simply a matter of making superficial adjustments. Updating survival strategies involves reviewing key life situations and bringing new resources into these experiences at several levels.

Promoting Generative Change

To transcend old survival strategies and achieve personal evolution and awakening, our mental maps of who we are and what is possible in the world must become broader, and we must perceive old limitations in a completely new way. This requires that we break through our old mind-set and "get outside of the box," learning at the level of what anthropologist and systems theorist Gregory Bateson called *Learning IV*—the creation of something "completely new" that has not existed before within an individual or species. Such a generative consciousness must both *include* and *expand* our previous knowledge and awareness.

True generativity, then, frequently requires a breakdown of current structure that is in place and has become overly rigid. This breakdown causes a regression to a more primordial and unintegrated state that brings us into more direct contact with both our "shadows" (behaviors and characteristics that we don't like and seek to avoid) but also new resources that have not previously been recognized or utilized. If we are able to stay centered in ourselves and connected to a larger field of awareness that holds all of these expressions, we can achieve a generative state of expansion, reorganization and greater integration. This allows us to attain a vastly improved level of performance.

The Adaptive Cycle

At the foundation of generative change and all levels of learning is the capacity for adaptation. Ecologist and environmental scientist C.S. Holling (1979, 1986) has developed a general model of systemic change that proposes an *adaptive cycle* composed of four phases: 1) growth, 2) conservation, 3) collapse, and 4) re-organization.

Derived from the comparative study of the dynamics of ecosystems, the model places attention upon the processes of destruction and reorganization as well as growth and conservation, providing a comprehensive view of the system dynamics behind adaptation, resilience and evolution.

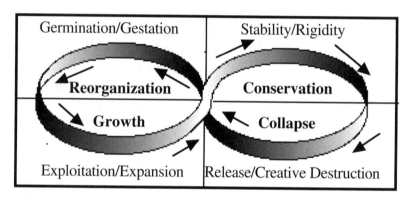

Holling's Adaptive Cycle Maps the Phases of Change in an Ecosystem

The traditional view of ecosystem development has been seen as the result of two primary functions: 1) growth and expansion, in which rapid escalation and exploitation of resources is emphasized; and 2) conservation and balance, in which accumulation, storage and thrifty use of resources is stressed.

In the field of ecology, species that succeed in the growth phase are known as "R-strategists." *R-strategists* are characterized by extensive dispersal ability and rapid growth in contexts where *scramble competition* succeeds (i.e., the first to get the prize wins).

Those who succeed in the conservation phase are called "K-strategists." *K-strategists* tend to conserve resources, have slower growth rates and flourish in an environment favoring *contest competition* (i.e., whoever outlasts the other wins).*

According to Holling, two additional functions are also key to the adaptive cycle. The first, *collapse*, or what the economist Joseph Schumpeter termed *creative destruction*, occurs when tightly contained accumulations of resources are suddenly "released" (in an ecosystem, for example, this may be the result of influences such as forest fires, drought, pests or periods of intense consuming).

Secondly, a *reorganization* phase typically follows this period of collapse or release. In such times, a system's boundaries and internal connections are tenuous and unstable. Such a loosely contained system can easily lose or gain resources and participants. During this period a system can easily be reorganized by small inputs (the so-called "butterfly effect") and the transient appearance or expansion of opportunistic actors or organisms is common. During this period, the future organization of the system can be shaped by chance events, and a system can become transformed into a new type of structure.

It is at this phase when new or exotic organisms or actors can enter and even eventually become dominant within an ecosystem. These new actors or elements can arise from growth of previously *suppressed* potentials within the system, from those which have been *germinating* and accumulating in unexploited areas, or those that have *migrated* from neighboring systems. It is at this stage when breakthrough innovation is most likely.

As the growth phase begins again, competitive processes (both scramble competition and contest competition) lead to a few species becoming dominant. The new system that emerges

---

* In ecosystem theory, R represents the instantaneous rate of growth of a population. K stands for the "carrying capacity" or maximum sustainable population size.

from these conditions may replicate aspects of the previous organization or it may be something entirely new. The lack of internal integration and control makes it difficult to predict exactly what type of form the new organization will take.

The growth phase also produces a new accumulation of resources. This, in turn, increases the potential for other kinds of ecosystems and new species of participants to emerge during the next collapse and reorganization cycle.

The generative stages of the adaptive cycle are the latter two stages, and they are frequently the most difficult stages to manage. The general steps of the process of moving through (a) *rigidity and stagnancy* to (b) *breakdown and regression* to (c) *discovering and adding new resources* to (d) *reorganization into a greater wholeness* involves the basic stages of:

1) *deconstructing*

2) *enriching* and then

3) *reconstructing*

To accomplish this on a personal level, Third Generation NLP practices and processes apply the following basic structure:

1. Beginning in a resourceful state in which you are grounded and centered in your body and in the present.

2. Identifying and revivifying the problematic experience or pattern.

3. Bringing new and increased awareness to the structure of the current "neurolinguistic" program associated with the problematic experience or pattern.

4. Getting outside of the influence of the program into a state in which you are centered and grounded in a state of awareness that includes but is larger than the problematic experience or pattern (as opposed to simply being in the polarity or antithesis of the problem state). As Einstein

said, "You cannot solve a problem with the same type of thinking that is creating the problem."

5. Viewing the program as part of a larger context or system and identifying its positive purpose within that context or system.

6. Connecting to a field of possibilities and resources that is larger than (beneath and beyond) the field associated with the problematic experience or pattern. This is achieved by accessing and aligning all three intelligences (cognitive, somatic, field) to become the best version of yourself possible at that moment.

7. Holding the current experience or pattern, and the program that produces and reinforces it, within the framework of the new resources and greater awareness.

8. Allowing new choices to emerge that include and transcend the current program or pattern, integrating it as a functional part of a larger whole.

This chapter will explore some applications through which Third Generation NLP can be used to facilitate generative change including:

- Establishing practices for remaining grounded and present in the face of uncertainty, vulnerability and difficult feelings.

- Developing the ability to accept and hold faults, in ourselves and others, without judgment.

- Learning to recognize and create a space for potential without expectation.

- Deepening and aligning levels of connection with ourselves and others.

- Expanding awareness of "fourth position" and the "field."

Choice

The notion of "choice" is fundamental to all NLP processes (of every generation) and is the foundation of generative change. Webster's Dictionary defines choice as the ability to "select between a number of alternatives, with free will and by exercise of judgment." The ability to choose is an integral component of freedom, intelligence and success. According to NLP, the ability to choose is at the core of human evolution—that is, the process of evolution is the process of having progressively more choice in one's life.

As NLP co-founders Richard Bandler and John Grinder pointed out in *The Structure of Magic Volume I* (1975), the difference between people who respond effectively as opposed to those who respond poorly in the world around them is largely a function of the choices they perceive available to them in their internal map of the world.

> [P]eople who respond creatively and cope effectively . . . are people who have a rich representation or model of their situation, in which they perceive a wide range of options in choosing their action. The other people experience themselves as having few options, none of which are attractive to them . . . . What we have found is not that the world is too limited or that there are no choices, but that these people block themselves from seeing those options and possibilities that are open to them since they are not available in their models of the world.

Thus, it is important to keep in mind that there is a subtle but significant difference between "alternatives" and "choices." *Alternatives* are external to a person. *Choices* are alternatives that have become a part of the person's map—those that a person can access through "free will" and "judgment." An individual could be given many options or alternatives but really have no choice. Choice and judgment involve having the capability and the contextual cues to be able to internally select and pursue the most appropriate option.

Choice is also intimately tied up with the notion of "ecology." One of the fundamental presuppositions of NLP is that people will make the best choice that they perceive available to them. That is, any behavior, regardless of how "evil," "crazy" or "bizarre" it seems, is or was the best choice available to the person, given his or her capabilities and model of the world at the time. NLP views all behaviors as potentially useful or necessary in some context. Even anger, frustration, jealousy, confusion, etc., can be appropriate and ecological choices under some circumstances.

Thus, it is important in NLP to add choices, not take them away. A basic assumption of NLP is that if someone truly has a better choice, he or she will automatically take it. The key is to find a choice that is genuinely "better" given the person's capabilities and situation.

In NLP, it is also considered important that the person possess more than one other alternative besides the undesired or problematic response. There is a saying in NLP that, "One choice is no choice at all. Two choices is a dilemma. It is not until a person has three possibilities that he or she is really able to legitimately choose." One of the missions of NLP is to constantly create and provide people with the capacity to generate more and more choices.

Choice may also be qualitative as opposed to quantitative. That is, rather than having "more" or "other" choices, one can have a choice about the quality with which one approaches or experiences a situation or event. Approaching a situation with "grace," "congruence" or a certain "focus of attention," for example, would be "qualitative" choices, which would influence how that situation was perceived and given meaning. Quantitative choices are typically at the levels of capabilities and behaviors, whereas qualitative choices are at the levels of beliefs, values and identity.

Awareness: the Basis for Choice

Choice and generative change become possible through the expansion of awareness. Awareness is naturally transformative. As transformational teacher Richard Moss points out, *whatever you can be aware of, there is something within you, beyond the object of awareness, that is being aware.* In this way, by becoming aware, you automatically become more than the object of awareness. If I am aware of one of my beliefs, for example, there is an "I" who is aware of the belief that is not the belief. If I am not aware, then the belief is running the show, like a type of autopilot. I have no real choice about it.

As an example, in the early days of NLP, author Robert Dilts was talking with a man who was struggling with a particular decision. Robert noticed that the man gave many of the behavioral cues associated with an internal voice that seemed to be creating a significant amount of interference. So Robert asked the man, "Are you talking to yourself about this decision?" The man repeated under his breath, "Am I talking to myself ?" and after a moment responded, "No, I don't do that. I don't talk to myself." A bit surprised, Robert continued, "Are you sure?" Again, the man repeated in a low voice, "Am I sure?" Then responded, "Yes. Quite sure." Robert went on, "I mean, if I ask you a question, do you repeat it to yourself?" "Do I repeat the question you ask me to myself?" the man said to himself. "No. I don't do that."

Obviously, the man was completely unaware of this aspect of his inner process. As a result he had no choice about it. When Robert finally succeeded in getting the man to become aware of his pattern of self-talk, the man was quite surprised. "Oh," he said, "That's an internal voice? I thought that was just reality."

This same dynamic happens with much of our "neurolinguistic programming." We are often not aware of the processes by which our inner experience and maps of the world are created, and this greatly limits our degree of choice with respect to them. As a result, we spend a good deal of time on "autopilot." This is not necessarily a problem, but it can become one if these programs no longer serve us and can interfere with our fitness for the future.

Unconscious Programming and Thought Viruses

The same thing can happen with "programming" in a group. Consider the following experiment. The process begins with a cage containing five monkeys and a specially rigged water system. In the cage, experimenters hang a banana on a string and put a set of stairs under it. Before long, a monkey will go to the stairs and start to climb towards the banana. As soon as he or she touches the stairs, however, the water system is activated and sprays *all* of the monkeys with cold water. After a while, another monkey makes an attempt with the same result—all the monkeys are again sprayed with cold water. Pretty soon, the monkeys make the connection and when any monkey begins to head for the stairs, the other monkeys will prevent it, using physical force if necessary. Eventually, the monkeys learn to completely avoid the stairs.

The experimenters then deactivate the cold-water spray mechanism. The monkeys never discover this, however, because they continue to avoid the stairs. (The territory has changed, but their map of it has not!)

Things become even more interesting when one monkey is removed from the cage and replaced with a new one. The new monkey sees the banana and wants to climb the stairs. To his surprise, as he approaches the stairs, all of the other monkeys rush up and restrain him. The more he struggles the more forceful the others become. After several attempts, he learns that if he tries to climb the stairs, he will be assaulted.

Later, another of the original five monkeys is removed and replaced with a new one. The newcomer goes to the stairs and is restrained by the group as well. The previous newcomer apparently joins the others with enthusiasm ("If I can't go on the stairs and get the banana, neither can you!"). The second replacement monkey also eventually learns that the stairs and banana are "taboo." After this, a third original monkey is replaced with a new one. When the new one moves to the stairs, he or she is restrained by all of the others as well. Two of the four monkeys that prevent him have no idea why they are not permitted to climb the stairs (they have never been sprayed with cold water). They are mirroring how they have been treated.

Ultimately, the fourth and fifth original monkeys are replaced. All the monkeys that had been sprayed with cold water are now gone and the cold water has been turned off for quite a while. Nevertheless, no monkey in the new group ever approaches the stairs. Why not? Because "that's the way it has always been."

This is an example of how what we call "thought viruses" are created. A *thought virus* is a limiting belief that has become dissociated from the experiences from which it was originally formed. For the first group of monkeys, the belief "you shouldn't go on the stairs to get the banana" was based on the uncomfortable personal experience that they all got sprayed when any one of them did it. The second group never had that experience. They learned "you should not go on the stairs to get the banana" from their social context.

In other experiments (Stephenson, G. R.; *Cultural acquisition of a specific learned response among rhesus monkeys,* 1967) researchers trained adult male and female rhesus monkeys to avoid handling an object using uncomfortable consequences as in the experiment above. They then placed individual naive monkeys in a cage with a conditioned individual of the same age and sex and the particular object the first one had been programmed to avoid. In one case, a previously conditioned male actually pulled his naive partner away from the object during their period of interaction. Even more interestingly, in other cases, previously conditioned monkeys exhibited what were described as "threat facial expressions while in a fear posture" when a naive animal approached the object, prompting their companion to avoid the object. Later, when alone in the cage with the object, naive males that had been paired with conditioned males almost completely avoided it. Naive monkeys that had not interacted with the conditioned monkeys, however, showed no difference in their interest in that object than any other object in the cage.

Such experiments show that these types of "programs" can be transmitted either directly through behavior (i.e., the one monkey pulling his partner away from the object) or through mirror neurons (as in the case of the monkeys showing threatening expressions and fearful postures when their partners approached the object). The result is that the belief becomes held and transmitted through the "field" of the monkey's interactions without any physical contact. It is interesting to speculate how much of our own programming is picked up through mirror neurons, especially at an early age.

Such beliefs or "thought viruses" can be difficult to change or correct for several reasons. One is that, because they are associated with avoidance, even when the conditions change (such as the water being shut off in the first experiment), the original group is not likely to discover it, as they never risk testing it. For the second group, there is another factor. Because the belief was not derived from their own direct experience of the uncomfortable consequences of their actions, the belief will not become automatically updated if the external conditions change. If the original group of monkeys in the first experiment discovers that the water has been turned off, they will cautiously approach the stairs again. For the second group, however, the water was never the reason to avoid it in the first place. It was just something that you "shouldn't do."

Bringing new awareness and new choices into such a situation is a major (and common) challenge, and one we will show several ways to address in this chapter.

Coaching with Next Generation NLP

The framework in which Next Generation NLP is primarily applied is that of coaching, a field that has emerged and grown tremendously since the origin of NLP in the 1970s. Many of the original formats and techniques of NLP were developed within the framework of psychotherapy. Coaching addresses a much broader range of everyday issues than psychotherapy, and can be applied to groups and even organizations as well as individuals.

In general, *coaching* is the process of helping people and teams to perform at the peak of their abilities. It involves drawing out people's strengths, helping them to bypass personal barriers and limits in order to achieve their personal best, and facilitating them to function more effectively as members of a team. Thus, effective coaching requires an emphasis on both task and relationship.

Coaching emphasizes generative change, concentrating on defining and achieving specific goals. Coaching methodologies are outcome-oriented rather than problem-oriented. They tend to be highly solution-focused, promoting the development of new strategies for thinking and acting as opposed to trying to resolve problems and past conflicts. Problem solving, or remedial change, is more associated with counseling and therapy.

Interestingly, the term "coach" comes from the name of a small Hungarian village, *Kocs*, where superior wagons, carts and carriages were built. Kocs lay on the main road along the Danube between Vienna and Budapest. These two great cities needed well-built, fast vehicles that would carry more than two people over the bumpy roads of the day in as much comfort as possible. One of the best of these multi-horse carts—a light, reasonably comfortable four-wheeled passenger wagon with a strap suspension—was called in Hungarian *kocsi szekér*, literally "a wagon from Kocs." It was so compact, elegant and sturdy that the design spread throughout Europe in the 15th and 16th centuries. The Viennese called the vehicle a *Kutsche* after the Hungarian town. In Paris, the French adapted the Austrian word to *coche*. In Rome it became *cocchio*. Eventually, the vehicle showed up in England and was called a *coach*.

Thus, a *coach* originally meant "a wagon or carriage" and still carries this meaning today—such as when a person travels "coach" on a railway or airline. A "coach" is literally *a vehicle that carries a person or group of people from some starting location to a desired location.*

A Coach was Originally a Vehicle that Transported People From Some Present State to a Desired State

The notion of coaching in the educational sense derived from the concept that the tutor "conveys" or "transports" the student through his or her examinations. An educational coach is defined as "a private tutor," "one who instructs or trains a performer or a team of performers," or "one who instructs players in the fundamentals of a competitive sport and directs team strategy." The process of being a coach is defined as "to train intensively (as by instruction and demonstration)."

In sports, the coach accompanies and observes the athletes while they practice, providing encouragement and feedback for them to give their best performance. A rowing coach, for instance, rides in a boat that moves along next to the rowers. The coach observes the rowers and directs their attention to various aspects of their performance both individually and as a team, saying things like, "Watch the knees of the person in front of you"; "Open your chest and keep your shoulders strong and soft."

**A Sports Coach Observes Athletes Providing
Encouragement and Feedback**

Coaching, then, is about supplying a vehicle by which a person or a group can move from their *present state* to some *desired state* along, hopefully, the most efficient and effective *path*. To accomplish this journey, key *resources* must be identified and put into place and potential *interferences* must also be identified and appropriately dealt with. We can summarize the basic coaching process in the following diagram.

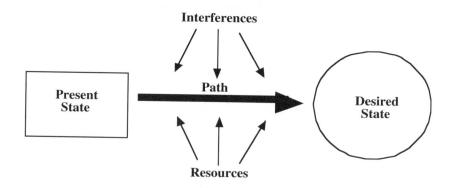

Diagram of the General Coaching Process

The skills and tools of all generations of NLP are uniquely suited for promoting effective coaching. NLP's focus on well-formed outcomes, its foundation in modeling exceptional performers, and its ability to produce step-by-step processes to promote excellence, make it an important and powerful resource for coaches of all types.

Common NLP skills, tools and techniques that support effective coaching include: establishing goals and well-formed outcomes, managing internal states, taking different perceptual positions, identifying moments of excellence, mapping across resources, and providing high quality feedback.

Large "C" and Small "c" Coaching

Historically, coaching has typically been focused toward achieving improvement with respect to a specific behavioral performance. An effective coach of this type (such as a "voice coach," an "acting coach," a "pitching coach") observes a person's behavior and gives him or her tips and guidance about how to improve in specific contexts and situations. This involves promoting the development of that person's behavioral competence through careful observation and feedback.

Coaching that promotes generative change, however, needs to provide support on a number of different levels: behaviors, capabilities, beliefs, values and even identity. We refer to this type of coaching as capital "C" Coaching (see *From Coach to Awakener,* R. Dilts, 2003).

Small "c" coaching is more focused at a behavioral level, referring to the process of helping another person to achieve or improve a particular behavioral performance. Small "c" coaching methods derive primarily from a sports training model, promoting conscious awareness of resources and abilities, and the development of conscious competence.

Large "C" Coaching or generative coaching, involves helping people effectively achieve outcomes on a range of levels.

It emphasizes generative change, concentrating on strengthening identity and values, and bringing dreams and goals into reality. This encompasses the skills of small "c" coaching, but also includes much more.

Large "C" Coaching is essentially about being an "awakener." *Awakening* others involves supporting them to develop awareness and grow at the level of vision, mission and spirit. An *awakener* supports another person to be the best version of himself or herself by providing contexts and experiences which bring out the best of that person's understanding and awareness of purpose, self, and his or her role within the larger systems of which he or she is a part.

It is obvious that it is not possible to awaken others if you yourself are still asleep. So the first task of the awakener is to wake up and stay awake. An awakener "awakens" others through his or her own integrity and congruence. An awakener puts other people in touch with their own missions and visions by being in full contact with his or her own vision and mission. In other words, we become awakeners by being the best version of ourselves.

Coaching and the "Inner Game"

The growth of coaching over the past 20 years has brought new awareness to what it takes to be successful in today's challenging and changing world. One of the major learnings is that helping people to develop their "Inner Game" is essential to optimal performance.

Mastering the *Outer Game* of any activity has to do with developing the capabilities necessary to effectively manage the behavioral and environmental aspects of that activity. In sports, this involves the physical aspects related to playing the game and using the equipment (tennis racket, skis, ball, bat, mitt, etc.). In a business environment, this has to do with applying the tools and implementing the procedures necessary to accomplish mission critical tasks and compete effectively in the marketplace.

The *Inner Game* has to do with your inner mental and emotional approach to what you are doing. This includes your attitude, your belief in yourself and your team, your ability to concentrate effectively, to deal with mistakes and pressure, and so on. The concept of the inner game was developed by Timothy Gallwey (1974, 2000) as a way of helping people to achieve excellence in various sports (e.g., tennis, golf, skiing, etc.), music and also business and management training.

According to Gallwey:

> *In every human endeavor there are two arenas of engagement: the outer and the inner. The outer game is played on an external arena to overcome external obstacles to reach an external goal. The inner game takes place within the mind of the player and is played against such obstacles as fear, self-doubt, lapses in focus, and limiting concepts or assumptions. The inner game is played to overcome the self-imposed obstacles that prevent an individual or team from accessing their full potential.*

A former captain of the Harvard University Tennis Team, Gallwey in the 1970s began to practice meditation techniques. He discovered that this enhanced his powers of awareness and concentration in a manner that spontaneously improved his tennis game. Gallwey's practice of the inner game is based upon certain principles in which an individual uses non-judgmental self-observation. By increasing awareness in this way, the person's body will adjust and correct automatically to achieve best performance.

When your outer game and inner game are working together, actions flow with a type of effortless excellence that is called "playing in the zone." Some indicators that you are focused and in *the zone* are:

- A feeling of confidence and the absence of anxiety and self-doubt

- No fear of failure or self-consciousness about achieving your goals

- A focus on performing beautifully and excellently

- A sense of "humble authority" – self-confidence without arrogance

- A state of relaxed readiness in the body and focused spaciousness in the mind

- Performance comes without effort and without having to think about it

The opposite of this state – anxiety, lack of confidence, low energy, fear, stress, mental paralysis – are responsible for many difficulties and challenges in any area of performance. To put it another way, *limitations in people limit their performance.*

Success in any area of performance involves using your mind together with your body. Preparing yourself mentally and emotionally to perform well is the essence of your inner game. From the perspective of Third Generation NLP, mastering the inner game is about mobilizing and aligning the intelligence from all three of our minds.

The Example of the "Miracle On The Hudson"

A good example of the importance of mastering of the inner game is the case of the captain and crew of the so-called "miracle on the Hudson" on January 15, 2009. US Airways flight 1549 was forced to land on the Hudson river in New York City after running into a flock of geese and losing all the power in both engines. Due to the capability of the captain and crew to stay calm and focused, all 155 occupants made it safely off of the airliner and were rescued by nearby watercraft.

Maintaining his composure and remaining within his zone of excellence in an unexpected and extremely challenging situation, Captain Chesley Sullenberger was able to glide the Airbus 320 to a successful emergency water landing. With no power at all in either engine, there were only three minutes between the time the birds hit the engines and the plane touched down on the water. Having twice walked the length of the cabin to confirm that no one remained inside after the plane had been evacuated, the captain was the last person to leave the aircraft.

Widely praised for his poise and calm demeanor during the crisis, the situation was clearly not an easy one for Sullenberger. In fact, it required that he play the inner game of his life. Had he not stayed in his inner zone of excellence and instead panicked or become lost in one of the survival strategies of fight, flight or freeze, it is clear that many lives could have been lost. It was the captain's ability to manage his inner state that was perhaps the major "difference that made the difference" in this incredible story.

Asked how he felt inside as his Airbus glided towards the water, the captain reported, "Calm on the outside, turmoil inside." Sullenberger claimed that he had never felt more nervous but managed to maintain his composure. The captain described his emotional state the moments before the landing as "the worst sickening, pit-of-your-stomach, falling-through-the-floor feeling" that he had ever experienced. In spite of that, Sullenberger was able to stay within his zone of excellence and pull off what has been called the most successful emergency landing in aviation history.

Sullenberger's description of calm in the presence of inner turmoil is what we refer to as the capacity for "holding" difficult feelings. When we are able to *hold* an intense internal response, we are able to be with it and allow it to be there from an inner state that is bigger and beyond the response. Instead of being lost in it, fighting against it or trying to control it, the response is allowed its place, and can even be utilized itself as a resource.

It seems evident that to pull off a "miracle" like that of flight 1549 requires the activation and alignment of the intelligence of all three minds: cognitive, somatic and field. Cognitive know-how and intelligence are necessary to skill-fully maneuver the aircraft, although the know-how is not enough if it is not "in the muscle." There are also very clearly the somatic factors related to the inner game of staying centered, calm, open and in the zone. Field factors have to do with being able to stimulate and organize the collective intelligence and competence of the team to form a collective zone of trust and excellence.

As an interesting demonstration of leadership, teamwork and perhaps the influence of mirror neurons, Sullenberger claimed that one of the reasons he was able to stay so calm was because his crew remained so cool and composed. The crew, however, claimed they were able to remain calm be-cause the captain was so confident and in control. Similarly, the passengers reported that the demeanor of the pilot and crew prompted them to remain calm. At the same time the crew acknowledged the passengers' calmness and coopera-tion as an influence on their own ability to remain composed.

A similar phenomenon has been reported by survivors of the September 11, 2001 catastrophe. By remaining calm and focused, and supporting each other to do so, many occupants of the Twin Towers were able to avoid panic, make it down many floors and out of the buildings to safety, significantly reducing the loss of life that could have been even greater in that disastrous event. This mutual support makes a type of field in which people are mutually reinforcing each other's capacity to stay within their zone of excellence. This is the positive side of the effect demonstrated in the monkey experiments cited earlier in which learned fear in a core group of monkeys created a thought virus of avoidance.

The Importance of Practice

The capacity to stay in one's zone and bring all three minds together, of course, requires much preparation and practice. As captain Sullenberger put it, "One way of looking at this might be that for 42 years, I've been making small, regular deposits in this bank of experience, through education and training. And on January 15 the balance was sufficient so that I could make a very large withdrawal."

The great Greek philosopher Aristotle maintained, "We are what we repeatedly do. Excellence then is not an act, but a habit." In his book *Outliers: The Story of Success* (2008), Malcolm Gladwell repeatedly mentions the "10,000-Hour Rule." Citing studies published by Anders Ericsson (2006), a psychologist who studies expertise and expert performance, Gladwell claims that the key to success in any field is, to a large extent, a matter of practicing for a total of around 10,000 hours.

"Outlier" is a scientific term to describe things or phenomena that lie outside normal experience. In his book Gladwell focuses on people who are *outliers*—exceptional men and women who have accomplished something quite outside of the ordinary. Gladwell claims that achieving such greatness requires an enormous investment of time in the form of practice. Drawing from examples as diverse as The Beatles, Bill Gates and Robert Oppenheimer, Gladwell shows how each met the "10,000-Hour Rule" as a prelude to their success.

The Beatles, for instance, performed live in Hamburg, Germany over 1,200 times from 1960 to 1964, amassing more than 10,000 hours of playing time, therefore meeting the 10,000-Hour Rule. Gladwell asserts that all of the time The Beatles spent performing shaped their talent, "so by the time they returned to England from Hamburg, Germany, 'they sounded like no one else. It was the making of them.'"

Bill Gates met the 10,000-Hour Rule when he gained access to a high school computer in 1968 at the age of 13, and spent 10,000 hours programming on it. In an interview for the book, Gates maintains that unique access to a computer at a time when they were not commonplace helped him succeed.

While 10,000 hours seems like a lot of time (it would be the equivalent of 20 hours of work a week for 10 years), it is a worthwhile investment when we truly seek evolution and transformation. As our colleague and friend Lynne Conwell points out, "You are what you practice."

It is also important to point out that 10,000 hours of practice is not required in order to achieve a basic, or even good, level of performance. We may be able to reach an acceptable threshold in much less time. It is good to keep in mind that practice of this type is not simply mindless, rote repetition. Rather than some tedious and boring activity, it is more like the iterative process through which a fractal is formed.

Furthermore, there is a growing body of research that shows that various types of "mental rehearsal" can accelerate our acquisition of skills. Other methodologies, such as self-hypnosis may also be able to create the possibility of mental rehearsal even while we are sleeping (thus potentially reducing the overall time it may take to reach 10,000 hours).

The point remains, however, that the foundation for excellence and high performance in any area begins with practice. Physical practice is what builds the skills of your outer game and puts them into "muscle memory" so you don't have to think about them during the game. Similarly, there are mental and somatic exercises that can help you to improve your inner game.

Practicing Being in the Zone:
COACHing Versus CRASHing

It is said that things are always changing, but not always progressing. During a time of transition and change, many challenges will present themselves such as meeting the fear of the unknown and the unfamiliar, dealing with loss, and a general sense of vulnerability. These can plunge us into unhelpful survival strategies: attack, escape or rigidity (fight, flight, freeze). This might result in temporary regression, inertia, ambivalence, the difficulty to let go, confusion and conflict.

When this happens we are likely to collapse into a stuck state that can be summarized by the letters in the word **CRASH**:

Contraction

Reaction

Analysis

Separation

Hurt

In order to progress through change, it is important to cultivate qualities such as flexibility and stability, balance, connection and the ability to let go. This comes from being centered and in your inner zone of excellence, connected with something beyond the confines of our egos. These processes are characterized by what we call the **COACH** state:

Centered

Open

Attending with Awareness

Connected

Holding

This state represents a state of coherence and alignment of all three of the minds we have been exploring in this book: somatic, cognitive and field.

It is important to have practices that help to create and strengthen our ability to be in the COACH state (our zone of excellence) and be the best of ourselves, especially when we are facing times of challenge and change. It is easy to stay balanced when life moves smoothly, but in order to maintain equilibrium during turbulent times, one must have developed these qualities until they are "in the muscle." Preparing for change requires durable practices to prepare you for moving through times of change with resourcefulness.

The earlier generations of NLP tended to place the most emphasis on techniques. Third Generation NLP focuses on the importance of practice as a key part of generative change and fitness for the future.

Finding Your Zone

The following exercise is based on a simple but profound inner game practice that we initially learned from our colleague John Welwood (author of *Toward a Psychology of Awakening* and *Journey of the Heart*). It was originally developed by his wife Jennifer as part of a meditation practice.

We have adapted and modified it a bit in order to include all of the elements of the COACH state. Its purpose is to access and align all three types of intelligence, moving from the somatic mind to include the cognitive mind and finally the field mind. As you will observe, it integrates a number of pieces and practices from earlier chapters.

1. Sit or stand in a comfortable position with both feet flat on the floor and your spine erect but relaxed (i.e., "in your vertical axis"). Check that your breathing is regular and from the belly. (Short, rapid breathing from the chest would indicate that you are in a stressed mode.)

2. Bring your attention to the soles of your feet (i.e., put your "mind" into your feet). Become aware of the universe of sensations in the bottoms of your feet. Feel the surface of your heels, toes, arches and the balls of your feet.

3. Begin to expand your awareness to include the physical volume (the three-dimensional space) of your feet and then move your awareness up through your lower legs, knees, thighs, pelvis and hips. Become aware of your belly center, breathe deeply into it and say to yourself: "I am here." "I am present." "I am centered."

4. Continuing to stay aware of your lower body, expand your awareness up through your solar plexus, spine, lungs, rib cage and chest. Bring awareness to your heart center in your upper chest, breathe into your chest and say to yourself: "I am open." "I am opening."

5. Now continue to expand your awareness up through your shoulders, upper arms, elbows, lower arms, wrists, hands and fingers, and up through your neck, throat and face. Be sure to include all of the senses in the head: the eyes, ears, nose, mouth and tongue. Bring your awareness to the skull, brain and the center in your head, behind your eyes. Breathe as if you are breathing into your head center, bringing in oxygen and energy, and say to yourself: "I am awake." "I am aware." "I am alert and clear."

6. Staying in contact with the ongoing physical sensations in your body, starting from your feet and including all three centers (belly, heart and head), become aware of all of the space below you, going into the center of the Earth; all the space above you, reaching into the sky; all of the space to your left; all of the space to your right; all of the space behind you; all of the space in front of you. Feel a deep sense of connection to your feet and the centers in your belly, heart and head, and to the environment and field around you. Be aware of the vast array of resources

available to you within yourself and in the field around you and say to yourself, "I am connected."

7. From this state you can hold all of the resources, strength, intelligence and wisdom available to you as well as disturbing energies such as fear, anger, sadness, etc. Acknowledge this capability by saying to yourself, "I am ready to hold whatever may emerge."

Practicing this COACH state of being in your zone will allow you to be able to hold more and more of your experience from a place of calm and clarity, just as captain Sullenberger was able to hold his fear from a place that was beyond the fear in the example of the "miracle on the Hudson."

As an example, author Robert Dilts was coaching a man who was a vice president at a major international bank. For a number of years he had been in charge of a large project in which he had invested a lot of time, energy and emotion. However, the top management had recently begun to make changes to the project that the man felt were taking it in the wrong direction and did not match his values. It reached a point where he scheduled a meeting with the board of directors to try to get the project back on track. If they did not make some key adjustments, he would feel compelled to leave the company.

In a very real sense, his position was on the line and he would clearly need to "play the inner game" of his career. When he had been in front of the board of directors previously, however, he had always struggled. As he put it, the atmosphere was so "heavy" that he felt tense, contracted, constrained and unable to express himself easily. By coaching him to practice finding and grounding in his inner zone of excellence, the manager was able to feel confident and calm and make a clear, compelling and charismatic presentation to the board. As a result, he was able to save his project, his integrity and ultimately his career.

Learning From Apple Juice

There is an amusing but instructive story told by Thich Nhat Hanh—Buddhist monk, teacher, poet and peace activist—that illustrates the benefits of this type of practice. He relates the story of a monk who went to live in France during the war in Viet Nam. While there, the monk would help other people arriving from that troubled part of the world by caring for the children while the parents went about the task of creating a new life.

One day the monk was taking care of a group of young children. After playing for a while, they came to the monk wanting something to drink. The monk had a bottle of home made apple juice. Not surprisingly, the juice had a lot of sediment in the bottom of the bottle.

The monk poured five glasses of apple juice for the children. A little girl got the last glass that consequently also had the most sediment. Upon seeing that the juice was so murky, the little girl decided she didn't want it after all and left to play with her friends.

Later, she became quite thirsty and returned to the house to get something to drink. She went to the sink and tried hard to reach and turn on the spigot for some water, but was too small to get it to work. The monk discovered her and asked what she was doing. The little girl replied that she was very thirsty and needed a drink.

The monk suggested that she try the apple juice from earlier. He had saved it for her. The little girl was just about to say "no" again when she noticed that the juice in the glass was now crystal clear. Surprised, she thought that it was different apple juice. The monk said no, it was the same apple juice, but that when it had the chance to sit still for a while, it naturally became clear because the sediment had a chance to settle to the bottom of the glass.

The little girl drank the apple juice and it was the best juice she had ever tasted. Turning to the monk she asked,

"Uncle monk, does that mean that the apple juice was meditating?" Smiling, the monk replied that the apple juice was not exactly meditating, but that we could learn even from apple juice how to center, settle and become clear.

We can liken the COACH state to the glass of juice in this story. The glass container includes both the sweet juice of the apple and the unappealing sediment. The juice can be viewed as our insights and resources and the sediment as the cloudy, difficult or disturbing feelings and energies (fear, frustration, anger, etc.). The act of holding them both from a state of stillness and calm allows the cloudy and disturbing emotions to settle down and the clarity and flavor to emerge (it is the juice that is closest to the sediment that is the most flavorful).

When we are able to learn to stay calm, clear and connected to a larger field, we are likely to be much more resourceful. The Buddhists like to use the relationship between the clouds and the sky above them and the Earth beneath them to illustrate this. If I identify with the clouds, I can get lost in changing, confusing and stormy contents of my experience. But if I center myself in the Earth beneath the clouds and open to the field of the sky beyond the cloud formations, I can let the clouds or contents of my thoughts and emotions pass through my awareness without becoming disturbed by them. Rather than getting lost in, fighting or trying to control or get rid of the experiential "clouds," I can be aware of the all the clouds, and let them pass through, holding them in an open field of awareness.

The Power of Presence

A key success factor for an effective coaching relationship is presence. Merriam-Webster's dictionary defines *presence* as "a quality of poise and effectiveness that enables a performer to achieve a close relationship with his or her audience." The abilities to be poised, effective and achieve a close connection to those with whom we are interacting are important resources for coaches, trainers, managers and professional communicators of all types.

As the definition above implies, poise and connectedness come from the capacity to be present, centered in yourself (the COACH state) and in relationship with those around you. Presence is associated with feelings of aliveness, connection, creativity, satisfaction and flow. When we are not present and are disconnected from ourselves and others, we can feel empty, out of control, distant and unavailable.

As the phenomena of mirror neurons and biomagnetic fields demonstrate, our physical presence and our internal state can have a powerful impact, either positively or negatively, on those with whom we are interacting, whether or not we directly engage them physically or verbally. The calming influence of the captain and crew of US Airways flight 1549 on the passengers is an example of the positive impact of presence and the COACH state. The influence of the fearful responses of the negatively conditioned monkeys on their naive companions is an example of how contracted, fear-driven presence can have the opposite impact.

Thus, our quality of presence is frequently the "difference that makes the difference" in our ability to enjoy life, collaborate generatively and contribute to the growth and transformation of others. When people are connected to themselves and present with each other, the natural feelings that emerge are compassion, empathy, genuine interest in each other, spontaneity, authenticity and joy. These feelings are the foundation for all effective personal and professional relationships.

Creating a COACHing Container™

From the perspective of Third Generation NLP, the COACH state helps us stay connected to the sources of all of our resources as we travel the path from our current state to our desired state. It also helps us to handle the interferences that can occur on the way, as dramatically illustrated in the case of captain Sullenberger and US Airways flight 1549.

Similar to the example of Sullenberger's influence on his crew (and vice versa), our rootedness in our own COACH state can become a resource for others. This is the essence of the *coaching relationship*. As a coach, one of our primary ways of supporting others as they travel their own paths from their present states to their desired states is to ground ourselves in our COACH state and help our coachees to remain in theirs as they perform each step, confront interferences and strive to progress. When we can do so, we create a field of resources between ourselves and others that simultaneously brings out the best of each other. As one executive said to his coach, "I really like who I am when I am around you."

We refer to this special relationship and the field it produces as the *COACHing Container™*. Creating a strong and rich COACHing Container™ is essential for accompanying and supporting others through times of challenge and change.

The COACHing Container™ is a form of holding environment. Psychologist Donald Winnicott developed the notion of *holding environment* to refer to the way a child is held physically, emotionally and psychologically by his or her primary caretakers. The way a child's behaviors, feelings and reactions are held and responded to by his or her primary caretakers in infancy and early childhood shapes the child's relationship with those behaviors, feelings and reactions in later life.

Developmental psychology has expanded the meaning of holding environment to describe the people, places, tools, and rituals that surround us at any given point in our lives. In coaching, a positive holding environment creates a "safe space" for people to talk about what is going on with themselves and their organizations. It is a space in which people can reflect openly with one another about the challenges they face, debate issues, and clarify assumptions, find resources, etc. A good holding environment offers the security we need to engage life and encourages us to take risks in order to grow. A poor holding environment provides insufficient support for life's challenges, stunts growth and triggers reactive behavior.

In a positive holding environment we are able to find our own resources and solutions and bring out the best of ourselves, even under very challenging circumstances (as in the case of the captain, crew and passengers in the miracle on the Hudson). Being able to stay within the zone of the COACH state thus creates a positive holding environment in which people can stay connected to their own creativity and resourcefulness and become empowered to find their own solutions.

The following simple exercise is a way to practice bringing the qualities of the COACH state into a coaching conversation. The purpose of this practice is to ensure that both coach and coachee begin their interaction from the best version of themselves, in order to get the most from the interaction. Just as athletes have warm-up practices that allow them to be the best of themselves during competition or practice, the COACHing Container™ prepares participants in a coaching interaction to get the best from one another.

Before beginning, it is useful to establish a set of non-verbal signals that serve as reminders for each element of the Coaching Container™:

 a. Center

 b. Breathe (Open)

 c. Slow down (Attend with awareness)

 d. Pause (Connect)

 e. Relax (Hold)

The purpose of these signals is for the coach to help remind the coachee to stay within his or her zone of excellence during the interaction. *Breathing,* for example, helps us to stay open to possibilities, resources and new ideas. *Slowing down,* especially when speaking, helps to ensure that we are actually aware of what we are saying and thinking while speaking and not just going on "autopilot," getting lost in our habitual neurolinguistic programming, internal "tape-loops" and stories. *Pausing* gives us an opportunity to connect with ourselves and make connections between what we are saying or thinking and its significance in our lives. *Relaxing* makes it easier to hold whatever thoughts or responses are being brought up by the conversation from a place of greater resourcefulness.

This results in being able to stay present and create enough space for greater awareness and movement to emerge naturally.

The signals should be in the form of simple, non-disruptive gestures that cue the coachee to move back into his or her zone of excellence but do not disturb the flow of the conversation. It is preferable for the coachee to chose the gestures he or she would like the coach to use.

When you are ready, begin the conversation with the following steps:

1. Stand or sit facing each other in a relaxed, aligned and balanced posture.

2. Bring your awareness into your body and your breath and become present. (A good way to do this is through the *Finding Your Zone* practice described earlier.)

3. Keeping eye contact, take turns making the following declarations to each other:
   I am present. I am centered.
   I am open.
   I am aware. I am awake, alert and clear.
   I am connected to myself, to you and to the field of resources within and around us.
   I am ready to hold what emerges from within myself and in the space of our interaction from the best of myself.

When done with authenticity and presence, this should create a strong and rich felt sense of rapport and resourcefulness between the participants in the interaction. This is what we call the field or "container." This container forms the holding environment for the rest of the conversation.

Moving from CRASH to COACH

Once the COACHing Container™ is established, the coachee can begin to reflect upon his or her present state, desired state and the path between them with access to all of his or her resources. In many ways, this is the essence of coaching. Like a rowing coach who accompanies his or her team providing encouragement and feedback for them to give their best performance, an executive coach or life coach accompanies his or her coachees as they prepare to face their life challenges, helping to keep them in their COACH state.

1. The coachee recounts his or her CRASH experience or pattern—i.e., the problem state or situation in which he or she involuntarily becomes contracted, reactive, overly analytical, separated from his or her resources, and caught in uncomfortable or hurtful feelings.

2. The coach gives the signals for "center", "breathe", "slow down", "pause" or "relax" as is appropriate to keep both the coachee and him/herself in the COACH state and maintain the quality of their field or container.

3. The coach then asks the coachee to describe his or her desired state within that context or situation. Again, the coach gives signals as is appropriate to keep both the coachee and him/herself within the zone of the COACH state.

4. The coachee is then asked to reflect upon the inner resources that he or she has that would allow him or her to achieve his or her desired state in that context or situation. Again, the coach continues to give signals as is

appropriate to keep both the coachee and him/herself within the zone of the COACH state.

When supported in this way with presence and intention, the coachee will be able to find his or her own solutions without the need for intervention or interference by the coach. As Milton Erickson liked to say, "You know far better what is appropriate for you than I could ever guess from the outside."

Rather than analyze or discuss particular solutions at the end of the session, the coach and coachee can share the symbols or metaphors that spontaneously emerge for them at the completion of the process.

The coach and coachee may end the interaction with an exchange of non-verbal gestures as expressions of gratitude to one another. This also serves as an anchor for the resources each will be taking with him or her as a result of the interaction. To do this ritual is a form of punctuation, similar to the end of a musical performance or play. In this way, awareness and connection are sustained from the beginning to the end of the process.

Bringing Archetypal Energies into the COACHing Container™

Once a strong COACHing Container™ has been established, additional resources may be introduced in the form of "archetypal energies." According to our friend and colleague Stephen Gilligan (2009), there are three fundamental *archetypal energies* required for generative change: *fierceness* (strength, force, intensity), *tenderness* (softness, openness, gentleness) and *playfulness* (humor, flexibility, creativity).

These energies may be called *archetypal* because all humans (and most mammals) possess them and they do not have to be learned. They "come with the equipment" and have evolved through many generations as a fundamental part of our somatic intelligence. From the time we are newborns we are able to express these energies in some way. When hungry or uncomfortable, a baby will show fierceness as it cries to be fed or cared for. Babies also naturally show tenderness, seeking love and connection. It is also clear that infants do not have to be taught how to play. Laughter and creativity are defining qualities of childhood that stay with us throughout life.

Each archetypal energy serves a purpose in supporting us to effectively address both life's challenges and opportunities. *Fierceness* is needed to stay committed and set boundaries. To take on any major task, you have to be able to have a fierce commitment - a deep, intense focus. It is the energy of the warrior.

Tenderness is needed to connect with others, have emotional wholeness and to effectively give and receive the nurturing necessary to grow and heal. If you're going to meet any deep challenge in life, you'll need to be connected to tenderness. It's what allows you to touch and be touched, to soothe, to calm and be calm, to feel empathy and sensitivity, etc. It is the energy of the mother and the healer.

Playfulness is necessary to find new perspectives, be creative and have fluidity. Humor and playfulness allow us to get outside of the box and sense things in many ways. When we are too serious, we can become rigidly attached to a particular perspective or point of view. Playfulness and humor can help to shake things up, keep them loose and moving, and create space for new possibilities. It is the energy of the shapeshifter. We have observed that in a coaching session there is frequently a turning point where the coachee starts to laugh or smile. It's a type of laugh of awakening. When this shift happens, the new awareness and expansion of consciousness releases into a laugh. This is one of the reasons there is considered to be a healing quality to laughter.

While each of these energies itself is archetypal and does not have to be taught, the way the energy is utilized and expressed becomes a matter of skill and a key part of our inner game. It is also possible that we lose touch with or repress these energies. As with all deep structures, there is a shadow side as well as a resource side to each archetypal pattern.

Positive or centered fierceness emerges when we are able to hold it and express ourselves from the COACH state. From this state, fierceness remains centered and can be integrated and balanced through contact with other resources. It comes out in the form of determination, clarity, strength, courage, commitment, boundaries, seeing through games and seductions, protecting life, both your own and others'. When we CRASH, that same energy becomes tense, contracted and reactive. Uncentered and unchecked fierceness, without softness and humor, comes out as violence and aggression.

Similarly, the positive expressions of tenderness take the forms of kindness, calmness, sweetness, gentleness, etc. But if you lose yourself in the energy of tenderness you can become too soft and sentimental. The shadow side of tenderness is weakness, lack of clear boundaries, dependency, etc.

Playfulness in its positive form helps us to stay loose, joyful, fluid and able to get outside of the box of rigid perspectives. Uncentered and ungrounded playfulness, disconnected from fierceness or tenderness, can become cynicism, superficiality, irresponsibility and trickery.

To deal effectively with life's challenges and opportunities, we need connection to all three of these archetypal energies. Think of these energies like the primary colors – red, blue and yellow. You can mix them in many different proportions to create an infinite number of possible expressions.

Sometimes bringing a missing archetypal energy into a situation can dramatically transform it. Consider the following example related by a policewoman who had been studying NLP.

While on duty in a rough neighborhood of a large city she received an urgent summons to a local residence to handle an incidence of domestic violence. As she approached the apartment she was on top alert, because it is in these types of situations that a police officer is actually in the most physical danger; even more so than in a robbery or murder. People, especially uncentered, angry people in the CRASH state, don't want the police interfering in their family affairs.

As she approached the scene of the unfolding incident, the police officer heard shouting and crying coming from inside the apartment. A man was yelling in a loud, angry voice. She could also hear the sound of various objects being broken along with the terrified screams of a woman. Suddenly, a television set came crashing through the front window, smashing into pieces on the ground in front of her. At the same time, the screaming escalated. The police officer rushed to the door and began to pound on it as hard as she could in order to get the attention of the occupants. A moment later, she heard an enraged male voice from inside the apartment shouting, "Who in the hell is that?!"

As a result of her many hours of practice of going into her zone of excellence during challenging moments, the police officer quickly dropped into her COACH state and opened to the field of possibilities. Spotting the pieces of the mangled television set spread over the ground, she quickly called back "Television repairman!"

After at least thirty seconds of dead silence inside the apartment, the man broke out in laughter. Shortly afterward, he opened the door and the police officer was able to make her intervention without physical confrontation or violence. She commented that those two words were more helpful for dealing with the situation than any amount of hand-to-hand combat.

Exploring the Influence of Archetypal Energies

According to Gilligan, it is necessary to maintain a balance of these three forces, and to "humanize" them by bringing them through your "center." The following exercise examines how to bring the positive forms of each archetypal energy and their combination into a challenging situation in order to explore what other choices they make possible. The exercise involves accessing each energy and expressing it through the COACH state and COACHing Container™ in order to experience the greatest and most appropriate benefit it can bring into a particular situation.

1. The coach guides him or herself and the Explorer into the COACH state in order to create a resourceful COACHing Container™.

2. The coachee steps into a location representing the "present state" and recounts a CRASH experience or pattern—i.e., a problem state or situation in which he or she involuntarily becomes contracted, reactive, overly analytical, separated from his or her resources, and caught in uncomfortable or hurtful feelings. The coachee relives the situation as fully as possible without getting caught in it: seeing what he or she sees in the situation, hearing what

he or she hears and feeling what he or she feels. In this way, the coachee brings awareness to his or her current reaction and the choices that he or she perceives available in the situation.

3. The coachee then changes locations and returns to his or her COACH state.

4. With the help of the coach, the coachee explores the impact of bringing the positive expression of each of the archetypal energies into the CRASH situation beginning with fierceness.

   a. Staying in the COACH state, the coachee accesses the energy through one of the following methods:

      1) Identify and relive a *reference experience* from some time in your life in which you strongly experienced the positive and resourceful expression of the energy.

      2) Identify a *positive role model* for the resourceful expression of the energy; i.e., a person who is able to consistently express the positive or centered version of the energy. Then, put yourself into that person's shoes (take 2nd position) in order to get a felt sense of that way of expressing the energy.

      3) Use your imagination to act *"as if"* you are in the centered and resourceful expression of the energy.

      4) Find a *symbol* for the positive expression of the energy and bring the symbol into your body so that it creates a felt sense of the energy.

   b. After connecting to a positive expression of the archetypal energy, the coachee returns to the CRASH location, bringing the archetypal energy into that situation. The coachee becomes aware of how the energy shifts his or her experience of the situation and notices what new choices become possible.

c. The coachee then returns to the COACH state location and repeats these steps for the energies of softness and playfulness.

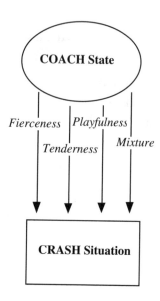

Bringing the Positive Forms of Archetypal Energies into a Challenging Situation Helps to Generate New Choices of Response and Behavior

5. After exploring the impact of the archetypal energies individually, the coachee connects with all three archetypal energies simultaneously, allows them to mix together and then re-enters the CRASH location. Again, the coachee is to experience how the combination of energies shifts his or her perception of the situation and notice what new choices become possible.

Holding Difficult Feelings

A key aspect of mastering one's inner game is the ability to acknowledge and transform difficult feelings that can be triggered by our life situations. One of the main factors that determines whether we CRASH into an unresourceful state or remain in the zone of the COACH state is our capacity to hold difficult feelings. Difficult feelings are frequently the uncentered or shadow forms of archetypal energies; i.e., rage, grief, frustration, panic, anxiety, etc.

Transformational teacher Richard Moss points out that *the distance between ourselves and others is precisely the distance between ourselves and ourselves.* This implies that the way we relate to others and to the world around us is a mirror for how we relate to ourselves. It is from this fundamental relationship with ourselves that our relationships with others and the external world emerge. This self-to-self relationship is frequently limited by those feelings that we don't know how to meet, accept, hold and love in ourselves.

Family therapist Virginia Satir frequently asked her clients two questions. The first was, "How do you feel?" A client might respond to this question by answering that he or she felt angry, sad, afraid, guilty, or some other type of difficult feeling. Then Virginia would ask a second question: "How do you feel about feeling that way?" The answer to this second question is quite significant and determines a lot about the impact and meaning the answer to the first question will have. There is quite a difference if someone feels calm or curious about feeling angry than if that person feels guilty or frustrated about feeling angry. It is these second feelings that determine the ease and quality with which we are able to stay present and hold the first feeling or set of feelings.

Captain Chesley Sullenberger's description of feeling "calm on the outside, turmoil inside" as he glided his engineless aircraft to the Hudson river is a powerful example of being able to hold difficult feelings.

"Holding" implies a relationship between two things: the thing holding and the thing being held. The metaphorical image of a mother holding a baby can help us to envision this relationship. The baby represents the primary somatic feeling, sensation or reaction that we are experiencing. The mother represents the response of the rest of our nervous system to this primary response.

If a baby is crying and the mother becomes tense, angry or nervous, the baby is likely to experience even more distress. If the mother is able to hold the baby from a state of nurturing support, the baby is more likely to be calmed by that presence (via mirror neurons) and move through the discomfort in a flowing way.

This same dynamic occurs with respect to our relationship with our own feelings. When we are fearful of them and refuse or fight them, we actually increase our degree of contraction, reaction, disconnection and discomfort. As it has been pointed out, "What you resist persists." When we can acknowledge and hold those feelings with centeredness, openness, awareness and connection, they are no longer a "problem," and their energy can either be released or transformed into a more resurceful expression.

We suggest that the following qualities are helpful for holding difficult feelings:

- non-reactivity
- unconditional acceptance of the feeling exactly as it is
- no agenda to change anything about the feeling
- patience, taking time
- unwavering attention to the feeling
- trust that all is well as it is, that the feeling has a positive intention and purpose
- a sense of being held in a field greater than oneself
- kindness toward the feeling
- a non-intrusive curiosity about the feeling

As Virginia Satir demonstrated, it is also useful to identify and acknowledge unresourceful feelings or attitudes about the difficult feelings. In this way, these feelings about the difficult feelings can also be included, transcended and held from a larger and more resourceful field of awareness. Such responses to the difficult feeling can include:

- wanting it to go away
- wanting it to be different, to change
- analyzing or explaining it
- identifying with it (getting lost in it)

As a coach, it is important to realize that the second feeling is as much a part of the problem state as is the first feeling. If we are not aware of this, we may find ourselves aligning with the second feeling to try to get rid of the first feeling. When we don't know how to be with a feeling, in one way or another, we want it to go away.

In summary, our difficult feelings, like a baby in distress, need more than anything else to be held. Through this holding, the feelings, like the baby, transform from a state of contraction and a sense of separation to relaxation and a sense of connection. Thus it is not a question of getting rid of difficult feelings, but rather of relating to them in a way that allows them to transform. The energy of the difficult feeling is then released back into the flow of our lives. We recuperate the energy that was previously spent in avoiding meeting the difficult feeling, allowing us to be more fully present with even more of ourselves available to engage in the present moment.

The purpose of the next exercise is to help you discover and apply the resources you need to stay present and hold difficult feelings that may arise and take you out of the present.

1. Identify a challenging situation in which you experience a difficult feeling that you are not able to hold and, consequently, takes you out of your "zone" into the CRASH state. Experience that feeling and sensations and allow your body to express it. Bring acknowledgement and awareness to the feelings and sensations without any attempt to change, analyze or explain them.

2. Step back from the location in which you were experiencing this difficult feeling and reflect upon the you who is experiencing the difficult feelings. How do you feel about those difficult feelings? How do you feel about yourself for feeling them? What is your relationship with those feelings and with yourself when you are feeling them? There may be a number of feelings about the first feeling (shame, guilt, despair, anger, helplessness, etc.). As in the previous step, bring acknowledgement and awareness to these feelings and sensations without judgment or any attempt to change them.

3. Now step back to a third location, shift your state by turning around, moving your body, shaking your arms and legs, etc. Take the time necessary to put yourself into a resourceful state in which you are centered, open, awake (the COACH state) and connected to a field that is bigger than you. What resources (e.g., trust, acceptance, curiosity, strength, love, etc.) could help you to more lovingly, respectfully and resourcefully hold the second set of feelings? Open to the larger field and allow yourself to receive the resources without thinking about it. Notice what emerges from the field. It may come in the form of images, symbols, feelings, movements, etc.

5. Bring the resources that have emerged from the field fully into your body and being. (If you need to, you can facilitate this by finding reference experiences for these resources and reliving them as fully as you can.) Find a symbol and a gesture or movement (somatic syntax) that expresses these resources and brings them present in your body. Allow the energy of these resources to flow fully through you both from the field and into the field around you.

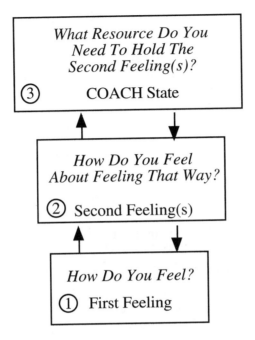

6. With these resources and their associated symbol fully present in your body and awareness, return to the second location (the feelings about the feelings). Don't attempt to change anything. Just hold the feelings and responses associated with the second location within the larger field of the resources. Make the gesture or movement associated with the resources you have received. Notice what shifts in your perception and attitude toward the second set of feelings.

7. Now step into the location in which you placed the original difficult feelings and bring with you the resources you have identified. Again, don't attempt to change anything. Just hold the difficult feelings and responses within the larger field of the resources. Make the gesture and movement associated with the resources you have received. How do you feel now about those difficult feelings? What changes in your ability to hold those difficult feelings?

Belief Barriers and Belief Bridges

It is also possible to identify, hold and transform limiting beliefs and "thought viruses" in a manner similar to holding difficult feelings. This can be done by:

- Centering and holding them within a larger field of resources
- Bringing greater awareness to the structure of the neurolinguistic programming which generates them
- Finding their positive intention or purpose
- Integrating them with other beliefs and programs

Beliefs are powerful influences in our lives. They are a classic example of neurolinguistic programming arising from an integration of both cognitive and somatic circuitry. They may also be held and transmitted through relational fields as illustrated in the examples of the monkey experiments cited earlier in this chapter. Beliefs are considered one of the most fundamental levels of change and learning in NLP and are one of the key components of our deep structure. They shape and create our surface structure in many ways. Beliefs determine how events are given meaning, and are at the core of motivation and culture. Our beliefs and values provide the reinforcement (*motivation* and *permission*) that supports or inhibits particular capabilities and behaviors.

It is common wisdom, for example, that if someone really believes he can do something he will do it, and if he believes something is impossible, no amount of effort will convince him that it can be accomplished. The power of beliefs was demonstrated in an enlightening study in which a group of 100 cancer "survivors" (patients who had reversed their symptoms for over 10 years) were interviewed about what they had done to achieve success. The interviews showed that no single treatment method stood out as being more effective than any other. Some had taken the standard medical treatment of chemotherapy and/or radiation, some had used a nutritional approach, others had followed a spiritual path, while others concentrated on a psychological approach and some did nothing at all. The only thing that was characteristic of the entire group was that they all believed that the approach they took would work.

As is illustrated by the above study and by phenomena such as the placebo effect, beliefs have a powerful self-fulfilling capacity.

Beliefs, however, are a "double edged sword." Limiting beliefs can be as persistent and influential as empowering beliefs. There is an old story about a patient who was being treated by a psychiatrist. The patient wouldn't eat or take care of himself, claiming that he was a corpse. The psychiatrist spent many hours arguing with the patient trying to convince him he wasn't a corpse. Finally the psychiatrist asked the patient if corpses bled. The patient replied, "Of course corpses don't bleed, all of their body functions have stopped." The psychiatrist then convinced the patient to try an experiment. The psychiatrist would carefully prick the patient with a pin and they would see if he started to bleed. The patient agreed. After all, he was a corpse. The psychiatrist gently pricked the patient's skin with a needle and, sure enough, he began to bleed. With a look of shock and amazement the patient gasped, *"I'll be darned...corpses **DO** bleed!"*

As the story above illustrates, beliefs are notoriously difficult to change through typical rules of logic or rational thinking. Furthermore, the most influential beliefs are often outside of our awareness (as with "thought viruses"). Consider, for example, the case of the monkeys mentioned earlier who conditioned the belief in their companions that a particular object was dangerous simply by their reaction to the behavior of their companions regarding that particular object. This demonstrates that beliefs can be held and transferred through a relational field as well as through direct communication and physical interaction.

The power of beliefs transmitted through this type of relational field was demonstrated in an enlightening study in which a group of children who were tested to have average intelligence was divided at random into two equal groups. One of the groups was assigned to a teacher who was told that the children were "gifted." The other group was given to a teacher who was told that the children were "slow learners." A year later the two groups were retested for intelligence. Not surprisingly, the majority of the group that was arbitrarily identified as "gifted" scored higher than they had previously, while the majority of the group that was labeled "slow" scored lower! It appears that the teacher's beliefs about the students affected their ability to learn.

In conclusion, we can liken the process of transforming limiting beliefs to the recipe for tiger stew: "Step one, catch the tiger." In the following inner game exercise, we explore how to "catch the tiger," but then, instead of killing the tiger, we turn it into a pussycat. The energy that was contained in the belief is liberated and transformed. The following process provides a way to discover and transform beliefs that create barriers to our connection with our resources, ourselves and others.

1. Think of a challenging situation in which it is important for you to be more fully present and more connected with yourself and others, but where instead you involuntarily become contracted, reactive, overly analytical, separated from your resources, and caught in uncomfortable or hurtful feelings (i.e., you become caught in a CRASH state). Create a physical location for that situation and step into it. Experience the situation the way you do now.

2. Step out of that situation and into a new location, and come fully into the COACH state. Define your desired state for the situation. How would you rather think, feel and respond? Experience this desired state as fully as you can in your body.

3. Keeping your attention on your felt sense of the desired state, begin to slowly walk toward the location representing the challenging situation. Pay attention to your physiology and your bodily sensations and stop as soon as you feel any change or contraction that begins to diminish, interfere with or bring you out of your resourceful state (the barrier). Stop, place your attention on those sensations and explore the question, "What beliefs are associated with those sensations that prevent me from being fully connected and resourceful in that situation?" Keep your attention on your body and the contracted sensations as you seek the beliefs instead of going up into your head to try to figure it out. As you discover the belief barriers also explore and acknowledge the positive intentions and purposes those beliefs serve.

4. Once you have identified the belief barriers, step back to the COACH state location where you can feel fully centered, present and resourceful. Ask yourself the questions, "Given what I have discovered about the belief barriers, what beliefs would I need in order to stay connected and resourceful in that situation anyway?" "What are the 'belief bridges' that would allow me to stay in the COACH state in that context?" Open to the larger field and allow yourself to receive the answers without analyzing or thinking about it. Notice what emerges from the field. "Neurolinguistically program" the beliefs by repeating them to yourself and experiencing the felt sense they create in your body. Where in your body do you most need to hold the beliefs? Create a physical gesture or movement (somatic syntax) that expresses the belief bridge.

5. Staying centered and present, hold the beliefs associated with the belief bridge in your body, heart and head. Step back into the challenging situation, using the gesture and maintaining your attention on these beliefs. Notice how your experience of that situation changes. What becomes possible through the presence of these beliefs in your nervous system?

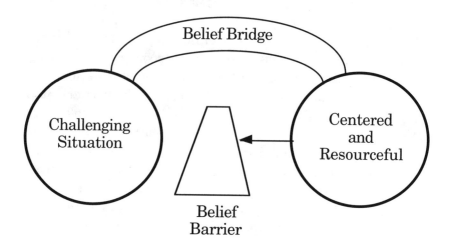

Creating a "Belief Bridge" Can Help You to Get Around "Belief Barriers" that Interfere with Your Connection to Yourself and Others

For more on working with beliefs using NLP, see *Beliefs: Pathways to Health and Well-Being* (Dilts, Hallbom, Smith, 1990), *Changing Beliefs With NLP* (Dilts, 1990), *From Coach to Awakener* (Dilts, 2003) and *The Encyclopedia of Systemic NLP and NLP New Coding* (Dilts & DeLozier, 2000).

Working With Archetypes of Transition

Belief issues and difficult feelings most frequently arise during times of transition (such as those that accompany the various stages of the adaptive cycle). Usually, the most difficult phase of transition for people to manage is that of collapse or creative destruction. It is this phase that generally brings the most disruption and upheaval.

Archetypically, this phase is portrayed in the symbol of the "dragon" which represents something huge, largely unknown and potentially dangerous. Some common "dragons" on the life path of our species include issues such as the arrival of adolescence, menopause, old age, career change, retirement, death of a loved one, loss, illness, and other major life transitions. When such transitions occur, we generally have common or archetypal reactions or responses such as denial, overwhelm, frustration, anger, determination, acceptance, etc. Each of these reactions or responses produces a certain relationship with the transition or dragon.

Carol Pearson (1992) has identified a series of archetypal responses to disruptive life transitions that symbolize various stages of our relationship with the mysterious and dangerous dragon.

- The Innocent (doesn't know the dragon exists)
- The Orphan (overwhelmed or consumed by the dragon)
- The Martyr (persecuted by the dragon)
- The Wanderer (avoids the dragon)
- The Warrior (fights the dragon)
- The Sorcerer (accepts and transforms the dragon)

As with all archetypal energies, each of the qualities represented in these symbolic roles has its gifts and its shadows:

The gifts of *innocence* are optimism, purity and simplicity. The shadow side is gullibility, inexperience and vulnerability.

The *Orphan* brings the gifts of compassion and the ability to let go. Its shadows are helplessness and despair.

The gifts of the *Martyr* include a sense of self-sacrifice and justice. The shadows produce victimization, judgment and a type of passive-aggressive reactivity.

The *Wanderer's* gifts are space, freedom and discovery. The shadow side brings avoidance and denial.

The resources associated with the *Warrior* are determination, courage and clarity. The shadows include aggression, violence and the imposition of a particular point of view.

The gifts of the *Sorcerer* have to do with acceptance, creativity and wisdom. The shadows come in the form of manipulation, trickery and illusion.

The key to dealing effectively with transition is obviously to be able to access and harness the gifts and resources each archetype brings through its relationship with the dragon. When the dragon can be held in the field of these resources, it becomes transformed—the problem becomes an opportunity; the wound becomes a source of learning and growth. The worst thing that ever happened to us becomes the best thing that ever happened to us.

We bring out the gifts of each archetype by connecting to them through the COACH state, thus producing the centered and integrated version of each response.

The following exercise combines the Next Generation NLP processes of spatial sorting, somatic syntax and connecting to the field mind through Pearson's archetypes as a way to resourcefully face times of upheaval and transition.

1. Define the dragon. Identify the life transition issue you are confronting. This can include key elements of the context or environment relating to the transition, such as the reactions of significant others or problematic details concerning the circumstances surrounding the transition.

2. Create a spatial location for the dragon and spatially sort each of the archetypes around the dragon in a circle in the sequence: a. Innocent, b. Orphan, c. Martyr, d. Wanderer, e. Warrior, f. Sorcerer. Include a location for the COACH state just outside the circle (a meta position).

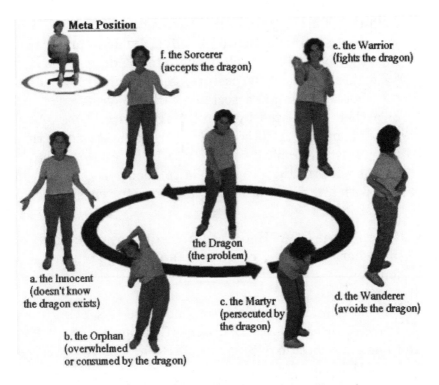

Layout for Archetypes of Transition Exercise

3. Starting at the location representing the Innocent, explore each archetype of transition in turn by taking on the attitude, energy, body posture and movements (i.e., Somatic Syntax) associated with that archetype. Experience the type of relationship each archetype has with the dragon. Notice both the gifts and shadows each relationship with the dragon brings up for you.

4. When you have moved through the entire sequence of archetypes, go to the meta position location and enter the COACH state as fully as possible. Connect to your zone of excellence and open to the wisdom of the larger field mind.

5. Holding this state in your body, physically move through each of the archetypes in the cycle again being sure that you receive and experience the gifts, resources and learnings they bring you in relationship to the dragon. Do this by exploring the body posture, gesture and movements (i.e., Somatic Syntax) associated with the positive version of archetype created by connecting it with the COACH state. Complete the process by returning to the space that feels most appropriate for you to be in at this time in relationship to the dragon. Notice that you can now do this with awareness of where you are in the entire cycle of transition.

6. Return to the COACH location in meta position and reflect on what you have discovered and learned from this journey.

For more information on this process, see *The Hero's Journey: A Voyage of Self-Discovery* (Gilligan & Dilts, 2009) and *The Encyclopedia of Systemic NLP and NLP New Coding* (Dilts & DeLozier, 2000).

Conclusion: Ego and Soul

We have reached the end of what we can present within the limits of this volume. Yet, in a way, this is only the beginning of our exploration of Next Generation NLP. There are many processes and techniques that we do not have the space to include here, and there are many more to come.

One of the major areas of application, for instance, of the principles and practices of this new generation of NLP is the area of identity coaching. Issues and transitions involving the level of identity are at the core of large "C" Coaching. We plan to cover this fascinating area in depth in our forthcoming book *Coaching at the Identity Level*.

The foundation of this work comes from viewing "identity" as composed of two complementary aspects: the ego and the soul. According to psychoanalysis, the *ego* is "the part of the psyche that mediates between the conscious and the unconscious and is responsible for reality testing and a sense of personal identity." Thus, the ego has to do with the development and preservation of our sense of a separate self, perceiving reality from its own individual perspective.

At the level of environment, the ego tends to focus on dangers and constraints, and the pursuit of short-term gain and pleasure. Consequently, at the level of behavior, the ego tends to be more reactive to external conditions. The capabilities associated with the ego are generally those connected with the cognitive intellect such as analysis and strategy. At the level of beliefs and values, the ego focuses on safety, security, approval, control, achievement and self-benefit. At the identity level, ego relates to our social roles and who we feel we should be or need to be. At the level of spirit or purpose, the ego is oriented toward survival, recognition and our ambition – the life we want to create for ourselves.

From the NLP perspective, the ego can be considered a cognitively constructed map or model of one's "self" and a

natural developmental process. These notions of "reality" and
"self" associated with the ego, however, are influenced by
external references such as social norms, cultural values and
family patterns. Like all maps or models, it is necessarily
shaped by the processes of deletion, distortion and generalization. When these distortions create too much separation from
the actual territory and potential of ourselves (our soul or
essence) they can create the "shadow" side of the ego. Some
characteristics of an unhealthy ego take the form of either *self-
inflation*—pride, arrogance, self-importance, narcissism and
self-infatuation—or *self-depreciation*—self-judgment, depression,
self-criticism, lack of self-worth and self-confidence, etc. These
can lead us to become overly gripped by greed, fear and survival
strategies (fight, flight, freeze).

The *soul* is the unique life force, essence or energy that we
come into the world with and that comes into the world
through us. As a newborn baby, for instance, we do not yet
have an ego, but we have a unique energy and being that are
the foundation for our identity. This energy is expressed
through our bodies and our interface with the larger fields
surrounding us. Because the soul is an energetic "deep
structure," it is not associated with any particular content—
and therefore is not constructed from influences such as
society, culture and family. It does, however, express itself in
the form of contribution to these larger fields. Thus, rather
than being an objectified or separate self, the soul is our
expression of an unfolding, connected self.

At the level of environment, the soul tends to focus on
opportunities for expression and growth. As a result, at the level
of behavior, the soul tends to respond more proactively to
external conditions. The capabilities associated with the soul
are generally those related to the perception and management
of energy and emotional intelligence. At the level of beliefs and
values, the soul focuses on internal motivations such as service,
contribution, connection, being, expansion and awakening. At
the identity level, soul relates to our mission and the unique

gifts that we bring into the world. At the level of spirit or purpose, the soul is oriented toward our vision of what we want to create in the world through us but that is beyond us.

Thus, we can say that while ego relates to the "content" of our experience, soul relates to the "container" that holds the content. Similarly, the ego functions through analysis while the soul operates through awareness. Some disciplines, like the Course In Miracles, maintain that there are two fundamental forces in the world, fear and love. From this perspective, we can view the ego as arising primarily from all of the variations of fear and the soul as arising primarily from all of the expressions of love. Clearly, both of these aspects of ourselves are necessary for a healthy and successful existence.

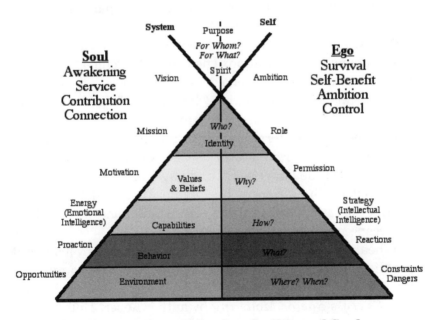

Levels of Expression for the Ego and Soul

When our body (somatic mind) and our intellect (cognitive mind) connect like two dancers responding to the music of life (the field), then the soul has a vehicle for expression and we find ourselves more alive, with greater joy, heightened intuition, and we feel more at home in the world. Charisma, passion and presence emerge naturally when these two forces (ego and soul; vision and ambition) are aligned. Optimum performance comes when the ego is in service of the soul.

The most powerful motivations are those that combine and align our vision, mission, ambition and values. When the ego and soul are out of alignment, and our ambition is at odds with our mission and vision, it produces conflict and struggle. If we "sell our soul" for ego benefits, we may have short-term success but are heading for a crisis in the long run. "Shadows" can emerge if our ambition creates arrogance or an "idealized self" and we begin to reject and supress other parts of ourself.

Understanding the dynamic between ego and soul and achieving a balance between them is an essential part of identity coaching and next generation NLP.

The dynamic between ego and soul operates in a similar way in a company or organization. The ego of the company is made up of the owners and shareholders, whose concern is with the survival, financial profitability ("bottom line") and return on investment. This is reflected by the ambition of the organization and its members in terms of status and level of performance. The soul of the organization is the value it provides for customers and the larger social and physical environment. This is created by the vision of the organization and the unique contribution and mission of the organization and its members with respect to the systems around it.

In healthy, thriving organizations, these forces are balanced and aligned. Some of the ways that the leaders of companies can achieve this alignment are covered in the forthcoming book *Success Factor Modeling* by author Robert Dilts and his late brother John Dilts. Success Factor Modeling™ (SFM) was developed by the two brothers as a method to identify and transfer the critical success factors necessary to promote the growth and impact of individuals, teams and organizations, and to help them be maximally prepared to create, recognize and take advantage of opportunities when they arise. By examining successful businesses, projects and initiatives and observing the behavior of high-performing individuals and teams, SFM™ helps people and organizations to quantify the factors that have created their legacy of success and to identify the trends necessary to extend that legacy into the future.

We hope you have enjoyed this journey so far into the next generation of NLP. It is our sincere wish that this book has been and will continue to be an effective road map and guidebook for you to reach your vision, mission, ambition and role with greater awareness, flexibility and confidence. As you can see, it is only the beginning. There is much more to come!

Afterword

The fertile field of NLP will continue to evolve new generations for years to come. If you are interested in exploring the principles and technology of Neuro-Linguistic Programming in more depth, other resources and tools exist to further develop and apply the distinctions, strategies and skills described within these pages.

NLP University is an organization committed to providing the highest quality trainings in basic and advanced NLP skills, and to promoting the development of new models and applications of NLP in the areas of health, business and organization, creativity and learning. Each Summer, NLP University holds residential programs at the University of California at Santa Cruz, offering extended residential courses on the skills of NLP, including those related to business consulting and coaching.

For more information please contact Teresa Epstein at:

NLP University

P.O. Box 1112

Ben Lomond, California 95005

Phone: (831) 336-3457

Fax: (831) 336-5854

E-Mail: Teresanlp@aol.com

Homepage: http://www.nlpu.com

In addition to the programs we offer at NLP University, we also travel internationally, presenting seminars and specialty programs on a variety of topics related to NLP and personal and professional development.

For more information on scheduled programs, please consult the NLP University website:

http://www.nlpu.com

or write to:

rdilts@nlpu.com

We have also written a number of other books and developed computer software and audio recordings based on the principles and distinctions of NLP.

For example, Robert has produced several software tools based on his modeling of Strategies of Genius: *Vision to Action*, *Imagineering Strategy* and *Journey to Genius Adventure*. He has also created audio recordings describing the creative processes of geniuses such as Mozart, Walt Disney and Leonardo Da Vinci.

For more information on these and other NLP-related products and resources, please contact:

Journey to Genius

P.O. Box 67448

Scotts Valley, CA 95067-7448

Phone (831) 438-8314

Fax (831) 438-8571

E-Mail: info@journeytogenius.com

Homepage: http://www.journeytogenius.com

Bibliography

Andreas, S. and Andreas, C., *Change Your Mind*, Real People Press, Moab, UT, 1987.

Andreas, C. and Andreas, S., *Heart of the Mind*, Real People Press, Moab, UT, 1989.

Andreas, C. and Andreas, T., *Core Transformation*, Real People Press, Moab, UT, 1994.

Aristotle, *On the Soul*, *Britannica Great Books*, Encyclopedia Britannica Inc., Chicago, Ill., 1979.

Aristotle, *Physics*, *Britannica Great Books*, Encyclopedia Britannica Inc., Chicago, Ill., 1979.

Armour, A., and Ardell, J., (Ed.), *Basic and Clinical Neurocardiology*, Oxford University Press, New York, NY, 2004.

Bandler, R. and Grinder, J., *The Structure of Magic Vol. I & II*, Science and Behavior Books, Palo Alto, CA, 1975, 1976.

Bandler, R. and Grinder, J., *Patterns of the Hypnotic Techniques of Milton H. Erickson, M.D., Vol. I & II*, Meta Publications, Capitola, CA, 1975, 1977.

Bandler, R., *Using Your Brain*, Real People Press, Moab, UT, 1984.

Bandler, R., *Time for a Change*, Meta Publications, Capitola, CA, 1993.

Bateson, G., *Steps To an Ecology of Mind*, Ballantine Books, New York, NY, 1972.

Bateson, G., *Mind and Nature*, E. P. Dutton, New York, NY, 1979.

Bateson, G. and Bateson, M. C., *Angels Fear: Towards an Epistemology of the Sacred*, Bantam Books, New York, N.Y., 1988.

Bateson, G., *A Sacred Unity*, HarperCollins Publishers, New York, NY, 1991.

Berman, M., *Coming to our Senses*, Simon and Schuster, New York, NY, 1989.

Childre, D. and Martin, H., *The HeartMath Solution*, HarperCollins Publishers, New York, NY, 2000.

Chomsky, N., *Syntactic Structures*, Mouton, The Hague, The Netherlands, 1957.

Chomsky, N., *Aspects of the Theory of Syntax*, The M.I.T. Press, Cambridge, MA, 1965.

Chomsky, N., *Language and Mind*, Harcourt Brace Jovanovich, Inc., New York, NY, 1968.

Darwin, C., *The Origin of Species*, Mentor Books, New York, NY, 1958.

DeLozier, J. and Grinder, J., *Turtles All The Way Down: Prerequisites to Personal Genius*, Metamorphous Press, Portland, OR, 1987.

Dilts, R., Grinder, J., Bandler, R., DeLozier, J., *Neuro-Linguistic Programming: The Study of the Structure of Subjective Experience, Volume I*, Meta Publications, Capitola, CA, 1980.

Dilts, R., *Roots of Neuro-Linguistic Programming: A reference guide to the technology of NLP*, Meta Publications, Capitola, CA, 1983.

Dilts, R., *Changing Belief Systems With NLP*, Meta Publications, Capitola, CA, 1990.

Dilts, R., Hallbom, T. and Smith, S., *Beliefs: Pathways to Health & Well-Being*, Metamorphous Press, Portland, OR, 1990.

Dilts, R. with Bonissone, G., *Skills for the Future*, Meta Publications, Capitola, CA, 1993.

Dilts, R., *Strategies of Genius Vols I, II & III*, Meta Publications, Capitola, CA, 1994-1995.

Dilts, R., *Visionary Leadership*, Meta Publications, Capitola, CA, 1996.

Dilts, R., *Time Lines*, *Anchor Point*, October, 1997.

Dilts, R. and McDonald, R., *Tools of the Spirit*, Meta Publications, Capitola, CA, 1997.

Dilts, R. and DeLozier, J., *Darwin's Thinking Path*, *Anchor Point*, February, 1997.

Dilts, R., *Modeling With NLP*, Meta Publications, Capitola, CA, 1998.

Dilts, R. and DeLozier, J., *The Evolution of Perceptual Positions*, *Anchor Point*, September, 1998.

Dilts, R., *Sleight of Mouth: The Magic of Conversational Belief Change*, Meta Publications, Capitola, CA, 1999.

Dilts, R. and DeLozier, J., *The Encyclopedia of Systemic NLP and NLP New Coding*, NLP University Press, Santa Cruz, CA, 2000.

Dilts, R., *From Coach to Awakener*, Meta Publications, Capitola, CA, 2003.

Einstein, A., *Out of My Later Years*, The Citadel Press, Secaucus, NJ, 1956.

Epstein, D., *The 12 Stages of Healing*, New World Library, Novato, CA, 1994.

Erickson, Milton H., *The Collected Papers of Milton H. Erickson Vol. IV*, Irvington Publishers Inc., New York, NY, 1980.

Ericsson, A.K., Charness, N., Feltovich, P., Hoffman, R.R., *Cambridge handbook on expertise and expert performance*, Cambridge University Press, Cambridge, UK, 2006.

Feldenkrais, M., *Awareness Through Movement*, Penguin Books, New York, NY, 1977.

Feldenkrais, M., *Body and Mature Behavior*, International Universities Press, New York, NY, 1981.

Freud, S., *An Autobiographical Study*, W. W. Norton & Company, Inc., New York, NY, 1964.

Gendlin, E., *Focusing*, Bantam Books, New York, NY, 1982.

Gershon, M., *The Second Brain: The Scientific Basis of Gut Instinct and a Groundbreaking New Understanding of Nervous Disorders of the Stomach and Intestines,* HarperCollins Publishers, New York, NY, 1999.

Gilligan, S., *The Courage to Love*, W. W. Norton & Co., New York, NY, 1997.

Gilligan, S. and Simon, D. (Ed.), *Walking in Two Worlds: The Relational Self in Theory, Practice and Community*, Zeig Tucker Publishers, Phoenix, AZ, 2004.

Gilligan, S. and Dilts, R., *The Hero's Journey: A Voyage of Self-Discovery*, Crowne House Publishers, London, 2009.

Gladwell, M., *Outliers: The Story of Success*, Back Bay Books, Little, Brown and Company, New York, NY, 2008.

Goleman, D., *The Multiple Personality Puzzle*, **New York Times**, June, 2, 1985.

Gallwey, T., *The Inner Game of Tennis*, Random House, New York, NY, 1974.

Gallwey, T., *The Inner Game of Work: Focus, Learning, Pleasure and Mobility in the Workplace*, Random House Trade Paperbacks, New York, NY, 2000.

Haley, J., *Uncommon Therapy: The Psychiatric Techniques of Milton H. Erickson M.D.*, W. W. Norton & Company, Inc., New York, NY, 1973.

Holling, C. S., *Adaptive environmental assessment and management*, John Wiley & Sons, London, 1978.

Holling, C. S., Gunderson, L. (Ed.), *Panarchy: understanding transformations in human and natural systems*, Island Press, Washington DC, 2002.

James, T. and Woodsmall, W., *Time Line Therapy and the Basis of Personality*, Meta Publications, Capitola, CA, 1987.

James, W., *Principles of Psychology*, *Britannica Great Books*, Encyclopedia Britannica Inc., Chicago, Ill., 1979.

Jung, C. G., *Memories, Dreams and Reflections*, Vintage Books, New York, NY, 1965.

Jung, C. G., *Psyche and Symbol*, Princeton University Press, Princeton, NJ, 1991.

Koestler, A., *The Act of Creation*, Hutchinson, London, 1964.

Korzybski, A., *Science and Sanity*, The International Non-Aristotelian Library Publishing Company, Lakeville, CT, 1980.

Laird, J. E., Rosenbloom, P. and Newell, A., *Chunking in SOAR; The Anatomy of a General Learning Mechanism*, *Machine Learning*, 1:11-46, 1986.

Laird, J. E., Rosenbloom, P. and Newell, A., *SOAR: An Architecture for General Intelligence*, *Artificial Intelligence*, 33:1-64, 1987.

Le Bon, G., *The Crowd: A Study of the Popular Mind*, Digireads.com Publishing, 2008 (1895).

Lovelock, J., *Gaia: A New Look at Life on Earth*, Oxford University Press, New York, NY, 1979.

Moss, R., *The Second Miracle*, Celestial Arts, Berkeley, CA, 1995.

Moss, R., *The Mandala of Being: Discovering the Power of Awareness,* New World Library, Novato, CA, 2007.

Pearsal, P., *The Heart's Code*, Crown Archetype, New York NY, 1998.

Pearson, C., *Awakening The Heroes Within*, HarperCollins Publishers, San Francisco, CA, 1991.

Rizzolatti, G., Craighero, L., *The Mirror-Neuron System*, *Annual Review of Neuroscience* **27**: 169-192, 2004.

Roth, G., *Maps to Ecstasy*, Nataraj Publishing, Mill Valley, CA, 1989.

Roth, G., *Sweat Your Prayers*, Penguin Putnam, Inc., New York, NY, 1997.

Roth, G., *Connections*, Jeremy P. Tarcher/Penguin, 2004.

Russell, P., *The Global Brain Awakens*, Global Brain, Inc., Palo Alto, CA, 1995.

Schilpp, P., *Albert Einstein, Philosopher-Scientist*, Northwestern University Press, Evanston, Ill., 1949.

Sheldrake, R., *A New Science of Life: The Hypothesis of Formative Causation*, Park Street Press, South Paris, ME, 2008 (1981).

Sheldrake, R., *The Presence of the Past: Morphic Resonance and the Habits of Nature*, Park Street Press, South Paris, ME, 2008 (1988).

Stephenson, G. R., *Cultural acquisition of a specific learned response among rhesus monkeys, in* **Progress in Primatology**, (Starek, D., Schneider, R. and Kuhn, H.J., Eds.), pp. 279-288, Fischer, Stuttgart, 1967.

Waldrop, M., *Toward a Unifying Theory of Cognition*, **Science**, Vol. 241, July, 1988.

Watson, L., **Lifetide**, Hodder & Stoughton Ltd., London, 1979.

Whitehead, A. N. and Russell, B., **Principia Mathematica**, 1910.

Wilber, K., **A Brief History of Everything**, Shambhala, Boston, MA, 1996.

Index

About the Authors

Judith DeLozier **Robert Dilts** **Deborah Bacon Dilts**

Robert Dilts has a global reputation as a leading developer, author, coach, trainer and consultant in the field of Neuro-Linguistic Programing (NLP). Robert worked closely with NLP co-founders John Grinder and Richard Bandler at the time of its creation and also studied personally with Milton H. Erickson, M.D., and Gregory Bateson. Robert pioneered the applications of NLP to education, creativity, health, leadership, belief systems and the development of what has become known as "Third Generation NLP".

Robert is the principal author of *Neuro-Linguistic Programming Vol. I*, which serves as the standard reference text for the field, and has authored or co-authored numerous other books on NLP including *Changing Belief Systems with NLP*, *Beliefs: Pathways to Health and Well Being*, *Tools of the Spirit* and *From Coach to Awakener*.

Robert's most recent book *The Hero's Journey: A Voyage of Self Discovery* (with Stephen Gilligan) is about how to how to embark on the path of learning and transformation that will reconnect you with your deepest calling, transform limiting beliefs and habits, heal emotional wounds and physical symptoms, deepen intimacy, and improve self-image.

Judith DeLozier has been a trainer, co-developer, and designer of training programs in the field of Neuro-Linguistic Programming since 1975. She is co-author of *Neuro-Linguistic Programming Vol. I* (1980), with Robert Dilts, John Grinder and Richard Bandler. A student of Milton Erickson, Judith modeled his tracking strategy for creating and utilizing trance states and metaphors. This work is described in *Patterns of the Hypnotic Techniques of Milton H. Erickson, M.D. Vol. II* (1976), which she co-authored with John Grinder and Richard Bandler.

In the book *Turtles All the Way Down: Prerequisites to Personal Genius* (1987), which she co-authored with John Grinder, Judith explored the interrelationships between NLP and the threads of culture, community, art, aesthetics and epistemology. The result of this work was the creation of *NLP New Coding*, which stimulated a movement toward a more systemic and relational approach to NLP, and a resurgence of interest in the work of Gregory Bateson.

Judith has been primarily responsible for bringing NLP to the area of transcultural competence, pioneering the application of NLP to the development of cross-cultural skills. Judith's background in ballet and Congolese dance has lead her to promote the use of dance and movement as a primary tool of NLP.

Deborah Bacon Dilts is a trainer in Psychosynthesis, Relaxation Therapy and Richard Moss' transformational and spiritual work. She is a teacher of Gabrielle Roth's 5 Rhythms® and is trained in Aquanima, a transpersonal body-psychotherapy approach based on Holotropic Breathwork™. She lives in France where she has also worked as a professional interpreter for trainers and teachers in the personal growth field for more than 20 years. She also shares a home in California with her husband Robert.

Deborah is the author of a number of articles (in French) including, *The sweat-lodge ritual - connecting with life*, *The earth - place of connection*, *Gabrielle Roth's 5 Rhythms®*, and a chapter on Richard Moss' Mandala of Being™ in a publication on transpersonal psychotherapy. Her work focuses on the body-mind connection and conscious relationship.

Deborah has been working with her husband Robert Dilts since 2005 to create programs blending Neuro-Linguistic Programming with movement and transpersonal approaches including: The Power of Presence; Coaching at the Identity Level; The Hero's Journey and the Five Rhythms; Crisis, Transition and Transformation: Tools for Managing Change; and Dynamic Teaming: Releasing the Generative Power of Groups and Teams. She is the co-author with Robert of the article *Coaching at the Identity Level*.